Microsoft Windows Server AppFabric Cookbook

60 recipes for getting the most out of WCF and WF services, including the latest capabilities in AppFabric 1.1 for Windows Server

Hammad Rajjoub

Rick G. Garibay

BIRMINGHAM - MUMBAI

Microsoft Windows Server AppFabric Cookbook

First published: July 2012

Production Reference: 1190712

Published by Packt Publishing Ltd.
Livery Place
35 Livery Street
Birmingham B3 2PB, UK.

ISBN 978-1-84968-418-7

www.packtpub.com

Cover Image by Artie Ng (artherng@yahoo.com.au)

Credits

Authors

Hammad Rajjoub

Rick G. Garibay

Reviewers

Adnan Masood

Zubair Ahmed

Alvin Lau

Acquisition Editors

Sarah Cullington

Kerry George

Lead Technical Editor

Azharuddin Sheikh

Technical Editors

Joyslita D'Souza

Unnati Shah

Project Coordinator

Joel Goveya

Proofreader

Aaron Nash

Indexer

Hemangini Bari

Graphics

Valentine D'silva

Manu Joseph

Production Coordinator

Nilesh R. Mohite

Cover Work

Nilesh R. Mohite

Foreword

Have you ever set foot in the kitchen with a certain hunger and found that you had no clue as to how to make that dish? At such a time a cookbook is a wonderful thing. That's why I appreciate this concept of a cookbook for workflows and services. At Microsoft when we build products they are often chocked full of little known but wonderful capabilities and guys like Hammad and Rick are just the sort of chefs that have what it takes to make you successful with it. AppFabric brings some terrific capabilities to Windows Server and IIS with distributed caching and terrific hosting features for WCF Services and WCF Workflow Services at no additional cost, so using it is a no-brainer but maximizing it will take the kind of insight you will find in this book. So break out the mixing bowls, spatulas, and turn on the oven... I can almost smell success from here.

Ron Jacobs

Senior Program Manager, Microsoft Corporation

About the Authors

Hammad Rajjoub works as an Architect Evangelist with Microsoft. Before joining Microsoft, he was awarded Microsoft's Most Valuable Professional award, seven years in a row. Along with being an MVP he was also a Microsoft Business Platform Technology Advisor. Being an MVP in Connected Systems gave him early access to Windows Communication Foundation, Windows Workflow Foundation, as well as Windows Server AppFabric. In his previous roles he has been a CTO at a technology startup, Vice President at one of the largest financial institutions, as well as a Solutions Architect at a leading consulting company.

He has over a decade of experience using Microsoft Technologies, especially .NET since its beta 1 release. He is a published author and a frequent speaker at technology conferences (including TechEd and Cloud Computing Asia). He has founded a number of developer and architect communities over the years and remains a passionate speaker and contributor at local technical communities in Singapore. He is also an active member of the International Association of Software Architects (IASA) - Singapore Chapter. His areas of interest include Cloud Computing, Enterprise Architecture, Design Patterns, and Quantum Computation.

At home he is a busy husband and father of twin girls and a baby boy. For more details visit his website at `http://www.hammadrajjoub.net` or on twitter: `@hammadrajjoub`.

Alhamdulillah - This work would not have been possible without the help and support from my family. Special thanks to my mother Noor and my wife Iman for being supportive and giving me time and help to complete this book. I would also like to express my gratitude to my friend and co-author of this book, Rick Garibay, for accepting my invitation to co-author this book and sharing his feedback throughout the lifecycle of this book. Also, special thanks to Adnan Masood, Zubair Ahmed, and Alvin Lau for technically reviewing the book, providing feedback, and correcting numerous mistakes. Last but not the least, thanks to the editorial and project team at Packt Publishing for giving me the opportunity to write this book, and also being patient and understanding through the process of writes, re-writes, technical edits, as well as cases of missed deadlines.

Rick G. Garibay is a developer, architect, speaker, and author on distributed technologies and is the General Manager of the national Connected Systems Practice at Neudesic. With over 13 years' experience delivering distributed solutions across industry sectors such as finance, transportation, hospitality, and gaming, he specializes in distributed technologies such as Microsoft .NET, Windows Communication Foundation, Workflow Foundation, and Windows Azure to help his clients deliver business value and drive revenue while reducing operational costs.

As a five-time Microsoft Connected Systems MVP, he is an active speaker, writer, and passionate community advocate and is the Co-Founder of the Phoenix Connected Systems User Group (pcsug.org), celebrating four years in operation. He serves as an advisor to Microsoft in a number of roles as a member of the Microsoft Application Platform Partner Advisory Council and long-time member of the Business Platform Advisors and Azure Technology Advisors groups.

Recent presentations include talks at the Microsoft SOA and Business Process Conference, Microsoft TechEd, Dev Connections, .NET Rocks, Desert Code Camp, and numerous Microsoft events and user groups throughout North America. He is a frequent contributor to industry publications such as CODE Magazine and maintains a blog at `http://rickgaribay.net`. You can catch up with Rick on Twitter `@rickggaribay`.

I would like to thank my loving, patient, and amazing wife Christie for being my rock and providing a foundation which has allowed us to grow a beautiful family while enduring the sometimes overbearing demands of my career. I'm also grateful to my wonderful children, Sarah and Ricky for tolerating the many lost nights and weekends holed up in my home office working on this book.

I would also like to thank Mickey Williams, VP Technology Platform Group at Neudesic for his support in taking on this project along with his words of encouragement and (always timely) sense of humor along the way.

Last but not least, I would like to thank my friend and co-author, Hammad Rajjoub for inviting me to participate in this project and trusting me to help carry out his vision for this book. Hammad and I both share a labor of love as it applies to the Microsoft distributed technology stack affectionately (and somewhat nostalgically) known as "Connected Systems" and this book is both a reflection and an acknowledgment of the tremendous work the WCF, WF, and Dublin teams have done in putting these tremendous capabilities within reach of developers tasked with solving tough distributed challenges today.

About the Reviewers

Adnan Masood is a Software Engineer and Architect with zeal for solving interesting algorithmic, business, and technology problems. With special interest in scalable architectures, algorithm design, application security, and software development, he has over a decade of hands-on experience in financial services and application service providers. He currently works as a System Architect for Green Dot Corporation, a leading pre-paid financial institution where he develops robust, scalable, and secure SOA based middle-tier architectures, distributed systems, and web applications. He is a Microsoft Certified Trainer and holds various technical certifications including MCPD (Enterprise Developer), MCSD .NET, and SCJP-II. He is attributed and published in print media and on the Web; he also taught Windows Communication Foundation (WCF) courses at the University of California, San Diego.

He regularly presents at local code camps and user groups. He is actively involved in the .NET community as Co-founder and President of the of San Gabriel Valley .NET Developers group and recipient of the INETA Community Champion Award for contributions to the developer community in Southern California.

He holds a Master's degree in Computer Science and is currently pursuing a doctorate in Machine Learning; specifically interestingness measures in outliers using belief networks. He also holds systems architecture certification from MIT and SOA Migration, Adoption, and Reuse Technique certificate from SEI, Carnegie Melon University. He can be reached at `adnan@nova.edu`.

Alhamdullilah - Thanks to my family for their constant support during the process of editing this book. I would also like to thank Hammad for the opportunity and both Hammad and Rick for putting up with my feedback and tech edits. Last but not least, thank you Joel for your great project coordination skills.

Zubair Ahmed is an experienced software developer, blogger, and technical presenter. His interests include software architecture, improving code quality, and keeping an eye on the latest technologies. He works as a Software Consultant for Infusion Development in Dubai. When he is not working he likes to spend time in front of his large monitor at home writing some code, go for long drives with his wife, or socialize with friends.

His technical blog is at `zubairahmed.net` and his tweet handle is `@zubairdotnet`.

For technology updates, subscribe to his Facebook page at `http://facebook.com/zubair.ahmed.public`.

www.PacktPub.com

Support files, eBooks, discount offers and more

You might want to visit www.PacktPub.com for support files and downloads related to your book.

Did you know that Packt offers eBook versions of every book published, with PDF and ePub files available? You can upgrade to the eBook version at www.PacktPub.com and as a print book customer, you are entitled to a discount on the eBook copy. Get in touch with us at service@packtpub.com for more details.

At www.PacktPub.com, you can also read a collection of free technical articles, sign up for a range of free newsletters and receive exclusive discounts and offers on Packt books and eBooks.

http://PacktLib.PacktPub.com

Do you need instant solutions to your IT questions? PacktLib is Packt's online digital book library. Here, you can access, read and search across Packt's entire library of books.

Why Subscribe?

- ▶ Fully searchable across every book published by Packt
- ▶ Copy and paste, print and bookmark content
- ▶ On demand and accessible via web browser

Free Access for Packt account holders

If you have an account with Packt at www.PacktPub.com, you can use this to access PacktLib today and view nine entirely free books. Simply use your login credentials for immediate access.

Instant Updates on New Packt Books

Get notified! Find out when new books are published by following @PacktEnterprise on Twitter, or the *Packt Enterprise* Facebook page.

Table of Contents

Preface

Windows Server AppFabric is an extension of the Application Server Role on the Windows Server Platform. In a nutshell, Windows Server AppFabric frees Windows Communication Foundation (WCF) and Windows Workflow Foundation (WF) Service developers from common infrastructure plumbing by providing a robust, secure, composable, and reliable platform which provides caching, hosting, and monitoring capabilities, including support for long running workflow services, all on the Windows Platform. As such, Windows Server AppFabric is an evolution of the Windows Server platform, providing essential building blocks for first-classing WCF (for code-based services) and WF (for declarative workflow services) that are built using the .NET Framework 4 and Visual Studio 2010.

As an extension to IIS and WAS, Windows Server AppFabric relies on IIS's proven capabilities for hosting and lifecycle management, adding additional useful capabilities for working with WCF and WF services. In addition, Windows Server AppFabric takes advantage of Windows Server's robust event tracing mechanism (also known as ETW). ETW provides optimized and high-performing kernel-level instrumentation which greatly minimizes impact on the performance of WCF and WF services hosted in IIS with Windows Server AppFabric.

Whether you are a developer who wants to avoid the same repetitive tasks when preparing your WCF and/or WF services for deployment, or an IT Pro who wants to avoid complex XML for configuring hosting and monitoring options for the services you manage, you will instantly benefit from Windows Server AppFabric. Best of all, Microsoft has made this key extension to the Windows Server Platform available free of charge.

Written by both a former MVP and now Architect Evangelist with Microsoft and a five-time Connected Systems Developer MVP, the authors of this book both worked very closely with Microsoft during the development of the product (then codenamed "Dublin") participating in Software Design Reviews and early incubation initiatives. Hammad and Rick have advised customers of all shapes and sizes and fielded these capabilities in countless projects across various verticals in the two years since its general availability.

This book is full of practical, step-by-step guidance including useful tips and techniques that will allow you to build scalable, reliable, and secure service-oriented applications on the Windows Server Platform with IIS and Windows Server AppFabric.

What this book covers

Chapter 1, Installing Windows Server AppFabric, covers setting up your development environment to use Windows Server AppFabric. You'll learn how to install hosting, persistence and monitoring capabilities, including provisioning repositories, choosing the appropriate storage options, making changes to configuration after installation, and troubleshooting common (and not so common) installation issues you might encounter along the way.

Chapter 2, Getting Started with AppFabric Caching, introduces Caching in Windows Server AppFabric, covering everything you need to get started with introducing this important capability to your composite applications and services. You will learn how to set up and use Caching using code and configuration options, as well as working with Caching within your applications. In addition, you'll learn how easily an existing application that relies on ASP.NET session state can immediately benefit from Windows Server AppFabric Cache, handling common error conditions, using PowerShell commandlets, and building a custom provider model.

Chapter 3, Windows Server AppFabric Caching – Advanced Use Cases, builds on the concepts in the previous chapter, covering the use of Regions and Tags as well as choosing the right concurrency mode and establishing expiration, eviction, and notification policies. You will also learn advanced monitoring concepts including the use of performance counters, configuring high availability, and common troubleshooting techniques for getting the most out of Windows Server AppFabric Cache.

Chapter 4, Windows Server AppFabric Hosting Fundamentals, introduces Windows Server AppFabric's hosting capabilities, covering common deployment, management, and hosting scenarios. You'll learn how to host WCF SOAP and REST services as well as simple WF services along with a number of tips and tricks for moving beyond the service template defaults.

Chapter 5, More Windows Server AppFabric Hosting Features, covers additional hosting topics, including supporting long-running WF services, how your services can benefit from the Auto-Start feature, properly hosting WCF services that take advantage of Windows Azure Service Bus Relay bindings for enabling modern, hybrid scenarios as well as common PowerShell commandlets for scripting many of the tasks covered in this and the previous chapter.

Chapter 6, Utilizing AppFabric Persistence, provides ample coverage of Windows Server AppFabric persistence capabilities, including configuring persistence for WF services, working with multiple persistence stores, and developing instance store, control, and query providers. This chapter also provides an in-depth walkthrough of development and configuration of custom instance, control, and query providers.

Chapter 7, Monitoring Windows Server AppFabric Deployment, provides an introduction to the monitoring capabilities provided by Windows Server AppFabric. Topics include collecting and viewing events from WCF and WF services, enabling tracing and configuring tracking profiles, and leveraging PowerShell cmdlets for monitoring WCF and WF services as well as the Caching service. In addition, you'll learn how to surface monitoring information to any user experience by following the sample recipe for building a custom monitoring dashboard using ASP.NET MVC and OData.

Chapter 8, Scaling AppFabric Hosting, Monitoring, and Persistence, covers a common scenario for scaling Windows Server AppFabric across multiple IIS hosts. You will learn how to prepare two hosts for clustering using Microsoft NLB as well as understand deployment, management, and administration of a multi-host Windows Server AppFabric deployment that shares a common, centralized persistence store.

Chapter 9, Configuring Windows Server AppFabric Security, covers what you need to know about planning and implementing a security model with Windows Server AppFabric. You will learn how to secure the caching, persistence, monitoring, and eventing (via ETW) subsystems of Windows Server AppFabric.

What you need for this book

This book assumes you have a solid foundation in messaging and workflow concepts and are proficient in developing web services with WCF 4.0 and WF 4.0, in addition to C#, the .NET Framework, and Visual Studio 2010. You will need a Windows 7 (or Windows Server 2008/R2) machine configured for IIS 7 along with SQL Server and Visual Studio 2010, as well as either Windows Server AppFabric or Microsoft AppFabric 1.1 for Windows Server.

To take advantage of the latest caching features introduced in AppFabric 1.1, it is recommended that you install Microsoft AppFabric 1.1. for Windows Server. Otherwise, Windows Server AppFabric (the first version of this release) will suffice and is the product name we use throughout this book.

Either version can be installed on Windows 7, Windows Server 2008, Windows Vista R2, or Windows Server 2008 R2 and they support both 32- and 64-bit architectures. You will also need Microsoft .NET Framework v4, IIS7, and Windows PowerShell 2.0. In terms of hardware, officially, any 1GHz+ CPU (900MHz+ for Dual Core and 700MHz+ for Quad Core) with 2 GB of RAM will be sufficient to get up and running. However, it is recommended that you have at least 4 GB of RAM to run Windows Server AppFabric or Microsoft AppFabric 1.1 for Windows Server.

Who this book is for

Whether you are an architect or developer designing and developing composite solutions with WCF and WF services or an IT Pro tasked with their deployment and maintenance; or designing and implementing a distributed caching strategy for your .NET services and applications, this book is for you.

This book does not assume any prior knowledge of Windows Server AppFabric; however, a basic understanding of .NET Framework 4.0, Windows Communication Foundation (WCF), and Windows Workflow Foundation (WF) technologies is required.

Conventions

In this book, you will find a number of styles of text that distinguish between different kinds of information. Here are some examples of these styles, and an explanation of their meaning.

Code words in text are shown as follows: "Once the Caching service is up and running, we can query it for the caches that are available in this cluster by using the `Get-Cache` command."

A block of code is set as follows:

```
internal enum AckNack
{
    Ack,
    Nack,
    Pending,
}
```

When we wish to draw your attention to a particular part of a code block, the relevant lines or items are set in bold:

```
<microsoft.applicationServer>
    <monitoring>
        <default
            enabled="true"
            connectionStringName="ConnectionString"
            monitoringLevel="Troubleshooting" />
    </monitoring>
</microsoft.applicationServer>
```

Any command-line input or output is written as follows:

```
Get-ASAppMonitoring -SiteName "Default Web Site" -VirtualPath
/ReservationService
```

New terms and **important words** are shown in bold. Words that you see on the screen, in menus or dialog boxes for example, appear in the text like this: "In IIS, click on the application and select **Features View**."

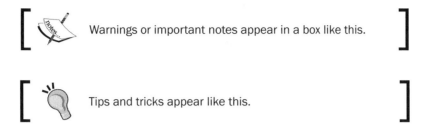

Warnings or important notes appear in a box like this.

Tips and tricks appear like this.

Reader feedback

Feedback from our readers is always welcome. Let us know what you think about this book—what you liked or may have disliked. Reader feedback is important for us to develop titles that you really get the most out of.

To send us general feedback, simply send an e-mail to feedback@packtpub.com, and mention the book title through the subject of your message.

If there is a topic that you have expertise in and you are interested in either writing or contributing to a book, see our author guide on www.packtpub.com/authors.

Customer support

Now that you are the proud owner of a Packt book, we have a number of things to help you to get the most from your purchase.

Downloading the example code

You can download the example code files for all Packt books you have purchased from your account at http://www.packtpub.com. If you purchased this book elsewhere, you can visit http://www.packtpub.com/support and register to have the files e-mailed directly to you.

Errata

Although we have taken every care to ensure the accuracy of our content, mistakes do happen. If you find a mistake in one of our books—maybe a mistake in the text or the code—we would be grateful if you would report this to us. By doing so, you can save other readers from frustration and help us improve subsequent versions of this book. If you find any errata, please report them by visiting `http://www.packtpub.com/support`, selecting your book, clicking on the **errata submission form** link, and entering the details of your errata. Once your errata are verified, your submission will be accepted and the errata will be uploaded to our website, or added to any list of existing errata, under the Errata section of that title.

Piracy

Piracy of copyright material on the Internet is an ongoing problem across all media. At Packt, we take the protection of our copyright and licenses very seriously. If you come across any illegal copies of our works, in any form, on the Internet, please provide us with the location address or website name immediately so that we can pursue a remedy.

Please contact us at `copyright@packtpub.com` with a link to the suspected pirated material.

We appreciate your help in protecting our authors, and our ability to bring you valuable content.

Questions

You can contact us at `questions@packtpub.com` if you are having a problem with any aspect of the book, and we will do our best to address it.

1
Installing Windows Server AppFabric

In this chapter, we will cover:

- ▶ Installing Windows Server AppFabric
- ▶ Configuring Windows Server AppFabric (hosting and monitoring)
- ▶ Configuring Windows Server AppFabric (caching)
- ▶ Installing caching Client Assemblies
- ▶ Changing the Windows Server AppFabric configuration after installation
- ▶ Starting a Caching service
- ▶ Troubleshooting Windows Server AppFabric – configuration errors
- ▶ Troubleshooting Windows Server AppFabric – auto restart issues

Introduction

Windows Server AppFabric is an extension of the Application server role on the Microsoft Platform. Windows Server AppFabric offers in-memory, super-fast, scalable caching capabilities for web applications and services. For applications built using Windows Communication Foundation (WCF) and Workflow Foundation (WF), Windows Server AppFabric provides streamlined hosting and monitoring capabilities that support composition scenarios.

Windows Server AppFabric is built on top of an existing set of technologies on the Windows platform including, but not limited to Internet Information Services (IIS), Windows Process Activation Service (WAS), .NET Framework v 4.0, and Event Tracing for Windows (ETW).

In this chapter, we will look at how to set up Windows Server AppFabric using the different configuration options. We will also see how the configuration of Windows Server AppFabric can be changed after the installation. Lastly, at the end of the chapter, we will see how to troubleshoot some common problems with Windows Server AppFabric installations.

Installing Windows Server AppFabric

Windows Server AppFabric is an extension of the Application Server role on the Windows platform. At the time of this writing there are two ways to install Windows Server AppFabric. One is the standard direct install and the other is using Microsoft's new and exciting **Web Platform Installer** (**WPI**).

In this recipe, we will go through the step-by-step instructions to install Windows Server AppFabric using WPI. Needless to say, if you already have Windows Server AppFabric installed on your machine, then you can skip this recipe.

 WPI is the preferred approach because it streamlines the installation process by smartly identifying and installing the prerequisite software.

Getting ready

Windows Server AppFabric can be installed on Windows 7, Windows Server 2008 SP 2, Windows Vista R2, and Windows Server 2008 R2 (it supports both 32 and 64 bit architectures). You will also need Microsoft .NET Framework v4, IIS7, and Windows PowerShell 2.0. In terms of hardware, officially, any 1GHz+ CPU (900MHz+ for Dual Core and 700MHz+ for Quad Core) with 2 GB of RAM will be sufficient to get up and running with Windows Server AppFabric. However, it is recommended that you have at least 4 GB of RAM to run Windows Server AppFabric.

 If you want to try Windows Server AppFabric before actually installing it on your host machine, it makes sense to use a virtual machine that has Windows Server AppFabric installed on it so that you can play with it. The good news is that Microsoft has made a preconfigured Windows Server AppFabric VM available on MSDN that can be downloaded and used with Microsoft's Virtual PC. This download is available as a part of Microsoft's training kit for Windows Server AppFabric. The download is available at: `http://www.microsoft.com/download/en/details.aspx?id=7956`.

How to do it...

WPI offers a highly streamlined package/software download installation mechanism. You can get WPI from Microsoft's website at: `http://www.microsoft.com/web/downloads/platform.aspx`. After downloading and installing WPI, you can use the following steps to launch Windows Server AppFabric Installer:

1. Under the **Start** menu, go to **All Programs**. If you are using Windows 7, type Web Platform Installer in the custom menu item, find the WPI as shown in the following screenshot, and launch it:

2. Accept the **User Account Control** (**UAC**) warning. This will allow WPI to make changes to your computer.

3. Click on **Next** at the bottom of the screen to get started with the WPI.

4. Type **AppFabric** in the search box (in the top right-hand corner of the screen) and press the *Enter* key:

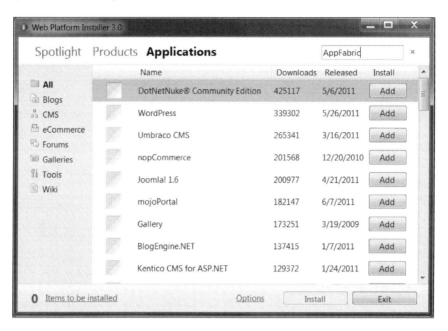

5. This will reveal a search result showing **Windows Server AppFabric**. Click on **Add** and then on **Install** to continue:

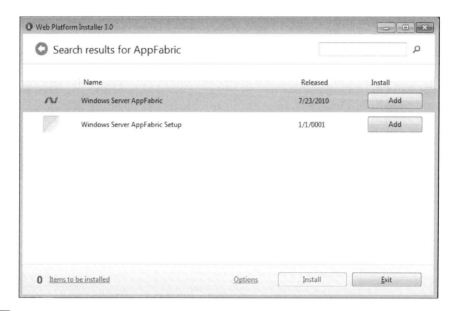

6. Now, WPI will ask to review the download and install of all the required software components to run Windows Server AppFabric. Select **I Accept** to continue.

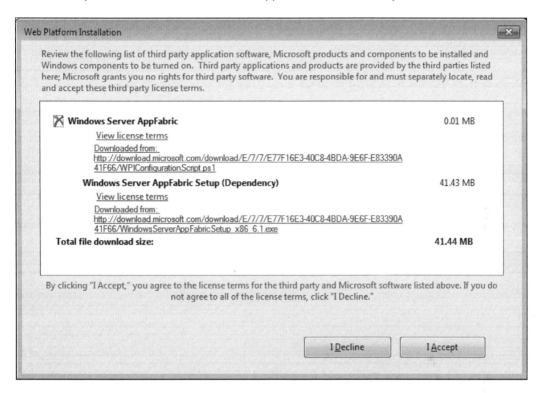

 The list of components, third-party application software, and Microsoft products will vary from machine to machine. WPI will determine the missing software and will list it on this screen.

7. Once you select **I Accept**, WPI will download and install all the required software components one by one. Sometimes this may result in multiple reboots for the host machine.

8. Once all the required software components are installed, the Windows Server AppFabric installation will be complete. Click on **Finish**:

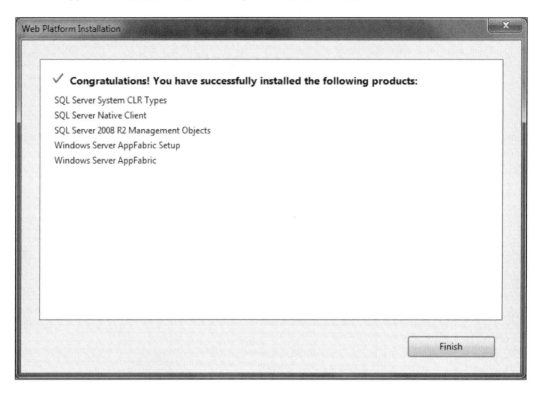

How it works...

The Windows Server AppFabric installation adds three new Windows services: **AppFabric Caching Service**, **AppFabric Event Collection Service**, and **AppFabric Workflow Management Service**, for caching, monitoring, and hosting scenarios respectively. These services can be seen when **the Services Snap-in** is launched from the **Control Panel** (or by typing `Services.msc` in the search box under the Windows Start menu).

As we can see in the preceding screenshot, only **AppFabric Event Collection Service** and **AppFabric Workflow Management Service** have **Status** as **Started** and have **Startup Type** defined as **Automatic**. By default, **Windows Server AppFabric Caching Service** is not available for use after a machine reboot.

 AppFabric Event Collection Service, **AppFabric Workflow Management Service**, and **Windows Server AppFabric Caching Service** form the heart of Windows Server AppFabric. These services work in the background and perform tasks such as collecting events, managing the workflow's life cycle, connecting to the cache cluster, and serving cache related requests.

Once Windows Server AppFabric is installed, the next step is to configure it using the Windows Server **AppFabric Configuration** wizard.

Configuring Windows Server AppFabric (hosting and monitoring)

There are a number of configuration options available when configuring Windows Server AppFabric, and in this recipe we will go through them. At this point, we should appreciate Microsoft's efforts in designing Windows Server AppFabric, as it allows a fair bit of customization.

Getting ready

Configuring Windows Server AppFabric is available via the Windows Server AppFabric Configuration wizard. It is a fairly simple task, but it requires careful consideration of a number of options and possibilities. We will need the following items ready in order to configure Windows Server AppFabric:

- Service accounts to run (with administrative privileges)
  - AppFabric Hosting's Event Collection service
  - AppFabric Hosting's Persistence service

- ▶ SQL server database for:

    - ❑ (SQL server based) monitoring provider

    - ❑ (SQL server based) persistence provider

    - ❑ AppFabric caching store service provider (if your machine is part of a domain)

- ▶ UNC file share for Windows Server AppFabric Caching service configuration provider (if the host machine is running in a workstation mode)

- ▶ Information on cluster set up (for a high-availability scenario)

> When **HA** (**High Availability**) is enabled Windows Server AppFabric Cache stores a copy of each cached object or region in a separate cache host. HA is discussed in detail in *Chapter 7, Monitoring Windows Server AppFabric Deployment*.

- ▶ Unique port numbers for cache, cluster, arbitration, and replication

> It should be noted that when you run the Windows Server AppFabric Configuration wizard and make changes to the configuration, it will overwrite any existing values.

How to do it...

To launch the Window Servers AppFabric Configuration wizard, go to **All programs** under the **Start** menu, find **AppFabric**, and then select **Configure AppFabric**.

The following is a sequence of steps that will take you through the configuration wizard for Windows Server AppFabric:

1. Run the **Configure AppFabric** wizard.

2. Accept the **User Account Control** (**UAC**) dialog, confirming that you will allow this program to make changes to your host machine:

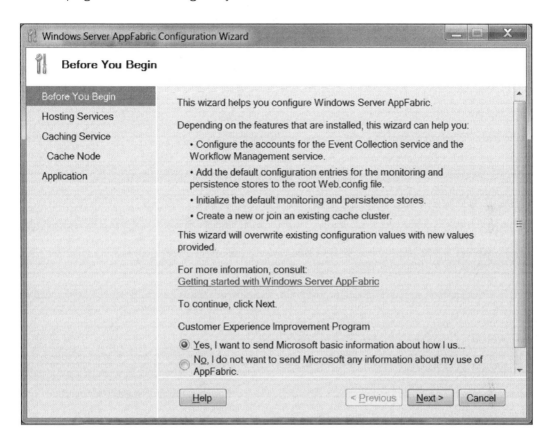

3. Click on **Next** at the bottom of the screen to start the configuration of Windows Server AppFabric.

4. Once you are at the **Configure Hosting Services** screen, select the box titled **Set monitoring configuration**:

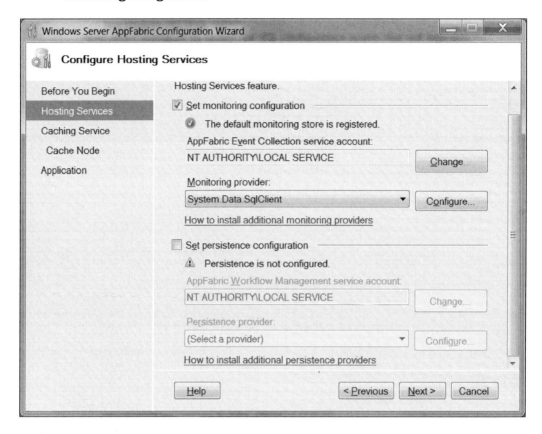

5. Select the service account required to run the **AppFabric Event Collection service** by clicking on **Change**.

6. If you do not have a ready-made account available for the event collection service, then you can leave the default value of **NT Authority\Local Service**, (as this can be modified later on). For more details on security, please refer to the *How it works...* section, as well as *Chapter 9, Configuring Windows Server AppFabric Security*.

7. Now select the **Monitoring provider**, as this will provide access to the monitoring database. (As there is only one default SQL-based implementation, select the **System.Data.SqlClient** option.)

 Windows Server AppFabric by design allows adding multiple providers for monitoring and persistence. Configuring multiple persistence providers is discussed in *Chapter 5, More Windows Server AppFabric Hosting Features.*

8. Now click on **Configure** to launch the SQL configuration screen to help you select/ configure the SQL server instance that will be used to store monitoring information.

9. Select **Register AppFabric monitoring store in root web.config**.

10. Select **Initialize monitoring store**.

11. Under **Connection String**, provide the SQL Server name, for example, `<HostServer Name>\<SQLInstanceName>`.

12. Provide the **Database** name for the SQL Server.

 The SQL database (specified above in steps 11 and 12) is used to store Windows Server AppFabric monitoring related information. The **Initialize monitoring store** option will initialize the database with the monitoring schema.

13. The first half of your configuration screen should appear as follows:

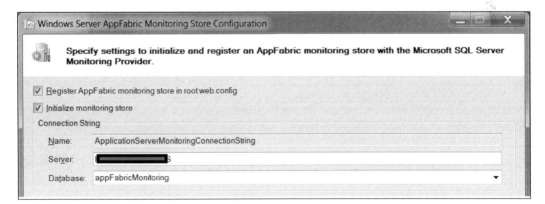

14. Now we will set up the **Security Configuration** to access the SQL Server database instance that we selected/created previously. For **Windows authentication**, if you have selected a complete install, then you will see default values for Administrators, Readers, and Writers in **Security Configuration**. If you already have roles defined and you have opted to initialize the **Monitoring Database**, then you can browse and select the appropriate roles. Otherwise, use the default values of **AS_Administrators** and **AS_Observers** as **Administrators/Writers** and **Readers** respectively. This is shown in the following screenshot:

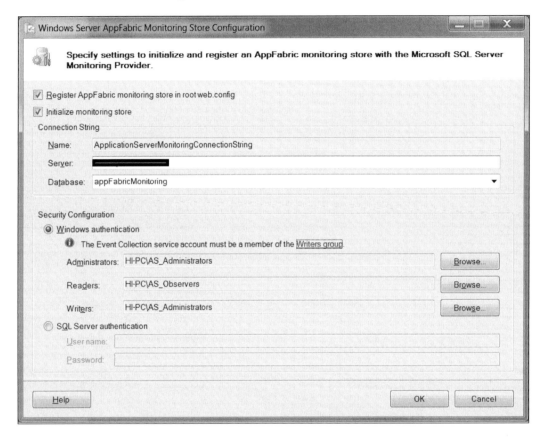

 Windows Server AppFabric's **AS_Administrators** is a conceptual and administrative role. As the name implies it allows full control over AppFabric's configuration, monitoring, and persistence capabilities. **Event Collection** and **Workflow Persistence** services run under this role.

Likewise, **AS_Observer** is also a conceptual and administrative role. It allows you to view the application and services configuration, monitor data, as well as view persisted instances, all without being able to modify anything.

15. However, if you wish to choose **SQL Server Authentication**, you will need to provide a username and password that will be used to connect to SQL Server database. In this recipe we will only use **Windows authentication**.

16. Once you click on **OK** you should see a confirmation dialog asking you to validate whether you want these settings to take effect:

17. Click on **Yes**, and the wizard will go ahead and create and initialize the monitoring store. Once completed, you should see a validation dialog advising you that the **Monitoring store was initialized and registered successfully**:

18. On the **Configure Hosting Services** screen, select **Set persistence configuration**.

19. Now, select an **AppFabric Workflow Management service account**. Just like the service account for monitoring, we will need a service account that has admin rights and can access the persistence provider/store. If you have an account already available for this then click on **Change** and select it. Otherwise, use the default value of the **NT AUTHORITY\LOCAL SERVICE** account:

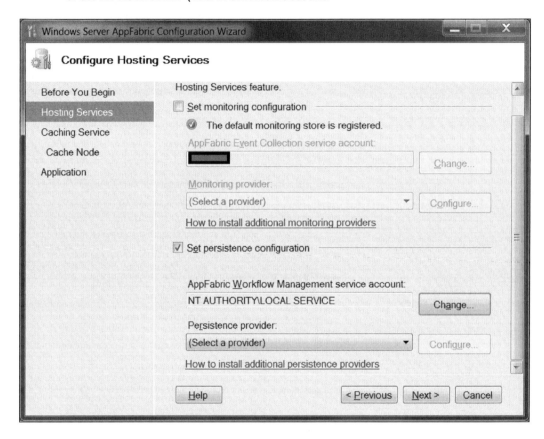

20. From the **Persistence provider** dropdown, select a **sqlStoreProvider** and then click on **Configure**. Now this screen should look familiar, as it is the same one we used to set up Windows Server AppFabric Monitoring earlier on. We will once again select **Register AppFabric persistence store in root web.config**. We will also select **Initialize persistence store** and provide the SQL **Server** and **Database** names:

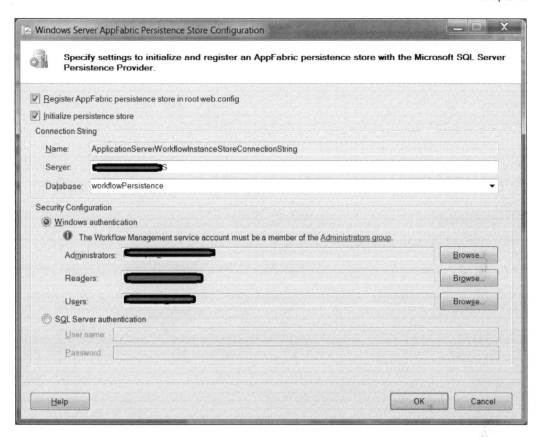

21. Just like we set up the **Security Configuration** for the Windows Server AppFabric Monitoring database, repeat the same steps and use built-in accounts for the persistence database.

22. Click on **OK** and proceed to confirm the changes. This will complete the configuration of the Hosting and Monitoring parts of Windows Server AppFabric.

How it works...

The configuration of Windows Server AppFabric provides contextual information to run Windows Server AppFabric services that are responsible for monitoring and hosting services. The values that we configured can be changed later, either by running the AppFabric Configuration wizard again or by using Windows Server AppFabric PowerShell commandlets (Cmdlets).

 Windows PowerShell is built on top of Microsoft.NET and offers a task based command-line shell and scripting language. Windows PowerShell has built in commands called Cmdlets (pronounced as commandlets). Cmdlets are lightweight commands and typically return a Microsoft.NET Framework object type to the next command in the pipeline.

It should be noted that monitoring and persistence services should be run under accounts with administrative privileges so that they can read and persist events to the preconfigured monitoring and persistence databases.

Configuring Windows Server AppFabric (caching)

Once you have finished configuring the Hosting Services as discussed in the preceding recipe, the next task is to configure the Caching Services for AppFabric. Just like in the preceding recipe, we will select a service account that should be part of the administrator group so that it has an administrative access to the caching configuration provider. Once again we will consider a workstation configuration and select a valid local system account.

We will see how to setup the **Caching Configuration Store Provider**. At the end of this recipe, we will also see how to join/create a new cache cluster (that this, the instance of Window Server AppFabric Cache is part of) along with the end point details (that is, port addresses) used by AppFabric services to communicate on the network.

Once we have configured Windows Server AppFabric Caching Services, we will be able to start using AppFabric Caching.

Getting ready

To begin this recipe, we will need the following in place:

- ▶ A service account for the AppFabric Caching service.
- ▶ A file share (UNC Server Share) to store XML based cache configurations or a SQL Server database for a SQL Server based AppFabric Configuration store. (This is required for configuring a High Availability Caching Service scenario that runs on Windows Server 2008.)

How to do it...

To set up Windows Server AppFabric Caching follow these steps:

1. Run the **AppFabric Configuration** wizard.

2. Accept the **User Account Control** (UAC) dialog, confirming that you will allow this program to make changes to your computer.

3. Click on **Next** on the **Before you Begin** and **Configure Hosting Services** screens to reach **Configure Caching Service**.

 You cannot directly select **Caching Service Configuration** from the left-hand navigation panel on the **Windows Server AppFabric Configuration Wizard**.

4. Once you are on the **Caching Service** screen of the Configure AppFabric wizard, select the **Set Caching Service configuration**.

5. Under **Caching Service Account**, click on **Change.** This will allow you to select the identity for the **Caching Service Account**.

6. If your machine is in workstation mode, then you cannot change the service account. Otherwise, you can browse and select a local account (that has administrative access to the Caching Configuration store).

7. Select **XML** from the **Caching Service configuration provider** dropdown.

8. The SQL Server based configuration is not available for the **Caching Configuration Service** in workstation mode. If you select **SQL provider** and click on **Configure**, you will get the following error message:

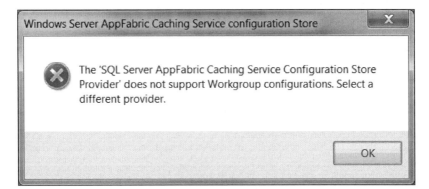

 We discuss the use of SQL Server AppFabric Caching Service Configuration Store Provider in more detail in *Chapter 7, Monitoring Windows Server AppFabric Deployment*.

9. Under **File Share**, provide a file path of an existing UNC file share. This will allow Windows Server AppFabric's Configuration Service to store and manage information stored as an XML file under this provided path. Your screen will appear as follows:

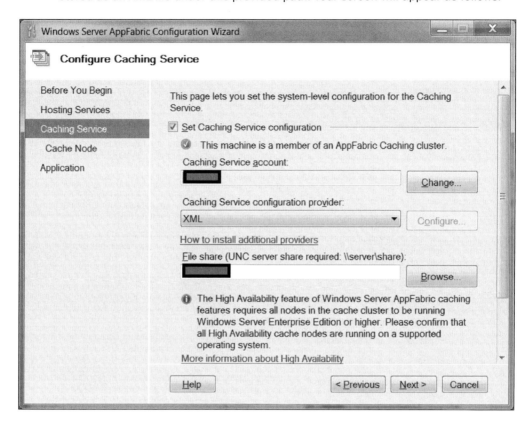

10. It should be noted that the **File share (UNC server share)** selection wizard will not allow you to create a new file share. As highlighted in the beginning of the recipe, it is required to have a UNC file share readily available. Under cluster information select **New Cluster** and click on **Next**.

11. Configure **AppFabric Cache Node** by providing a unique port number value (numbers must be between 1024 and 65535) for the **Cache port**, **Cluster port**, **Arbitration port**, and **Replication port**.

> The Cache port is used for transmitting data between Cache Clients and Cache Hosts. The Cluster port enables Cache Cluster formation and Management. The Arbitration port is used to double check if the Cache Host is unavailable. Arbitration is used when the Cache Host fails. The Replication Host is used to move data between the Cache Hosts. Replication is used when Cache is configured for High Availability.

12. Configure **Windows firewall exceptions** by selecting the rules for **Windows Server AppFabric Caching Service** and **Remote Service Management**. Your screen should appear similar to the following:

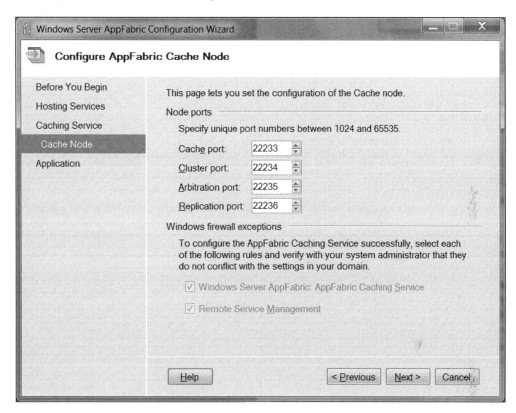

> If you are using any third-party (non-Microsoft) firewall then you will need to manually update the firewall rules. This must be done to allow Windows Server AppFabric to use the ports that were specified during its configuration.

13. After clicking on **Next**, click on **Yes** on the **Windows Server AppFabric Configuration Wizard** dialog box and you will come to the end of the wizard with an option to launch IIS to further manage Windows Server AppFabric. Click on **Finish** to close the wizard.

14. Congratulations! You have fully configured Windows Server AppFabric. Click on **Finish**.

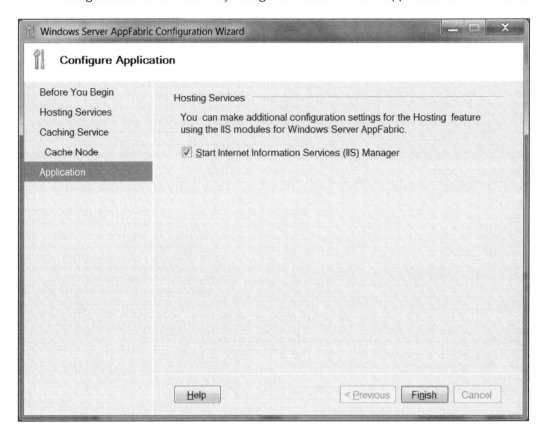

 The High Availability feature of Windows Server AppFabric Caching can only be enabled on Enterprise versions of Windows Server 2008/2008 R2. This implies that all the nodes in the cluster must have enterprise editions of Windows Server 2008/2008 R2. For more information you may refer to: http://go.microsoft.com/fwlink/?LinkId=164929.

How it works...

The Windows Server AppFabric Caching Service requires a service account to run its Windows service as well as a configuration provider where it can store its configuration. As the caching service runs under the identity of the provided account, the account must have administrative privileges so that it can access and modify the configuration.

The Windows Server AppFabric Caching Service needs to identify which ports to connect to in order to communicate with the other hosts in the cluster. Once the port numbers are specified, ensure that any software or hardware firewalls are not blocking these ports.

As we experienced in this recipe, the Windows Server AppFabric Caching Service is highly configurable and the configuration wizard makes it extremely easy to set up (or change) the existing configuration.

Now that we have configured Services for AppFabric and all the services are up and running under valid service accounts along with firewall rule definitions, we can now start coding to test and start consuming the caching service.

Installing Cache Client Assemblies

For non-production/client environments, we do not need to install the complete Windows Server AppFabric. Instead, we can use Client Assemblies to connect to an instance of AppFabric. In this recipe, we will see how to set up a Client Machine that can connect to and communicate with Windows Server AppFabric. Once we have set up the Client Assemblies, then we can use Visual Studio, for example, to write applications that can use Windows Server AppFabric Caching capabilities.

 Cache Client, as the name implies, refers to the applications or services that can access and modify cached items by connecting to a configured or specified cache cluster.

Getting ready

To set up the Cache Client, you will need the following assemblies:

- `Microsoft.ApplicationServer.Caching.Core.dll`
- `Microsoft.ApplicationServer.Caching.Client.dll`
- `Microsoft.WindowsFabric.Common.dll`
- `Microsoft.WindowsFabric.Data.Common.dll`

 For the Windows Server AppFabric Caching Client to be able connect to the Windows Server AppFabric Caching Service, it is required that Client Binaries are of the same version number as that of the Cache Service.

How to do it...

Setting up the Client Caching environment is a very simple task; it is just a matter of copying the binaries highlighted at the start of the recipe to a particular location. These binaries can be obtained by installing Windows Server AppFabric on a workstation. You will need the Caching feature installation to get the required Caching binaries. The default location for these assemblies is `.\Windows\System32\AppFabric`:

1. On Windows 7, type `C:\Windows\System32\AppFabric` in the custom menu; you should be able to see a number of binaries and the configuration file:

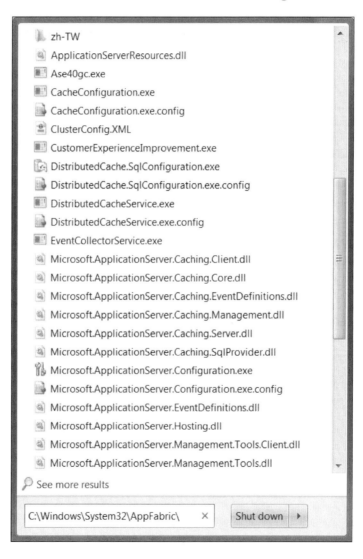

2. Obtain the following assemblies from the Windows Server AppFabric Cache installation:

    ❑   `Microsoft.ApplicationServer.Caching.Core.dll`

    ❑   `Microsoft.ApplicationServer.Caching.Client.dll`

    ❑   `Microsoft.WindowsFabric.Common.dll`

    ❑   `Microsoft.WindowsFabric.Data.Common.dll`

3. Copy the assemblies mentioned in step 2 to a place where they are available under a known path to your Client application.

To cache-enable an application server, you will need to install the Windows Server AppFabric Caching Assemblies on it. It is as simple as having an application/service installed on the server along with the AppFabric Caching assemblies. As long as your application installation copies the AppFabric Cache Assemblies and has a valid configuration in place, your application server is Cache enabled.

How it works...

The Windows Server AppFabric Caching Client application requires an API to talk to the Caching Service. This API (provided as a set of assemblies highlighted earlier in this recipe) must be available for the client to program against it. By copying these assemblies on the client machine, we ensure that the client does not need to do a complete installation of Windows Server AppFabric.

Once the Client Assemblies are available, we can write applications that can use AppFabric's Caching capabilities and connect to the AppFabric Caching cluster.

Changing the Windows Server AppFabric configuration after installation

Once Windows Server AppFabric is configured, it is still possible to change its configuration.

There could be a number of reasons for changing the configuration of an existing deployment. The following are some of the most common scenarios that would require such changes:

▸   Changes database repository (SQL instance for example)

▸   Changes to system accounts (for security reasons)

▸   Port number related changes for caching.

You can use the Windows Server AppFabric configuration wizard and make the required changes as they are required. In this recipe, we will see how to re-configure Windows Server AppFabric after installation.

Getting ready

You will need an existing instance of AppFabric that has been installed and configured to get started with this recipe. In this recipe, we will learn how to change Windows Server AppFabric configuration after it has been installed on the host OS.

How to do it...

To begin, launch the AppFabric Configuration wizard to go through the configuration options on an existing installation of AppFabric to easily select the options that we want to change.

1. Start the **Window Server AppFabric Configuration** wizard.

2. Accept the **User Account Control** (UAC) warning. Click on **Next** at the bottom of the screen to get started with the configuration.

3. Give the wizard a few seconds while it loads the existing configuration. The screen should look as follows:

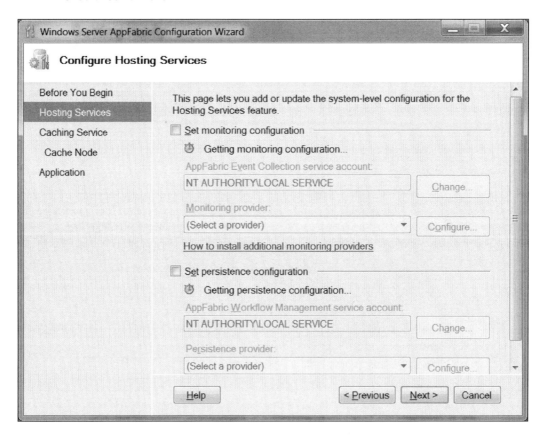

Once the configuration is loaded, you will notice that the green tick under the monitoring and persistence configurations states that the default monitoring store is registered.

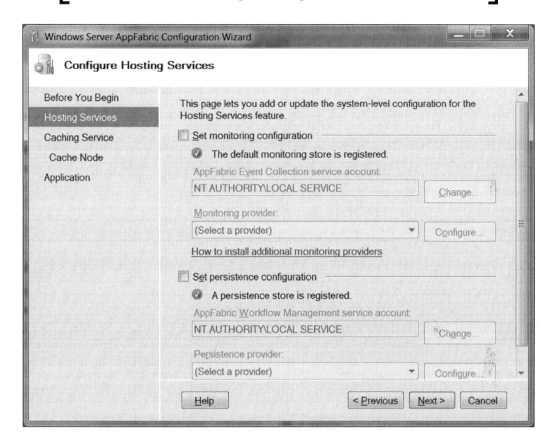

4. We can now go ahead and change the monitoring configuration by selecting **Set monitoring configuration** and clicking on **Change**.

5. This will launch a **Windows Server AppFabric Monitoring Store Configuration** wizard that we have already used in the recipe *Configuring Windows Server AppFabric (hosting and monitoring)* earlier in this chapter.

6. By selecting **Register AppFabric monitoring store in root web.config**, we can specify the **Server** and **Database** name.

 Registering the monitoring or persistence store in the configuration implies that that the connection string (with the name = `ApplicationServerMonitoringConnectionString`) is placed in the root `Web.Config` file and is made available to all subsequent websites.

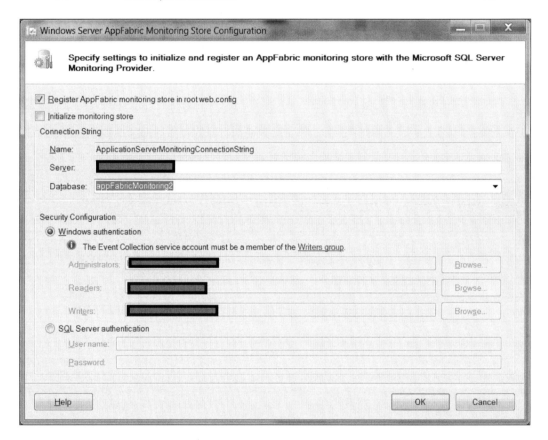

 The **Initialize monitoring store** option will create a new database (if it does not already exist) and it will also initialize the schema and the structure of the database (based on the Microsoft SQL Server provider for the **AppFabric monitoring site**).

It should also be noted that if you skip the **Register AppFabric monitoring store in root web.config** option, then the monitoring database will not be available on this computer.

7. We can repeat steps 4, 5, and 6 by selecting **Set persistence configuration**.

8. Next move to **Caching Service** and select **Set Caching Service configuration**, as shown in the following screenshot:

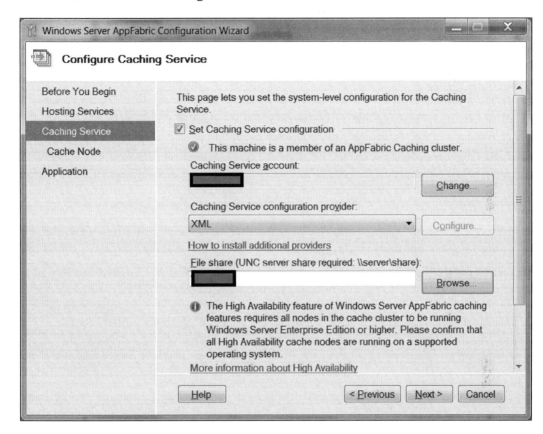

9. Change the **Caching Service account** by selecting **Change** and opting for a relevant account.

10. Change the **File share** (**UNC server share**) by browsing and selecting the appropriate share that we want to store the XML configuration file.

11. Join an existing cluster (as opposed to creating a new one) by selecting the **Join cluster** option, as shown in the following screenshot:

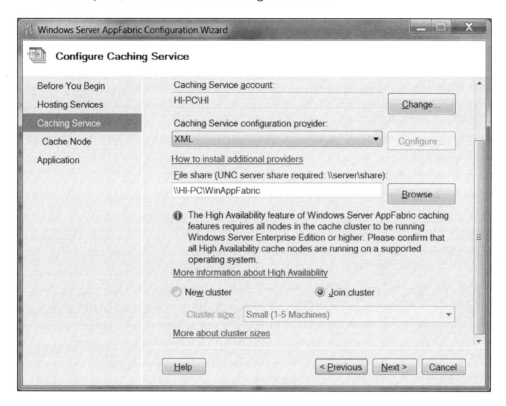

 If the configuration already exists, then this caching service instance will become part of an existing cluster.

12. If you are joining an existing cluster, you will not be able to change the cluster size.

 It should be noted that the cluster size does not dictate the possible number of machines in the cluster; however, it does optimize the whole cluster based on the size selected. So for example, you can add seven machines to a cluster that is defined as "Small" (1-5 machines). However, Windows Server AppFabric will optimize the caching configuration based on cluster configuration of 1-5 machines.

13. To change port numbers for caching, click on **Next** and change the values as required.

> In case of changing port numbers you must ensure that firewall level exceptions have already been defined for the newly selected port numbers. Otherwise, Windows Server AppFabric Cache will not be able to function properly.

How it works...

One of the best things about Windows Server AppFabric is that it is highly configurable. Configuration can be changed in a variety of ways. For example, in this recipe our changes were driven by the Windows Server AppFabric configuration wizard; however, we could have achieved similar results using AppFabric PowerShell commandlets. We will learn more about PowerShell commandlets in the following chapters.

Another possible way to change configuration is to modify the configuration manually. For example, when using the XML provider, we can always go to the file share and modify the `ClusterConfig.xml` file.

```
1   <?xml version="1.0" encoding="utf-8"?>
2   <configuration>
3       <configSections>
4           <section name="dataCache" type="Microsoft.ApplicationServer.Caching.DataCacheSection, Microsoft.ApplicationServer.Caching
5       </configSections>
6       <dataCache size="Small">
7           <hosts>
8               <host replicationPort="22236" arbitrationPort="22235" clusterPort="22234"
9                   hostId="1489712553" size="2047" leadHost="true" account="        "
10                  cacheHostName="AppFabricCachingService" name="       " cachePort="22233" />
11          </hosts>
12      </dataCache>
13  </configuration>
```

Windows Server AppFabric uses providers to abstract the implementation details of its Cache configuration as well as persistence and monitoring stores. In this recipe we used out of the box providers, but configuration storage and management can be further extended to implement a custom provider.

At runtime, Windows Server AppFabric looks up the registered configuration provider. Based on the provider it then accesses a specific configuration store. The configuration store is then used to fetch relevant information for that provider. For example, with the Caching configuration provider, the configuration store will store information such as port numbers, service accounts, and so on. Similarly, for the persistence and monitoring configuration providers, the configuration store will maintain information relevant to monitoring and persistence stores such as connection strings, for example.

Starting a Caching service

Windows PowerShell plays an extremely important role in the overall management of Windows Server AppFabric. There are hundreds of cmdlets and functions available that allow administrators (and developers alike) to perform day-to-day management tasks on AppFabric. As Caching is one of the biggest features in Windows Server AppFabric, it is no surprise that AppFabric Caching has a dedicated set of PowerShell cmdlets that allow developers and administrators to interact with the distributed Cache environments in an interactive and streamlined manner.

In this recipe, we will look at how to use PowerShell cmdlets to interact with the AppFabric Caching service.

> There are two ways that you can configure your Windows Server AppFabric installation/environment. One option is to use the Windows Server AppFabric Configuration wizard (that we have extensively used in this chapter) and another option is to use the Windows Server AppFabric PowerShell cmdlets. Using PowerShell to manage AppFabric Caching introduces a number of useful possibilities, including but not limited to automating build and deployment scenarios, and enabling command line monitoring and troubleshooting.

Getting ready

Assuming that you have the Windows Server AppFabric administration feature installed, you can launch the AppFabric PowerShell console via Administrative tools (available under **Start | Control Panel | Administrative Tools**) or by going to the Windows Server AppFabric folder under **Program Files** and selecting **Caching Administration Windows PowerShell**:

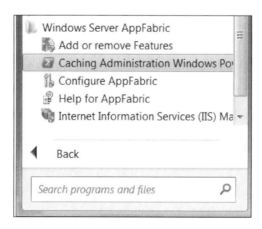

On Windows 7 and Windows Server 2008, you must run Caching Administration Windows PowerShell with administrative privileges, otherwise some commands will not work.

How to do it...

After starting the **Caching Administration Windows Powershell** console with administrative privileges, we can start our Cache Cluster for the first time:

1. To set the context of the Windows PowerShell session, we will execute the
    `use-CacheCluster` command first.

     The `Use-CacheCluster` command sets the context for Windows PowerShell. Considering that this is being executed on the host computer, we do not need to provide the configuration, as the parameters are extracted from the local computer.

2. Once the context has been set, we will execute the `start-CacheCluster` command. This should result in a status that shows that the Caching Service is up and running:

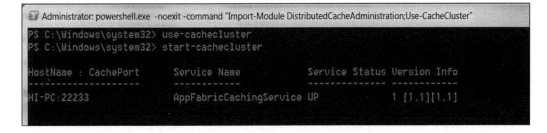

 The `Start-CacheCluster` commandlet starts the caching service on all the servers that are part of the cluster with the lead hosts starting before non-lead hosts.

3. Once the Caching Service is up and running, we can query it for the caches that are available in this cluster by using the Get-Cache command.

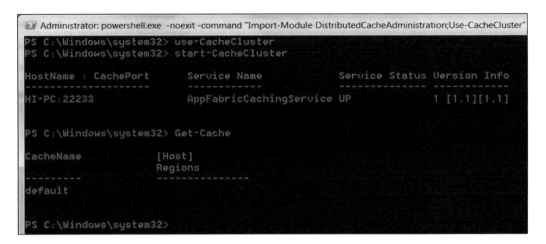

 This shows that the cluster is up and running and there is a default cache instance running on the cluster.

How it works...

The Caching Administration PowerShell commandlets give us complete control for managing an AppFabric Cache Cluster. When starting PowerShell sessions and running on a non-host computer, you must provide the -Provider (xml or System.Data.SqlClient) and ConnectionString (file path for XML or connection string for database).

Note that Cache services do not automatically start after a system reboot, so the Start-CacheCluster command must be invoked. We can also use the Start-CacheHost command with HostName and Port parameters to start a particular host in the cluster.

We will see much more on each of these PowerShell commands in the following chapters of this book.

Troubleshooting Windows Server AppFabric – configuration errors

It is not too uncommon to come across errors while installing and configuring Windows Server AppFabric. As long as we know where something wrong, most installation related errors are fairly trivial to fix.

In this recipe we will troubleshoot some common Windows Server AppFabric installation and configuration errors.

How to do it...

The first thing to do is to find the log file under the `%temp%` folder and then search for errors. Once error(s) are found, we can look up in MSDN for the error details as well as their corresponding resolutions.

1. To find installation related errors, find a log file created by the AppFabric installer available in the `%temp%` folder with the file name: `AppServerSetup(yyyy-MM-dd H-mm-ss).log`.

2. These errors can either be viewed by clicking on the link in the last page of the installation wizard by or by browsing to the file and then opening it with Notepad (or your favorite text editor).

3. Search for `errors` in the text file. Note the error codes and look up their reasons and associated workarounds at this URL: `http://msdn.microsoft.com/en-us/library/aa368542(VS.85).aspx`.

> When using an automated installer, log file options can be provided by using `/logfile` or `/l switch` and specifying the file path where the log file should be placed.

4. Likewise, for configuration errors, find a file under the `%temp%` folder with the name: `Microsoft.ApplicationServer.Configuration(yyyy-MM-dd H-mm-ss) <process code>.log`.

5. Errors mentioned in the configuration log can be looked up for details along with possible remediation at: `http://msdn.microsoft.com/en-us/library/ms681381(v=VS.85).aspx`.

> Configuration errors are AppFabric specific but descriptive enough to point you in the right direction; providing information that let's you know the issue is related to network resource, firewalls, and so on. It is also worth noting that you can see all PowerShell commands that are executed by the wizard logged in this file as well.

How it works...

Windows Server AppFabric uses a very detailed logging mechanism, and writes log entries for configuration and installation related errors in separate physical log files available under the `%temp%` folder.

Troubleshooting configuration errors revolves around going to a relevant log file and finding the error entries and then looking up each error on the corresponding MSDN help page (as highlighted in the *How to do it...* section) to find a solution for each issue reported.

For more information on error codes please visit the following MSDN links:

▸ `http://msdn.microsoft.com/en-us/library/ms681381(v=VS.85).aspx`

▸ `http://msdn.microsoft.com/en-us/library/aa368542(VS.85).aspx`

Troubleshooting Windows Server AppFabric – auto restart issues

When a cache host is rebooted, Windows Server AppFabric does not start the caching services by default. Although services can always be started manually using the PowerShell commandlets, this intervention is far from ideal. Furthermore, this lack of auto-start for caching services is problematic because even when the host is backed up its caching services are not available to the cluster. In this recipe, we will learn about two possible workarounds that will allow caching services to be available after a host has been rebooted.

How to do it...

We will first set the **Startup type** of the **AppFabricCachingService** to be automatic so that the Caching Service is started every time a cache host is rebooted:

1. Set the **AppFabric Caching Service's Startup type** to be **Automatic**, as shown in the following screenshot:

>
> To get to **AppFabric Caching Service Properties** launch `services.msc` (available under **Start | Control Panel | Administrative Tools**), select **AppFarbric Caching Service**, and then click on **Action** followed by the **Properties** menu item.

2. Another option is to schedule a startup task to execute the `Use-CacheCluster` and `Start-CacheHost` commands.

>
> For more details on how to configure a startup task in Windows 7, visit: `http://windows.microsoft.com/en-US/windows7/schedule-a-task`.

How it works...

Every time a Cache Host is rebooted, by default it is necessary to restart the AppFabric Caching Service manually. This is because Windows Server AppFabric Caching Services do not have a built-in mechanism for auto-start. By setting the service to start automatically, we worked around the limitation, but it is important to note that doing so carries some important caveats.

The reason Microsoft chose to require a manual restart of the caching service by default is that under certain conditions, waiting for the service to start can result in significantly longer boot times (sometimes several minutes).

On development machines, it can be useful to configure the service to start automatically so that you aren't pulling you hair out when caching all of a sudden stops working. However, if you experience excessive boot times, or errors resulting from applying this tip, it is probably best to skip it all together.

As we discussed, another option is to schedule a startup task which is a better approach as it still uses the same Windows Server AppFabric PowerShell cmdlets including `Use-CacheCluster` and `Start-CacheHost`, and you can define the trigger most appropriate to your environment for executing the start up task.

 It must be noted that these potential workarounds and not recommended by Microsoft.

2
Getting Started with AppFabric Caching

In this chapter, we will cover:

- ► Initializing Cache Client using code
- ► Initializing Cache Client using configuration
- ► Programming AppFabric Cache Client
- ► Using AppFabric Cache via the ASP.NET provider model
- ► Using AppFabric local cache
- ► Using the AppFabric cache management tool
- ► Building a custom provider model
- ► Handling common Windows Server AppFabric caching errors

Introduction

In distributed applications, object caching offers significant performance gains compared to direct database access. Historically, we have come to believe that performance and scalability are like two faces of the same coin; one can either get the system to perform better or have it optimized for scalability.

The use of distributed in-memory caching not only helps with performance, but also with scalability. If you cannot scale up then you have to scale out and that is exactly how distributed in-memory caching works for Windows Server AppFabric.

 Scale out, or the horizontal scaling, refers to the scalability approach that allows adding of new (compute and/or storage) nodes to the deployment to handle additional load; whereas with the traditional scale up approach to handle additional workload we add more memory and compute power to the existing compute node (server).

In Windows Server AppFabric Cache, the data is kept in-memory, but instead of limiting it to one server node, it has the capability of scaling out to hundreds of nodes, on demand, seamlessly.

This distributed in-memory architecture offers a possibility of dynamically scalable and highly available cache. This cache can then be used for storing large amounts of data in memory and as a result, applications and services perform faster and become more reliable.

Windows Server AppFabric uses a notion of a Cache Cluster to represent a logical collection of a number of Cache Hosts (nodes). Cache is transparently distributed across the hosts. Each host may contain zero or more named cache regions. The good thing is that the Cache Client is abstracted from the details of distributed architecture. The following diagram is a schematic representation of a Cache Cluster in Windows Server AppFabric:

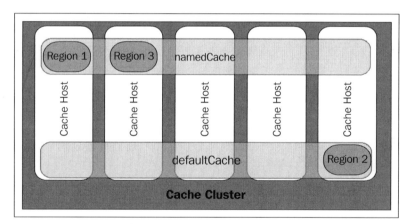

In this chapter we will go through some of the most common caching-related scenarios for Windows Server AppFabric Cache.

We will start with initializing Windows Server AppFabric Cache using code.

Initializing Cache Client using code

In the preceding chapter, we looked at the Client Libraries required for using Windows Server AppFabric's caching capabilities. Once these libraries are available, it is fairly straightforward to get started with common cache-related programming scenarios.

Windows Server AppFabric Caching Client needs connection settings to connect to a particular instance of a Cache Host. There are two ways a Cache Client can specify these settings:

- **Code based**: Using Windows Server AppFabric's Cache Client API to specify connection details programmatically
- **Configuration based**: Using the configuration file of a Cache Client to specify connection settings declaratively

In this recipe we will cover code-based configuration.

 To be able to program the AppFabric Cache Client, we need to make sure that AppFabric Caching Assemblies are available.

Getting ready

To be able to connect to Windows Server AppFabric Cache using the Client API, we need to ensure that the Cache Host we want to talk to is available. By using Windows Server AppFabric commandlets in PowerShell, we can identify and ensure that the particular instance is available for caching.

We will use the following AppFabric commands to check and see if the AppFabric Host is up and running.

 To be able to use AppFabric commandlets, PowerShell must be launched as the administrator. This will ensure that PowerShell has enough privileges to execute AppFabric commandlets.

You will need to launch AppFabric's Caching Administration Windows PowerShell tool with Admin privileges and run the following commands:

- ▶ `Use-CacheCluster`: To set the context for PowerShell.
- ▶ `Start-CacheHost`: To start the cache host (if the cache host is already up and running, then we can skip this command), OR
- ▶ `Start-CacheCluster`: To start the cache cluster. If you have only one node (for example, in Development environment) this is the same as `Start-CacheHost`.
- ▶ `Get-Cache`: To see if there is any cache defined on this host.

```
Administrator: powershell.exe  -noexit -command "Import-Module DistributedCacheAdministration;Use-CacheCluster
PS C:\Windows\system32> Use-CacheCluster
PS C:\Windows\system32> Start-CacheCluster

HostName : CachePort       Service Name            Service Status Version Info
-------------------        ------------            -------------- ------------
HI-PC:22233                AppFabricCachingService UP              1 [1,1][1,1]


PS C:\Windows\system32> Get-Cache

CacheName               [Host]
                        Regions
---------               ---------------
default


PS C:\Windows\system32>
```

How to do it...

We will use Visual Studio 2010 to write programs against the AppFabric Caching API. Before we actually initialize the cache using the AppFabric API, we will quickly go through the following steps which will help us set up the development environment:

1. Launch Visual Studio 2010 with administrative privileges.

2. Start a new project using the C# Console Application project template and assign **InitializeCacheWithCode** as **Solution name**:

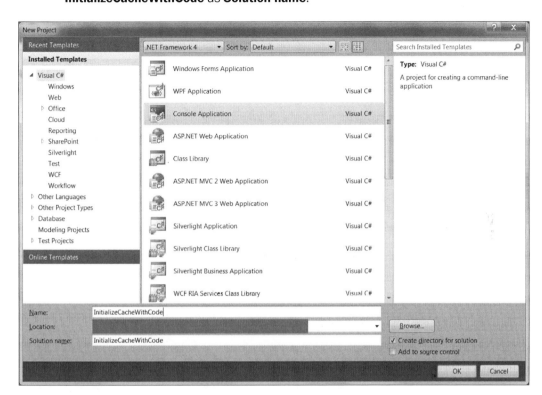

 This can be done using Visual Studio 2008 as well. You will need to make sure that you use .NET Framework 2.0 or above.

3. Once the project is created, right-click on **References** and select **Add Reference**.

4. Browse to `.Windows\System32\AppFabric` and add the following two assemblies:

   ❑ `Microsoft.ApplicationServer.Caching.Core.dll`
   ❑ `Microsoft.ApplicationServer.Caching.Client.dll`

 On a 64-bit OS, you may not be able to access the AppFabric folder directly using System32. However, AppFabric should still be available under `.\Windows\SysNative\AppFabric`.

5. Initialize the `DataCacheServerEndPoint` array with an instance that has server name = `'your-host'` and `port='22233'` (or your own configured cache port):

```
var cacheServerEndPoints = new[]
{
    new DataCacheServerEndpoint("yourServerHost", 22233)
};
```

> Your server host should be the cache Host Name as shown in the `Start-CacheCluster` command. You will also need to add the following `using` statement to access AppFabric's caching related classes: `using Microsoft.ApplicationServer.Caching;`.

6. Create an instance of `DataCacheFactoryConfiguration` and pass it an object of `DataCacheServerEndPoint`:

```
var cacheConfiguration = new DataCacheFactoryConfiguration {
Servers = cacheServerEndPoints };
```

Downloading the example code

You can download the example code files for all Packt books you have purchased from your account at `http://www.packtpub.com`. If you purchased this book elsewhere, you can visit `http://www.packtpub.com/support` and register to have the files e-mailed directly to you.

7. Create an instance of `DataCacheFactory`, passing `DataCacheFactoryConfiguration` to the constructor:

```
var cacheFactory = new DataCacheFactory(cacheConfiguration);
```

8. Invoke `GetCache` on `DataCacheFactory` by providing the name of the cache. The following code snippet shows a utility method showing the creation of `DataCache`:

```
private static DataCache InitializeCache(string cacheName)
{
    var cacheEndPoints = new[]
    {
        new DataCacheServerEndpoint("yourServerHost",
        22233)
    };
```

```
var cacheConfiguration = new
DataCacheFactoryConfiguration
{ Servers = cacheEndPoints };

var cacheFactory = new
DataCacheFactory(cacheConfiguration);

return cacheFactory.GetCache(cacheName);
```

    }

9. The calling client can simply pass the name of the cache and the rest of the details around cache initialization can be handled by the method just defined:

```
DataCache cache = InitializeCache("referenceData");

Debug.Assert(cache != null);
```

 This may seem like a complex way of initializing a cache instance, but this complexity is worth it because of the highly configurable nature of the Windows Server AppFabric Cache API.

How it works...

DataCacheFactory is responsible for providing access to DataCache instances. DataCacheFactory requires a configuration object of type DataCacheFactoryConfiguration, which in turn requires an instance of array of DataCacheServerEndPoint. The following is a schematic representation of the composition of DataCacheFactory with respect to DataCacheFactoryConfiguration and DataCacheServerEndPoint(s):

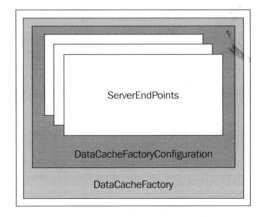

To be able to access `DataCache`, we will need to create an array of `DataCacheServerEndPoints`. Initialize it and assign it to an instance of the `DataCacheFactoryConfiguration` class. We can then pass the `DataCacheFactoryConfiguraiton` instance to our `DataCacheFactory` class so that it can read the configuration via server end points and get the appropriate cache instance.

 Instantiation of `DataCacheFactory` is a compute/resource extensive operation. Think about establishing network connections with server end points to start with. Considering this, it is recommended that you minimize the instantiation of `DataCacheFactory` objects. Ideally, it makes sense to have only one instance of `DataCacheFactory` available throughout the application lifecycle. Use of the Singleton design pattern is highly recommended to control the access to, and lifecycle of, `DataCacheFactory` objects.

See also

In this recipe, we saw the use of the object model to construct a DataCache instance. In the following recipe we will once again create a DataCache instance, but without interacting with the detailed object model.

Initializing Cache Client using configuration

In this recipe, we will go about doing exactly what we did in the previous recipe, that is, initializing Windows Server AppFabric Cache client, but using XML configuration instead of code.

Cache Client requires an end point to connect to the Windows Server AppFabric. More specifically, we need to tell the `DataCacheFactory` which host and port number to connect to for cache connection. In this recipe, we will use the application configuration XML file to specify these details. We will also write a similar simple application (this time without the `DataCacheServerConfiguration` related details).

Getting ready

Just as seen in the preceding recipe, we will need to ensure that Windows Server AppFabric Cache is available by using PowerShell commandlets. Once we know the end point details (the host name and port number), Windows Server AppFabric cache is ready; we can get started with the following steps.

We will also need to:

▶ Create an empty C# Console Project

▶ Add the following AppFabric Cache assemblies:

  ❑ `Microsoft.ApplicationServer.Caching.Core.dll`

  ❑ `Microsoft.ApplicationServer.Caching.Client.dll`

How to do it...

After creating the empty C# project and adding references we will need to add an application configuration file. We will then proceed with updating this configuration file with additional entries for Windows Server AppFabric Cache.

1. Select **Add New Item** from the **File** menu, select **Application configuration file**, and click on **Add**:

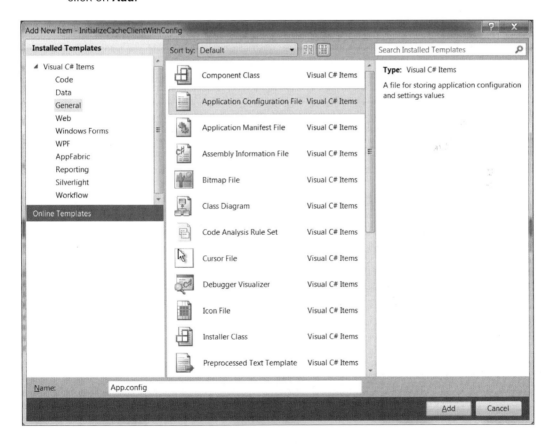

2. Open the `App.Config` file and add the following configuration section for Windows Server AppFabric Data Cache Client (make sure that `configSections` is the first entry in the configuration file):

```
<configSections>
  <section name="dataCacheClient"
      type="Microsoft.ApplicationServer.Caching.
          DataCacheClientSection,
          Microsoft.ApplicationServer.Caching.Core,
          Version=1.0.0.0,
          Culture=neutral, PublicKeyToken=31bf3856ad364e35"
      allowLocation="true"
      allowDefinition="Everywhere"/>
</configSections>
```

3. Now that we have the configuration section defined, we can add configuration settings under the `dataCacheClient` section:

```
<dataCacheClient>
    <hosts>
      <host
          name="cacheHost1"
          cachePort="22233"/>
    </hosts>
</dataCacheClient>
```

4. Instantiate `DataCacheFactory` without providing an instance of `DataCacheServerConfiguration`.

> When `DataCacheFactory` is invoked without setting `DataCacheServerConfiguration`, it uses an internal initialization mechanism to read end point details from the configuration file.

5. Call `GetCache` on `DataCacheFactory` by passing the name of the cache. Your initialization code should look as follows:

```
private static void InitializeWithConfiguration()
{
    DataCacheFactory cacheFactory = new
        DataCacheFactory();
    DataCache cache =
        cacheFactory.GetCache("default");
    Debug.Assert(cache != null);
}
```

How it works...

`DataCacheFactory` needs to know which end points to connect to, and there are different ways we can provide this information. If you don't specify `DataCacheFactoryConfiguration` while creating `DataCacheFactory`, then it will go ahead and try to create it internally by finding the `dataCacheClient` section in the application configuration file. It will read property values, for example, `host name` and `cachePort`. Using these values it will internally create the instance `DataCacheFactoryConfiguration` and use it to initialize `DataCache`.

Configuration based setup makes code look cleaner. It also gives you an opportunity to change end point related details without changing the code, avoiding the need for recompiling the application.

Programming AppFabric Cache Client

Windows Server AppFabric in Version 1 was built for cache-aside patterns, which implies that all the applications and services relying on AppFabric cache are responsible for loading data into the AppFabric Cache themselves. With v1.1, Windows Server AppFabric has added support for Read-Through and Write-Behind scenarios. There are more details on these caching patterns in *Chapter 3, Windows Server AppFabric Caching – Advanced Use Cases*.

Data can be loaded in cache if and only when it is needed by the calling client. This is called **Lazy Loading**. The data can also be loaded in the cache when the application starts. This is called **Eager Loading**. Both approaches have their pros and cons.

In this recipe we will go through some of the common use-cases of adding, retrieving, and updating data from the Windows Server AppFabric Cache.

Getting ready

We will need the AppFabric Cache to be available (verifiable via running the cache cmdlets as highlighted in the preceding recipe) as well as a C# console application with necessary AppFabric assemblies added to its reference.

How to do it...

After initializing the cache (from configuration or programmatically), we can access the `DataCache` object to add/update/remove data. We will start with adding data to the cache first.

 Any .NET serializable object can be cached in AppFabric.

1. In the `DataCache` object (assuming that the cache is initialized and it is up and running) invoke the `Add` method and pass the key-value pair of the item to be stored.

2. Likewise, once the item is in the cache it is very simple to retrieve it by invoking a `Get` method on the Cache object. The following code shows the usage of `Add` and `Get`:

```
private static void AddAndRetrieveFromCache(DataCache cache)
{
        Console.WriteLine("Adding simple string key-value
            pair to the cache");

        cache.Add("key1", "value1");
        Console.WriteLine("Added key = {0} and value - {1}
            ", "key1", "value1");
        cache.Add("key2", "value1");
        Console.WriteLine("Added key = {0} and value - {1}
            ", "key2", "value2");

        Console.WriteLine("Retreving values from the cache");

        object value = cache.Get("key1");
        Console.WriteLine("Got back from cache, key = {0}
            and value- {1} ", "key1", value);
        value = cache.Get("key2");
        Console.WriteLine("Got back from cache, key = {0}
            and value- {1} ", "key2", value);
}
```

 If you try and add items with the same key, AppFabric Cache will raise an exception with an error message an attempt is being made to create an object with the key that already exists in the cache. As expected, the keys are unique. We will learn in more detail about exceptions (and their handling) later in this chapter.

3. However, to update an existing item in the cache, AppFabric Cache provides a `Put` method that overrides an existing value (or creates a new one, if it was not available in the first place). The following code snippet shows the usage of the `Put` and `Get` methods:

```
private static void PutAndRetrieveFromCache(DataCache cache)
{
    Console.WriteLine("Putting simple string key-value
        pair into the cache");

    Console.WriteLine("Put key = {0} and value - {1} ",
        "key1", "anotherValue2");
    cache.Put("key1", "anotherValue2");
    Console.WriteLine("Added key = {0} and value - {1}
        ", "key2", "anotherValue2");
    cache.Put("key2", "anotherValue2");

    Console.WriteLine("Retreving values from the cache");

    object value = cache.Get("key1");
    Console.WriteLine("Got back from cache, key = {0}
        and value- {1} ", "key1", value);
    value = cache.Get("key2");
    Console.WriteLine("Got back from cache, key = {0}
        and value- {1} ", "key2", value);
}
```

 AppFabric Cache returns a `DataCacheItemVersion` object every time `Add` or `Put` is invoked. `DataCacheItemVersion` is updated every time the `Cache` object is updated for that particular key. `DataCacheItemVersion` plays an important part when it comes to comparing the versions of cached items. This will be discussed in detail when covering notifications in a recipe titled *Setting up notifications* in the next chapter.

4. The indexer or the `Item` property of the `DataCache` instance can also be used to set and get objects from the cache (as shown in the following code snippet):

```
private static void UseIndexerToPutAndRetrieve(DataCache cache)
{
    Console.WriteLine("Putting simple string key-value
        pair into the cache using Indexer/Item")
    Console.WriteLine("Put key = {0} and value - {1} ",
        "key1", "anotherValue3");
```

```
cache["key1"] = "anotherValue3";
Console.WriteLine("Added key = {0} and value - {1}
    ", "key2", "anotherValue3");
cache["key2"] = "anotherValue3";

Console.WriteLine("Retreving values from the cache");

object value = cache["key1"];
Console.WriteLine("Got back from cache, key = {0}
    and value- {1} ", "key1", value);
value = cache["key2"];
Console.WriteLine("Got back from cache, key = {0}
    and value- {1} ", "key2", value);
}
```

5. To remove an item from the cache, we can call the `Remove` method on the `DataCache` object by providing a key for the item to be removed:

```
private static void RemoveFromTheCache(DataCache cache)
{
    Console.WriteLine("Removing Items from the cache ");
    cache.Remove("key1");
    Console.WriteLine("Removed key 1");
    cache.Remove("key2");
    Console.WriteLine("Removed key 2");

    Console.WriteLine("Trying to retrieve values again
        to see if remove worked correctly or not.");

    Console.WriteLine("Value for Key1 = {0}",
        cache["key1"] ?? "NULL");
    Console.WriteLine("Value for Key2 = {0}",
        cache["key2"] ?? "NULL");
}
```

 Once the item is removed from the cache, the subsequent get calls for that key will return null.

How it works...

`DataCacheFactory` is responsible for setting up the infrastructure (reading configuration, setting up end points, and so on), whereas `DataCache` is responsible for abstracting distributed the in-memory Caching Service of Windows Server AppFabric. `DataCache` (or Cache Client as it is normally called) provides a means to interact with the cache as if it was running locally on the client.

It is important to understand that under the hood, `DataCacheFactory` creates and returns an instance of `RoutingClient` when `GetCache` is invoked. `DataCache` is an abstract class, whereas `RoutingClient` is an implementation.

 Communication between the Cache Client and the Cache Host is carried out using Windows Communication Foundation (WCF) and uses the net.Tcp binding on default port 22233 as the underlying communication mechanism.

For all the `Get`, `Add`, `Put`, `Remove`, and other calls to the cache, `DataCache` uses an internal mechanism for communicating with cache cluster. It uses a notion of API Execution which abstracts the communication level details. This is done by passing request objects of type `RequestBody` with different request types. Some of the common request types are listed as follows:

```
internal enum ReqType
  {
    ADD,
    PUT,
    GET,
    GET_CACHE_ITEM,
    GET_ALL,
    GET_AND_LOCK,
    GET_NEXT_BATCH,
    GET_IF_NEWER,
//..more enums
```

 `RequestBody` implements `MessageBody` and serves as a `DataContract`. It is worth highlighting that all the communication under-the-hood is based on WCF and the notion of the `DataContract` attribute is applied to the request body.

Using AppFabric Cache via the ASP.NET provider model

Web applications and services are classic candidates for caching when it comes to maintaining application states, for example, keeping session state in-memory. This helps to keep frequently accessed data in memory and thus achieves the aim of overall performance gain. This holds true as long as we are talking about web applications deployed on a single node.

As soon as we start considering distributed architectures where web servers are clustered in a scale-out web farm scenario, things start to get interesting. More specifically for ASP.NET session state caching, when used in a clustered deployment presents a couple of subtle and interesting challenges:

▶ **Sticky sessions**: Ensuring that a particular (returning) client gets routed to a particular server node is critical because that's where the session information is stored for that user

▶ **Performance**: If the data/state is persisted in SQL Server repository (to avoid sticky routing), then we have to account for performance lag (for additional database calls)

Windows Server AppFabric Cache tackles these challenges by offering in-memory distributed object cache so that it can be plugged into ASP.NET as a session state provider. In this recipe, we will cover how to use AppFabric Cache as ASP.NET's session state provider.

> ASP.NET's custom provider model for session state has been implemented in the industry over the years for a number of reasons, including but not limited to a lack of support for other database technologies such as MySQL and Oracle, as well as a wrapper around existing third-party caching products. The Windows Server AppFabric team must be commended for considering it and providing an out of the box session state provider for ASP.NET.

Getting ready

Utilizing Windows Server AppFabric Caching as an ASP.NET session state provider requires a two-step process:

1. Set up configuration (in `web.config`).
2. Grant permission using a PowerShell commandlet.

The beauty of this solution is that, for an existing web application, there is ZERO code change required. This implies that setting up AppFabric caching as an ASP.NET session provider practically becomes an infrastructure level detail and code is abstracted from it.

How to do it...

We will now set up the web configuration by adding details for AppFabric caching and then allow the IIS user to have access to the AppFabric configuration store provider:

1. Open the `web.config` file of an existing web application (or create a new one using Visual Studio's new website template).

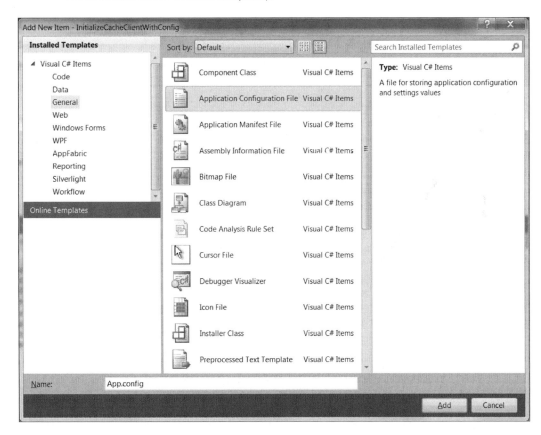

2. Add the following assemblies to the project:
   - `Microsoft.ApplicationServer.Caching.Core.dll`
   - `Microsoft.ApplicationServer.Caching.Client.dll`

3. Add the following configuration entry at the top of your `web.config` file (under the configuration element):

```
<configuration>
  <configSections>
    <section name="dataCacheClient"
        type="Microsoft.ApplicationServer.Caching.
            DataCacheClientSection,
            Microsoft.ApplicationServer.Caching.Core,
            Version=1.0.0.0,
            Culture=neutral, PublicKeyToken=31bf3856ad364e35"
        allowLocation="true"
        allowDefinition="Everywhere"/>
  </configSections>
```

4. Add the following entries in the web configuration file for data cache client configuration:

```
<dataCacheClient>
  <hosts>
    <host
        name="HostNameHere"
        cachePort="22233"/>
  </hosts>
</dataCacheClient>
```

5. Add the following custom session state provider in the `web.config` file:

```
<sessionState mode="Custom" customProvider="AppFabricCacheSessionS
toreProvider">
        <providers>
          <add
            name="AppFabricCacheSessionStoreProvider"
            type="Microsoft.ApplicationServer.Caching.
            DataCacheSessionStoreProvider"
            cacheName="cacheNameHere"
            sharedId="SharedApp"/>
        </providers>
</sessionState>
```

6. Grant permission using `Grant-CacheAllowedClientAccount` to the identity under which your application (app) pool is running:

```
Administrator: powershell.exe  -noexit -command "Import-Module DistributedCacheAdministration;Use-CacheCluster"
PS C:\Windows\system32> grant-cacheAllowedClientAccount |
```

7. The application should now be configured and ready to use. If it was a default ASP. NET website you should be able to browse the home page:

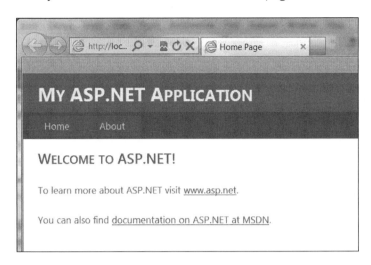

How it works...

ASP.NET's provider model allows AppFabric's cache to be plugged in as a custom session provider. This works seamlessly with existing websites and offers a quick win when it comes to improving the performance of a given web application. High availability scenarios must be considered for mission critical web applications.

Note that the cache name must be a valid cache name defined at the AppFabric cache host stated via the data cache client configuration entry.

 To find out the identity under which your application (app) pool is running, you can go to **IIS Manager** and select **Application Pools** from the left-hand menu under your machine name (as shown in the following screenshot).

Using AppFabric local cache

Along with server side in-memory caching, AppFabric also supports in-process client caching scenarios.

AppFabric local cache works as follows:

- ▸ Local caching is configured on the client
- ▸ Client requests for an object to be returned from a cache (for example, a `Get` call)
- ▸ If the object is available in the local cache then a reference to the object is directly sent to the calling client (without looking up the server cache)
- ▸ If the object is not available in-memory, then it is pulled from the server and it is placed in the local cache as well as returned back to the calling client
- ▸ Any subsequent request to the same object will result in the object being retrieved from the local cache
- ▸ The only exception, where the object will be requested from the server for the second time, is when it is invalidated from the local cache

It must be considered that once the object is placed in the AppFabric's local cache, all the subsequent calls will use this version of the object, regardless of the fact that the original copy of the data might have changed at the server. Although Windows Server AppFabric Local Cache supports the notion of invalidation, it is generally advisable to use local caching for data that changes less frequently.

Some of the common motivations behind using AppFabric Local Caching include the following:

- ▸ **Client-server communication channel latency**: Consider a client-server use case where the service is hosted in America and the clients running the application are based in Asia-Pacific. In such cases, there will always be latency due to the nature of physics involved. Use of local caching will reduce round trips to the server and hence improve performance of the application considerably.

- ▸ **The cost of bandwidth between the client and the server**: For scenarios where bandwidth consumption between the client and server is a concern, it is advisable to make as few data-intensive calls as possible and take advantage of local caching to use local copies of data.

- ▸ **Cost associated with # of calls to the server**: If there is a performance cost associated with the number of calls that are made to the service, it makes sense to use client caching.
- ▸ **Reference data that is mostly static**: If the data in question is mostly static, then it makes sense to place it in local cache and control its lifetime based on the invalidations scheme of your choice.

In this recipe, we will see how to configure AppFabric to set up local caching for Windows Server AppFabric Caching client.

Getting ready

We will use a simple C# console application to enable Windows Server AppFabric Client Cache. We will start with an empty C# console project. We will also need to make sure that Windows Server AppFabric caching services are available and the hosts are up and running.

How to do it...

Windows Server AppFabric offers two options to configure client caching.

The following steps will help with setting up the Windows Server AppFabric local cache programmatically:

1. Create an instance of `DataCacheLocalCacheProperites` by passing it an object count, time out, as well as an enumeration of `DataCacheLocalCacheInvalidationPolicy`. Here's how the constructor should look:

```
DataCacheLocalCacheProperties localCacheProperties = new
        DataCacheLocalCacheProperties(
                1000, //object count
                new TimeSpan(0, 0, 30), // 30 seconds
                DataCacheLocalCacheInvalidationPolicy.TimeoutBased
                );
```

2. Create server end points as shown in the following snippet:

```
var serverEndpoints = new[]
{
    new DataCacheServerEndpoint("yourServerHost", 22233)
};
```

3. Create an instance of `DataCacheFactoryConfiguration` and assign it the values for `DataCacheLocalCacheProperites` as well as `DataCacheServerEndpoint[]`. Your code should look like as follows:

```
DataCacheFactoryConfiguration cacheFactoryConfiguration = new
    DataCacheFactoryConfiguration()
{
    LocalCacheProperties = localCacheProperties,
    Servers = serverEndpoints
};
```

4. Create an instance of `DataCacheFactory` by passing an instance of `DataCacheFactoryConfiguration` and invoke `GetDefaultCache()`.

```
DataCacheFactory cacheFactory = new
    DataCacheFactory(cacheFactoryConfiguration);
DataCache cache = cacheFactory.GetDefaultCache();
```

For configuration (XML) based set up, use the following steps:

1. Open the **App.Config** file and add the following configuration section for Windows Server AppFabric Data Cache Client (make sure that `configSections` is the first entry in the configuration file):

```
<configSections>
  <section name="dataCacheClient"
      type="Microsoft.ApplicationServer.Caching.
          DataCacheClientSection,
          Microsoft.ApplicationServer.Caching.Core,
          Version=1.0.0.0,
          Culture=neutral, PublicKeyToken=31bf3856ad364e35"
      allowLocation="true"
      allowDefinition="Everywhere"/>
</configSections>
```

2. Add the following configuration settings under the `dataCacheClient` section:

```
<dataCacheClient>
    <hosts>
      <host
          name="cacheHost1"
          cachePort="22233"/>
    </hosts>
</dataCacheClient>
```

3. Add the following `localCache` element under the `dataCacheClient` element:

```
<localCache
isEnabled="true"
sync="TimeoutBased"
objectCount="10000"
ttlValue="300" />
```

4. Call `GetCache` on `DataCacheFactory` by passing the name of the cache, for example `CacheHost1`. Your initialization code should look as follows:

```
DataCacheFactory cacheFactory = new DataCacheFactory();
DataCache cache = cacheFactory.GetDefaultCache();
```

How it works...

When local cache is enabled (via configuration or programmatically) Windows Server AppFabric Cache Client stores objects in memory (until the data is invalidated or evicted, based on the selected invalidation mechanism).

The `TimeoutBased` invalidation copy of the object in the local cache is maintained as long as it has not exceeded its timeout limit. Once timeout is reached, the subsequent request for the object will be fetched from the server and the local cache will be refreshed with the latest copy of the object.

 `TimeoutBased` policies should be used with care as too small a timeout will reduce the benefits of local cache (that is, frequent server calls) and too long a value for timeout may cause the client to end up using the stale copy of an object (while it has been changed on the server).

With `NotificationBased` invalidation, Windows Server AppFabric's Client Cache checks with the server for data updates on configurable time intervals (called polling interval and has a default value of 300 seconds). If and when the updates are available on the server, local cache is updated.

 For the `NotificationBased` invalidation policy we will also need to specify the polling interval in a separate element under the `dataCacheClient` configuration section.

```
<clientNotification pollInterval="500" />
```

For multi-threaded applications it must be considered that all the threads will be accessing and modifying the same object reference and that there will be potential issues with object (data) consistency.

Using the AppFabric cache management tool

Windows Server AppFabric's PowerShell commandlets offer an extremely powerful tool to configure and manage AppFabric's caching features. There is a PowerShell commandlet for setting each and every option and configuration option available in Windows Server AppFabric cache.

However, the user experience lacks the interactivity of a modern UI-based management console. This is something that most end users have come to expect from a technology like Windows Server AppFabric.

IIS is Microsoft's dashboard and management console for Windows Server AppFabric, but it does not offer any of the cache management tasks.

This has left room for a developer community to:

▸ Ask Microsoft for a better experience for managing Windows Server AppFabric caching features

▸ Develop their own management console

In this recipe, we will see one developer community effort that has resulted in a very useful tool that helps in managing Windows Server AppFabric's Caching via the streamlined Management Console.

It is worth mentioning that any tool that is built for managing and configuring AppFabric is in fact, under the hood, using AppFabric's PowerShell comandlets. Also, it is not an "either/or" scenario between a fully fledged GUI tool versus PowerShell comandlets. As a matter of fact, both are required to work efficiently while managing Windows Server AppFabric's caching configurations.

Getting ready

The AppFabric Caching Admin tool is available for download at Microsoft's Codeplex via
`http://mdcadmintool.codeplex.com/`. If you have Windows Server AppFabric installed
on your PC, then it is just a matter of downloading binaries from Codeplex and launching the
tool (`MDCAdminTool.exe`) with administrative privileges:

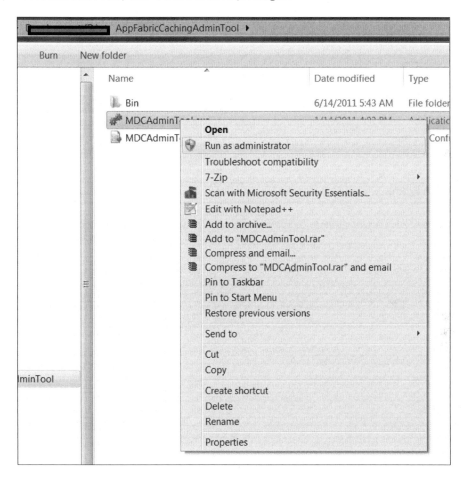

As of now, the AppFabric Caching Admin offers support for the following caching related commands:

Category	Cache command
Cache Cluster Related	Stat Cache Cluster
	Stop Cache Cluster
	Restart Cache Cluster
	Export Config Cache Cluster
	Import Config Cache Cluster
Cache Host Related	Stat Cache Host
	Stop Cache Host
	Statistics
	Get / Set Config
Cache Related	Add Cache Name
	Remove Cache Name
	Statistics
	Get / Set Config
	Add / Remove Region
	Add Data Cache Item for test

The AppFabric Caching Admin also offers some visualizations/reports that provide a useful representation of data available via PowerShell commands. The reports that are available, as of the writing of this book, include the following:

- Cache Host Stats Report
- Cache Name Stats Report
- Cache Host Size by Cache Name Report
- Cache Cluster Size Report

How to do it...

The AppFabric Caching Admin tool is very intuitive and lets you do simple cache related tasks with just the click of a button. We will not go through all the details; instead, we will highlight a couple of useful scenarios and will leave it with the user to explore the tool further:

1. As soon as the AppFabric Cache Admin tool is launched, it executes the `Use-CacheCluster` and `Start-CacheCluster` commands to set the context for the tool.

2. All the PowerShell commandlets are viewable via the PowerShell output window:

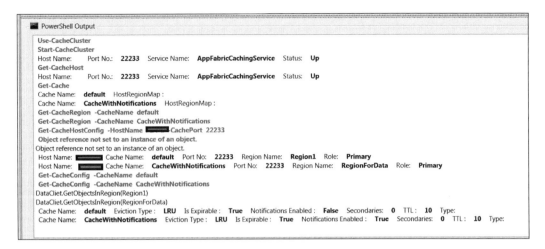

3. You should be able see a nice hierarchical representation of the cluster's cache configuration (as shown in the following screenshot):

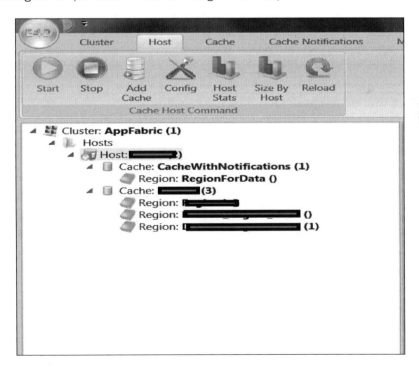

4. To update the cache configuration, double-click on the cache and it will show its configuration on the right-hand side of the application (in a tab).

5. Update the values and click on **Save**. This will trigger the execution of the
   `Set-CacheConfig` command and the changes will be persisted accordingly.

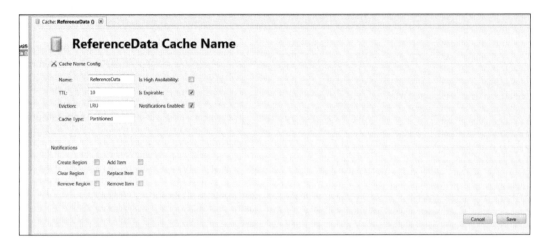

6. To view the statistics, select the desired cache and click on **Cache Stats** from the
   ribbon menu:

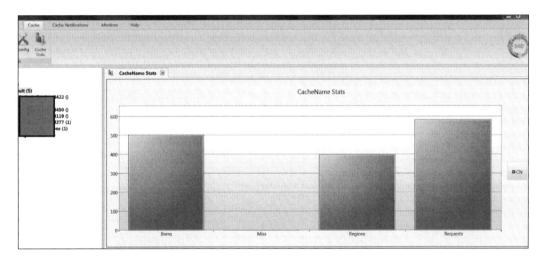

How it works...

The AppFabric Cache Admin Tool runs on top of Windows Server AppFabric's PowerShell
commandlets and provides a streamlined UI experience for executing common day-to-day
tasks for cache management and configuration.

Building a custom provider model

In this recipe we will implement an abstraction on top of Windows Server AppFabric Cache. The idea is to support:

▸ Multiple implementations of a Cache provider

▸ Ability to switch providers via configuration

As Windows Server AppFabric Cache is an external subsystem, it makes sense to have an abstraction around it and have the capability to plug in a suitable implementation at runtime.

Consider a scenario for an ISV (Independent Software Vendor) where their application is built using Windows Server AppFabric Cache. One of their customers does not have Windows Server 2008 so they cannot install Windows Server AppFabric Cache. If ISV was able to implement a provider model such that they could switch Cache implementations via a configuration switch (for example, replacing Windows Server AppFabric Cache with ASP.NET's HttpCache) they would still be able to sell their product to this customer.

Of course, there is a feature cost associated with this type of generalization. For example, ASP.NET's HttpCache may be light-weight, but is no match for Windows Server AppFabric Cache when it comes to feature sets. This is a type of trade-off generally associated with the flexibility of choosing one implementation over the other at runtime.

Getting ready

To begin this recipe we will need to have an instance of Visual Studio running (with administrative privileges). We will also need Windows Server AppFabric's cache cluster to be up and running.

We will also need access to Windows Server AppFabric's cache client libraries (as highlighted in the first recipe of this chapter, *Initializing Cache Client using code*).

Optionally, if you have the latest version of NUnit (available to download from http://www.nunit.org/?p=download#dev) then you will be able to run the test cases to cover the functionality of this recipe.

How to do it...

We will define a custom interface that represents caching operations. In this recipe, we will implement this interface twice. The implementations will be based on Windows Server AppFabric Cache and ASP.NET's HttpCache respectively. These implementations will be further tested via unit tests in this recipe.

> This is a very basic level of abstraction and it probably does not cover real-world requirements. However, this implementation should be sufficient to show how the provider model can be used to implement an abstraction on top of Windows Server AppFabric Cache.

1. Add a new interface called `ICacheProvider` using the following code:

   ```
   public interface ICacheProvider
   {
           object Add(string key, object value);
           object Get(string key);
           object Put(string key, object value);
           bool Delete(string key);
           object this[string key] { get; set; }
   }
   ```

2. Add a new class called `CustomHttpCache` that implements the `ICacheProvider` interface and uses ASP.NET's `HttpCache` internally for caching. The code is shown in the following snippet:

   ```
   public class CustomHttpCache : ICacheProvider
   {
           private readonly Cache cache;
           private readonly TimeSpan minutesToExpire;

           public CustomHttpCache(int minutesToExpire)
           {

               cache = HttpRuntime.Cache;
               this.minutesToExpire =
                   TimeSpan.FromMinutes(minutesToExpire);
           }

           public object Add(string key, object value)
           {
               return cache.Add(key, value, null,
                   DateTime.Now.Add(minutesToExpire), TimeSpan.Zero,
                   CacheItemPriority.Normal, null);
           }
   ```

```
        public object Get(string key)
        {
            return cache.Get(key);
        }

        public object Put(string key, object value)
        {
            cache.Insert(key,value);
            return cache[key];
        }

        public bool Delete(string key)
        {
            return cache.Remove(key) != null;
        }

        public object this[string key]
        {
            get { return cache[key]; }
            set { cache[key] = value; }
        }
    }
```

3. Add another class called `WindowsServerAppFabricCache` that implements the `ICacheProvider` interface and uses Windows Server AppFabric internally for caching. The code is as follows:

```
    public class WindowsServerAppFabricCache : ICacheProvider
    {
        private readonly DataCache dataCache;

        public WindowsServerAppFabricCache(string hostName,
            int portNumber, string cacheName)
        {
            var cacheEndPoints = new[]
            {
                    new DataCacheServerEndpoint(hostName,
                    portNumber)
            };

            var cacheConfiguration = new
                DataCacheFactoryConfiguration { Servers =
                    cacheEndPoints };

            var cacheFactory = new
                DataCacheFactory(cacheConfiguration);
```

```
                dataCache = cacheFactory.GetCache(cacheName);
        }

        public object Add(string key, object value)
        {
            return dataCache.Add(key, value);
        }

        public object Get(string key)
        {
            return dataCache.Get(key);
        }

        public object Put(string key, object value)
        {
            return dataCache.Put(key,value);
        }

        public bool Delete(string key)
        {
            return dataCache.Remove(key);
        }

        public object this[string key]
        {
            get
            {
                return dataCache[key];
            }
            set
            {
                dataCache[key] = value;
            }
        }
    }
```

4. Add an enumeration for cache types, shown as follows:

```
    public enum CacheProviders : byte
    {
        CustomHttpCache = 0,
        WindowsServerAppFabricCache = 1
    }
```

5. Implement a provider factory to abstract the creation of cache implementations, shown as follows:

```
public static class CacheProviderFactory
{
        public static ICacheProvider GetCache(CacheProviders
                                                        cacheProvider)
        {
            if(cacheProvider == CacheProviders.CustomHttpCache)
                return new CustomHttpCache(timeInMinutes);

            return cacheProvider ==
                CacheProviders.WindowsServerAppFabricCache ? new
                WindowsServerAppFabricCache(hostName, portNumber,
                cacheName) : null;
        }

}
```

6. Add the following unit test to check if the cache instance is created successfully by providing the `CacheProvider` enumeration:

```
[Test]
public void ShouldCreateCustomHttpCache()
{
        CacheProvider cacheProvider=
            CacheProviderFactory.GetCache
            (CacheProviders.CustomHttpCache);
        Assert.IsNotNull(cacheProvider);
}
```

7. Add the following unit test to insert and retrieve a value from the cache:

```
[Test]
public void ShouldAddAndGetFromCustomHttpCache()
{
        ICacheProvider cacheProvider=
            CacheProviderFactory.GetCache
            (CacheProviders.CustomHttpCache);
        Assert.IsNotNull(cacheProvider);
        cacheProvider.Add("key", "value");
        var result = cacheProvider.Get("key");
        Assert.IsTrue("value".Equals((string)
            result,StringComparison.OrdinalIgnoreCase));
}
```

8. Add the following test case and assert the successful instantiation of the `WindowsServerAppFabricCache` based cache provider:

```
[Test]
public void ShouldCreateWindowsServerAppFabricCache()
{
    ICacheProvider cache =
        CacheProviderFactory.GetCache
        (CacheProviders.WindowsServerAppFabricCache);
    Assert.IsNotNull(cache);
}
```

9. Add the following test case for `WindowsServerAppFabricCache` and assert that putting and retrieving an item works fine:

```
[Test]
public void ShouldPutAndGetFromCustomHttpCache()
{
    ICacheProvider cacheProvider =
        CacheProviderFactory.GetCache
        (CacheProviders.WindowsServerAppFabricCache);
    Assert.IsNotNull(cacheProvider);
    cacheProvider.Put("key", "value");
    var result = cacheProvider.Get("key");
    Assert.IsTrue("value".Equals((string)
        result,StringComparison.OrdinalIgnoreCase));
}
```

How it works...

By using the `ICacheProvider` interface and `CacheProviderFactory` implementation we have abstracted the client code from the underlying cache provider. The client is free to choose whatever implementation they want without affecting the cache usage throughout the code base.

The factory implementation shown in this recipe is fairly trivial and it can be further improved with the use of an **Inversion of Control** (**IoC**) container that takes care of resolving all the dependencies and creating the cache provider.

 Discussing IoC containers and how to use them to abstract implementation details and the creation of complex object graphs is beyond the scope of this book. But we can very easily simplify and further abstract the cache provider's creation by using an IoC (for example, like Ninject or Microsoft's Unity) container.

Handling common Windows Server AppFabric caching errors

Windows Server AppFabric Cache raises exceptions whenever it encounters errors while executing commands issued by its calling clients. Windows Server AppFabric Cache Exceptions also provide additional details (such as error code, and so on) as part of its exception message. These exception details and error codes are used by calling clients to decide their execution path.

 A system should continue to work even if it encounters problems with its caching subsystem. Apart from getting data directly from the source, caching clients should also be able to handle caching related exceptions gracefully.

Windows Server AppFabric Cache uses `DataCacheException` to raise exceptions. `DataCacheException` exposes `ErrorCode` and `SubStatus` properties that provide additional information about the error.

The `DataCacheException` class looks as follows:

```
[Serializable]
public class DataCacheException : Exception, ISerializable
{
    private int _errorCode = -1;
    private int _substatus = -1;
    private const string _helpLink = "http://go.microsoft.com/
    fwlink/?LinkId=164049";

    public int ErrorCode
    {
        get
        {
            return this._errorCode;
        }
    }

    public int SubStatus
    {
        get
        {
            return this._substatus;
        }
    }
}
```

```
public override string HelpLink
{
    get
    {
        return "http://go.microsoft.com/fwlink/?LinkId=164049";
    }
    set
    {
        throw new InvalidOperationException();
    }
}

public override string Message
{
    get
    {
        StringBuilder stringBuilder = new StringBuilder();
            //logic to build error message goes here..
        return ((object) stringBuilder).ToString();
    }
}

public DataCacheException()
{
}

public DataCacheException(string message)
    : base(message)
{
}

public DataCacheException(string message, Exception
innerException)
    : base(message, innerException)
{
}
// more code
```

The following are three of the most common types of errors encountered by an AppFabric cache client:

- ▶ RetryLater
- ▶ TimeOut
- ▶ ConnectionTerminated

RetryLater

The `RetryLater` error is raised to highlight a temporary failure and the Windows Server AppFabric Cache Client is asked to retry later. There are a number of reasons why this error could be raised. Generally, these reasons are highlighted via the `SubStatus` property. Here are some common examples along with their `DataCacheErrorSubStatus` codes:

Sub status	Common reasons
CacheServerUnavailable	▸ Identity of cache client is not authenticated and authorized on the cache cluster.
	▸ Firewall is not properly configured and it is preventing requests from being routed to the cache cluster.
	▸ Cache host/cluster is down.
Throttled	▸ Windows Server AppFabric Cache hosts are low on memory
NotPrimary	▸ Cache client tries to get data from the cache host that is not primary. This generally happens in High Availability scenarios.
	▸ One of the cache hosts is rebooted; the client may get this error.

TimeOut

The `TimeOut` error is raised when a Windows Server AppFabric Caching Client does not get a response back within its timeout limit while trying to connect to the cache cluster. The `TimeOut` error can be raised for a number of reasons including but not limited to network latency issues, load on server, or smaller `requestTimeOut` settings.

More importantly, with the `TimeOut` error Windows Server AppFabric Cache is trying to tell the caching client that the cache cluster did not respond within the configured timespan.

 The `TimeOut` error does not necessarily mean that the client's request was not processed by the Windows Server AppFabric Cache.

ConnectionTerminated

If the cluster is shutting down or if the network is unavailable, the cache client will receive a `ConnectionTerminated` error.

Getting ready

We will use our sample console application to add some exception handling code.

How to do it...

We will now simulate these errors and then follow up with their resolutions one by one:

1. Launch Caching Administration Windows PowerShell with administrative privileges.

2. Invoke `Stop-CacheCluster`. Ensure that the service status is **DOWN**, as shown in the following screenshot:

```
PS C:\Windows\system32> stop-cachecluster

HostName : CachePort      Service Name              Service Status Version Info
-------------------       ------------              -------------- ------------
                          AppFabricCachingService   DOWN            1 [1.1][1.1]
```

3. Launch Visual Studio with administrative privileges and create an empty C# console application.

4. Add references for Windows Server AppFabric Cache assemblies (as highlighted earlier in the recipe *Initializing Cache Client using code*):

5. Add the following method to the code to initialize the cache.

```
private static DataCache InitializeCache(string cacheName)
{
    var cacheEndPoints = new[]
    {
        new DataCacheServerEndpoint("serverName", 22233)
    };
    var cacheConfiguration = new DataCacheFactoryConfiguration
        { Servers = cacheEndPoints };

    var cacheFactory = new DataCacheFactory(cacheConfiguration);
    var cache = cacheFactory.GetCache(cacheName);

    Debug.Assert(cache != null);

    return cache;
}
```

6. In the `Main` method, invoke the `InitializeCache` method and have exception handling (`try-catch` block) around it as follows:

```
try
{
DataCache cache = InitializeCache("default");
Debug.Assert(cache != null);
}
catch (DataCacheException cacheException)
{
        if (cacheException.SubStatus ==
            DataCacheErrorSubStatus.CacheServerUnavailable)
        {
            Console.Error.WriteLine(
                "Cache Server is unavailable. Exception
                details are = {0}, error code = {1} ",
                cacheException.Message,
                cacheException.ErrorCode);
        }
}
```

7. Run the application.

8. Since the cache cluster is not running the `DataCache` exception with `RetryLater`, an error code will be thrown:

9. A quick console dump of the exception from the application should look as follows:

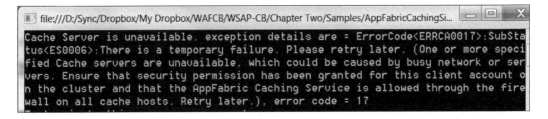

We handcrafted a situation to raise this `DataCacheException` so that we can explore its different properties. In real-world scenarios, there are a number of reasons for a `RetryLater` (`CacheServerUnavailable`) error. This error is most commonly raised due to security related aspects. To resolve this error (assuming it was raised due to security related aspects) we will need to check if the account running the client application has been authorized to access the cache cluster or not.

10. Execute `Get-CacheAllowedClientAccounts`. Windows Server AppFabric's service account should be in the list of authorized accounts that are allowed to the access cache host:

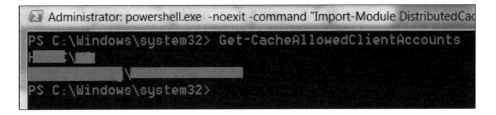

11. Run the application again and see if the problem is resolved.

12. If this doesn't solve the problem, then check if you have specified the correct hostname and port number (in configuration or programmatically) while initializing the `DataCache` client object.

13. If host names are valid and this still doesn't solve the problem, then we will need to do server level troubleshooting to identify the health and availability of hosts in the cache cluster. We will cover this in *Chapter 6, Utilizing AppFabric Persistence* in more detail.

14. If you get an exception that has `SubStatus == DataCacheErrorSubStatus.` `Throttled` then make sure the eviction policies are set up appropriately so that enough memory is available for caching. (More detail on setting up eviction policies is provided in the next chapter.)

15. If you still get the `DataCacheErrorSubStatus.Throttled` error, then check if the items in the cache are locked. Locking can cause throttled errors as well, as the locked items are always in memory regardless of their expiry status.

> When Windows Server AppFabric Cache runs out of available physical memory it raises this throttled error. There are more details on throttling in the next chapter under the *Troubleshooting throttling* recipe.

16. Instead if you are getting `cacheException.SubStatus == DataCacheErrorSubStatus.NotPrimary`, then you need to check whether cache hosts are available and that they are not going through the reconfiguration scenario in High Availability configuration.

> We will discuss High Availability configuration later on in the book (covered in full detail in *Chapter 8, Scaling AppFabric Hosting, Monitoring, and Persistence*); for now, consider that if the primary cache host goes down, Windows Server AppFabric will reconfigure the secondary host to take the primary role. If a cache client tries to connect while configuration is in progress it may temporarily receive this error.
>
> The best way to implement a work around for a `Retry` (and perhaps `ConnectionTerminated` as well as `TimeOut`) error is to use a notion of "retry" to your cache client code such that your code retries "n" number of times by waiting "x" unit of time between each retry before giving up and raising an exception, such that x and n should be configurable. Unfortunately, C# does not provide any out of the box implementation of this use case as a language construct, but that should not stop you from implementing your own.

How it works...

At the API level, all of the `DataCacheException` instances are based on a response received from the cache cluster. This response is implemented as a class called `ResponseBody`. `ResponseBody` is a WCF based `DataContract` implementation. The following is a brief snapshot of `ResponseBody` implementation:

```
[DataContract(Name = "ResponseBody", Namespace = "http://schemas.
microsoft.com/velocity/namespace")]
    internal class ResponseBody : MessageBody
    {
        [DataMember]
        public AckNack Ack;
        [DataMember]
        public ErrStatus ResponseCode;
// more properties...
```

`AckNack` is an enumeration which, as the name implies, tells us whether the server has acknowledged the request:

```
internal enum AckNack
{
    Ack,
    Nack,
    Pending,
}
```

It is the `Nack` enum value along with the `ErrorCode` enumeration that causes the `DataCache` client to raise an exception. Here is what the code that is responsible for throwing the exception looks like:

```
switch (respBody.ResponseCode)
{
        case ErrStatus.INTERNAL_ERROR:
        case ErrStatus.REPLICATION_FAILED:
        case ErrStatus.REGIONID_NOT_FOUND:
          errCode = 17;
          break;
        case ErrStatus.NO_WRITE_QUORUM:
          substatus = 2;
          errCode = 17;
          break;
        case ErrStatus.TIMEOUT:
          errCode = 18;
          break;
        case ErrStatus.SERVER_DEAD:
          substatus = 5;
          errCode = 17;
          break;
        case ErrStatus.REPLICATION_QUEUE_FULL:
          substatus = 3;
          errCode = 17;
          break;
        case ErrStatus.KEY_LATCHED:
          substatus = 4;
          errCode = 17;
          break;
        case ErrStatus.NOT_PRIMARY:
          substatus = 1;
          errCode = 17;
          break;
        case ErrStatus.CONNECTION_TERMINATED:
```

```
            errCode = 16;
            break;
        case ErrStatus.THROTTLED:
            substatus = 6;
            errCode = 17;
            break;
    // more codes..
```

There's more...

In this recipe, we saw some of the most common errors that a Windows Server AppFabric Cache Client can come across. All of these errors are well documented and once you develop an understanding of these codes you can program defensively against them.

Here is a short list of some other common error codes worth looking at:

ErrorCode	ErrorCode String	SubStatus	SubStatus String
RetryLater	ERRCA0017	CacheServerUnavailable	ES0006
RetryLater	ERRCA0017	Throttled	ES0007
RetryLater	ERRCA0017	NotPrimary	ES0002
RetryLater	ERRCA0017	NoWriteQuorum	ES0003
Timeout	ERRCA0018	None	ES0001
ConnectionTerminated	ERRCA0016	None	ES0001

3
Windows Server AppFabric Caching – Advanced Use Cases

In this chapter, we will cover:

- ▶ Using regions in cache
- ▶ Using tags in cache
- ▶ Using optimistic concurrency
- ▶ Using pessimistic concurrency
- ▶ Setting up expiration
- ▶ Setting up eviction
- ▶ Setting up notifications
- ▶ Using performance counters
- ▶ Troubleshooting throttling
- ▶ Troubleshooting eviction
- ▶ Setting up read through – write behind

Introduction

In the previous chapter, we went through some of the most common caching related scenarios for Windows Server AppFabric Cache. In this chapter, we will continue working with Windows Server AppFabric Cache. But, this time we will drill down to some of the more advanced use cases.

Windows Server AppFabric Cache is feature rich and enables advanced use cases that empower development of smart applications and services. For example, Tags and Regions features allow different levels of logical and physical grouping of cached data. Optimistic and Pessimistic Concurrency allows developers to pick and choose relevant concurrency mechanisms. Windows Server AppFabric also provides means of controlling the lifecycle of cache items through its Expiration and Eviction mechanisms. In this chapter, we will cover all of these exciting features.

This chapter also includes a recipe covering Windows Server AppFabric v1.1's new and exciting feature that allows a Read-Through and Write Behind Caching Model. Last but not least, towards the end we will also see how to troubleshoot when things go wrong with your Windows Server AppFabric Cache deployments.

Using regions in cache

Windows Server AppFabric, for the most part, manages the logical and physical distribution of data implicitly. It controls where the cache item is stored when added for the first time. It also manages how to move data around different hosts (within the cluster—based on cache configuration) throughout its lifecycle. Most of the time we would want to leave cache item management (especially in terms of where data is being placed and how it is grouped together) with Windows Server AppFabric.

However, there are times when developing real-world applications that we would like to control the organization of a set of cache items. One of the most common use cases that requires the control of cache item grouping is when we have a logical collection of data and we may not know the keys of cache items at runtime.

Windows Server AppFabric allows logical (and to an extent physical) organization of data via **named regions**. By using named regions we can tell Windows Server AppFabric Cache to store all the items together so that we can query them (without even knowing the individual cache item keys).

When data is added to the Windows Server AppFabric Cache, it distributes the payload across all the available nodes in the cluster. This is done transparently to the user and the calling client does not know where the data is stored. However, with named regions, Windows Server AppFabric does not distribute the portions of data across multiple hosts available in a cache cluster. Instead, cache items in a named region are all bundled together and placed on a single cache host.

In this recipe, we will see how to program for named regions in Windows Server AppFabric.

Getting ready

We will need to launch Visual Studio 2010 with administrative privileges, create a new C# console application, and add a reference to Windows Server AppFabric assemblies.

You will need to have a valid instance of the `DataCache` class (which can easily be created using either configuration or code as described in the first two recipes of *Chapter 2, Getting Started with AppFabric Caching*) available to work on the following recipe.

Last but not least, the cache cluster should be up and running.

How to do it...

We will simply create a new named cache region first and then we will add and retrieve items from the region using an instance of the `DataCache` class:

1. To create a named region, invoke the `CreateRegion` method on an instance of the `DataCache` class by passing the region name:

    ```
    public static void CreateRegion(DataCache cache, string
    regionName)
    {
        cache.CreateRegion(regionName);
    }
    ```

 The `DataCache` client throws an `ArgumentNullException` if the `regionName` is passed as null. The `DataCache` client also throws an `ArgumentException` when an empty string is passed as a `regionName`.

2. Create a `static` method called `AddItemsToTheRegion`, as shown in the following code. Note that we are adding currency names along with their symbols to a named region.

```
private static void AddItemsToTheRegion(DataCache cache, string
regionName)
{
    cache.Add("USD", "$",regionName);
    cache.Add("GBP", "£", regionName);
    cache.Add("JPY", "¥", regionName);
}
```

 The preceding currency example is used to show the Windows Server AppFabric Cache API usage. In a real world scenario, understandably, similar implementations will never be hard coded.

3. To query all the objects (cache items) within a region, invoke the `GetObjectsByRegion` method on an instance of `DataCache`. The following code shows that `GetObjectsByRegion` returns an `IEnumerable<KeyValuePair<string, object>>`, which can be iterated over to get the key-value pairs.

```
foreach (var cacheItem in cache.GetObjectsInRegion(regionName))
{
    Console.WriteLine("Key={0} -- Value ={1}",
        cacheItem.Key,cacheItem.Value);
}
```

4. For cache items within regions, instead of using the `Get` method, invoke the `GetCacheItem` method. The `GetCacheItem` method returns an instance on the `DataCacheItem`. `DataCacheItem` has a number of additional properties. This is shown in the following `PrintCacheItem` method:

```
private static void PrintDataCacheItems(DataCache cache, string
regionName)
{
    PrintCacheItem(cache.GetCacheItem("USD",regionName));
    PrintCacheItem(cache.GetCacheItem("GBP", regionName));
    PrintCacheItem(cache.GetCacheItem("JPY", regionName));
}

private static void PrintCacheItem(DataCacheItemcacheItem
cacheItem)
{
    Console.WriteLine("Key={0}, Value={1}, Version={2},
    RegionName = {3}, TimeOut = {4}", cacheItem.Key,
    cacheItem.Value, cacheItem.Version,
    cacheItem.RegionName, cacheItem.Timeout);
```

`DataCacheItem` has a number of additional properties available, along with the cache item value. Some of the most important properties apart from `Key – Value`, include `Tags`, `Version`, `RegionName`, `CacheName`, `TimeOut` values. The `Value` is the representation of the cache item (as you would have retrieved it via the `Get` method). We will learn more about version, tags, and timeouts later in this chapter under recipes titled *Using tags in cache* and *Setting up eviction*.

5. To clear the cache items from the cache's named region, invoke a method called `ClearRegion` on `DataCache`:

```
cache.ClearRegion(regionName);
```

How it works...

Windows Server AppFabric regions are stored locally on the cache host. These regions are different from a **Named Cache**, in the sense that the cache is distributed across the cluster, whereas a region is stored locally on the host.

Regions are stored locally on the cache and are lost if the host goes down. The only exception is when Windows Server AppFabric is configured in High Availability (HA) mode. We will discuss HA in more details in *Chapter 8, Scaling AppFabric Hosting, Monitoring, and Persistence*.

The following logical architecture diagram shows how named cache (or just Cache), default cache, and regions are distributed in a Windows Server AppFabric cluster. We can see that **Region1**, **Region2**, and **Region3** are stored locally on cache hosts, whereas the named caches, **namedCache** and **defaultCache**, are distributed across the Windows Server AppFabric Cache Cluster.

Named cache, also referred to as cache, is a unit of storage that is distributed across the Windows Server AppFabric Cache Cluster.

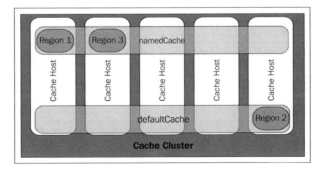

Windows Server AppFabric uses two types of regions:

- ▸ System regions
- ▸ Named regions

System regions are used by Windows Server AppFabric implicitly to distribute data across different hosts in the cluster. These regions have names starting with `Default_Region`. System regions are transparent to the end user, and client applications do not have to concern themselves with these regions at all. In fact, system regions are not available for general access. Windows Server AppFabric raises an `ArgumentException` when a system region name is passed to access a cache item. The following code shows how this validation is carried out internally by the `DataCache` client:

```
if (region != null && RegionNameProvider.IsSystemRegion(region))
        throw new ArgumentException(GlobalResour
ceLoader.GetString(CultureInfo.CurrentUICulture,
"NotPermittedForDefaultRegion"), "region");
```

 `IsSystemRegion` is a helper method in the `RegionProvider` class in the `Microsoft.ApplicationServer.Caching` namespace.

`IsSystemRegion` checks if the passed region name starts with `Default_Region_`, as shown in the following code:

```
internal static boolIsSystemRegion(string regionName)
{
    return regionName.StartsWith("Default_Region_",
    StringComparison.Ordinal);
}
```

Named regions are defined and populated with data explicitly.

There's more...

To get a system region name for any given cache item, use `GetSystemRegionName`:

```
public string GetSystemRegionName(string key)
```

To get all the available system regions, invoke `GetSystemRegions`:

```
public IEnumerable<string> GetSystemRegions()
```

Using tags in cache

We saw in the previous recipe that regions in Windows Server AppFabric cache offer a mechanism for organizing a set of objects on a particular cache host. Tags add another layer of association on top of regions.

In a nutshell, tags are (one or more) strings associated with a cache item. At the API level, tags can only be associated with cache items in a particular region. This implies that tags are only used on cache items that are explicitly stored in a region. The following diagram shows how tags are associated with cache items within a named region:

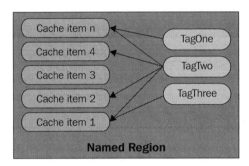

In this recipe, we will see how to associate tags with cached items as well as how to retrieve cached items based on tags.

Getting ready

The requirements for getting started with this recipe are exactly the same as those of the previous recipe titled *Using regions in cache*. You will need to do the following:

1. Launch Visual Studio 2010 (using administrative privileges).
2. Create an empty C# console project.
3. Add references to Windows Server AppFabric binaries.
4. Ensure Windows Server AppFabric Cache is up and running.

How to do it...

We will add and retrieve items associated with `DataCacheTag` to the region:

1. To associate `DataCacheTag` to a cache item being added to the cache, create an instance of `IEnumerable<DataCacheTag>`. For example, continuing with our currency based example, we will define a `DataCacheTag` with the value = `Exotic`:

    ```
    var tags = new List<DataCacheTag>
    {
        newDataCacheTag("Exotic")
    };
    ```

     It should be noted that most of the methods that deal with `DataCacheTag` work on the collection of `DataCacheTag` that is `IEnumerable<DataCacheTag>`. This implies the one-to-many relationship between a cache item and the associated tags such that a cache item can have multiple tags associated to it.

2. Add two more items to the cache by using an overload of `Add` method that accepts the `IEnumerable<DataCacheTag>` and `region` as shown below:

    ```
    cache.Add("ARS", "$",tags, regionName);
    ```

3. Add a couple more items using the same tags and region name:

    ```
    cache.Add("IDR", "Rp", tags, regionName);
    cache.Add("MYR", "RM", tags, regionName);
    ```

4. Retrieve the newly added items using `GetObjectsByAllTags`. This method returns a list of cache items (that match all the provided tags) as `IEnumerable<KeyValuePair<string, object>>`:

    ```
    foreach (var cache Item in cache.GetObjectsByAllTags(tags,
    regionName))
    {
        Console.WriteLine("Key={0} -- Value ={1}",
        cacheItem.Key, cacheItem.Value);
    }
    ```

How it works...

Tagging should be thought of as a means of attaching additional metadata so that it can be used to retrieve objects based on this association.

A closer look at the `DataCacheTag` class's definition reveals that it is mostly an abstraction on top of a string value:

```
[DataContract(Name="DataCacheTag", Namespace="http://schemas.
microsoft.com/velocity/namespace")]
public class DataCacheTag
{
    public DataCacheTag(string tag);
    public override bool Equals(object obj);
    public override int GetHashCode();
    public override string ToString();
//more code here
}
```

This abstraction via the `DataCacheTag` class allows Microsoft to provide additional means of tagging cache items for future releases of Windows Server AppFabric.

Windows Server AppFabric internally uses a `GetByTagsOperation` enumeration to identify a strategy for retrieving cache items based on tags. The `GetObjectsByAllTags` method uses `GetByTagsOperation.ByIntersection`, whereas the `GetObjectsByAnyTag` method uses `GetByTagsOperation.ByUnion` and `GetObjectByTag` uses `GetByTagsOperation.ByNone`.

Using optimistic concurrency

Windows Server AppFabric allows cache clients (as long as they are authorized) to access and modify the cache concurrently. Concurrent cache read-access works just fine and the cache cluster (scale-out) generally helps with demands on the scalability. However, the real challenge is to handle concurrent writes to the cache.

To understand concurrency issues, consider a scenario where we have two cache clients, let's call them client A and client B. Let us assume that client A and client B both have copies of the same data (retrieved against the same key from Windows Server AppFabric Cache). Imagine that client A updates the data in the cache. Now what would happen if client B tried to update the same data in the cache? Should client B override the value in the cache? Or should an exception be raised?

Windows Server AppFabric caching supports two modes to handle concurrency scenarios, namely **Optimistic Concurrency** and **Pessimistic Concurrency**. In this recipe, we will learn to program the Windows Server AppFabric cache for optimistic concurrency.

Getting ready

We will need the AppFabric cache to be available as well as a C# console application with the necessary AppFabric assemblies added to its reference.

How to do it...

We will need to initialize the cache (from configuration or programmatically) first. Then we will create two instances of the `DataCache` class to simulate the concurrency scenario we described at the beginning of this recipe.

1. Create two instances of the `DataCache` class and name them `cacheA` and `cacheB` respectively:

   ```
   var cacheA = InitializeCache("default");
   var cacheB = InitializeCache("default");
   ```

    Note that we are using our own custom utility method to create an instance of `DataCache` class.

2. Define the following variables as follows:

   ```
   var key = "key";
   var value = "value";
   var value2 = "value2";
   ```

3. Add items to `cacheA` as follows:

   ```
   if(cacheA.GetCacheItem(key) == null)
           cacheA.Add(key, value);
   ```

4. Get the cache items (for the key defined above) from `cacheA` and `cacheB` and store them in two separate instances of the `DataCacheItem` class called `cacheItemFromCacheA` and `CacheItemFromCacheB`:

   ```
   var cacheItemFromCacheA  = cacheA.GetCacheItem(key);

   Console.WriteLine("Get item for the cache instance.
   cacheInstance={0}, key={1}, value={2} and version ={3}", "cacheA",
   cacheItemFromCacheA.Key,
   cacheItemFromCacheA.Value,
   cacheItemFromCacheA.Version);

   var cacheItemFromCacheB  = cacheB.GetCacheItem(key);
   ```

```
Console.WriteLine("Get item for the cache instance.
cacheInstance={0}, key={1}, value={2} and version ={3}", "cacheB",
cacheItemFromCacheB.Key,
cacheItemFromCacheB.Value,
cacheItemFromCacheB.Version);
```

5. Update the cache item (using `cacheA`) with a new value using the previously retrieved `cacheItemFromCacheAversion` and `key`.

```
cacheA.Put(cacheItemFromCacheA.Key, value2, cacheItemFromCacheA.
Version);
```

 Note the use of `Put` overload that takes the `key`, `value`, and `DataCacheItemVersion` number for updating data cache items.

6. It should be noted that the cache item has been updated by `cacheA` via its previous `Put` call. As Windows Server AppFabric Cache updates the cache item's version number after each update this leaves `cacheB` with an older version of the cache item.

7. Now, if `cacheB` tries to update the same cache item, it will get an exception:

```
cacheB.Put(cacheItemFromCacheB.Key, value2, cacheItemFromCacheB.
Version);
```

 Windows Server AppFabric will raise an exception complaining about version number mismatch with the following error message:

```
ErrorCode<ERRCA0001>:SubStatus<ES0001>:Client
referring to the object has an older version of
the object. Latest version of the objects should
be fetched for this client operation.
```

How it works...

In optimistic concurrency implementations, there are no locks on the cache items as opposed to pessimistic concurrency, which is based on a locking mechanism.

Every time an object in the cache is updated, the Windows Server AppFabric cache will increase its version number. These version numbers act as a mechanism for providing optimistic concurrency checks. If and when the cache item being updated has a version number smaller than that in the cache, the Windows Server AppFabric cache will raise an exception.

In the next recipe, we will see how to implement pessimistic concurrency in the Windows Server AppFabric cache.

There's more...

For more details on the API that supports optimistic concurrency in Windows Server AppFabric caching, visit: `http://msdn.microsoft.com/en-us/library/ee790915.aspx`.

Using pessimistic concurrency

Windows Server AppFabric caching supports the notion of pessimistic concurrency implementation by placing locks on the cache items that are expected to be within the scope of subsequent updates by more than one possible caching client. This is in total contrast to optimistic concurrency, where there are no locks and each cache client is allowed to modify the cache item. Of course, this is only as long as there is no cache item version number mismatch.

The following are three key API calls available on `DataCache` that support pessimistic concurrency (via locks):

- `GetAndLock`
- `PutAndLock`
- `UnLock`

When the lock is acquired, it returns a (lock) handle to the cache client. For example, for `GetAndLock` calls, once a particular cache client has a lock handle, no other cache client will be able to invoke a `GetAndLock` call (for as long as the lock is valid and alive–there is a timeout associated with each lock and we will discuss this later in the recipe).

It should be noted that regular `Get` (that is without the lock) will always succeed as these calls are not blocking a Windows Server AppFabric cache. However, it gets more interesting when a regular `Put` call is invoked on a cache item that has a valid lock handle against it. It may come as a surprise, but locked objects can still be updated via a `Put` call.

 A Windows Server AppFabric cache expects the client to use locks via `PutAndLock` consistently when using pessimistic concurrency.

In this recipe, we will learn how to implement pessimistic concurrency in the Windows Server AppFabric cache.

Getting ready

We will need the AppFabric cache to be up and running as well as a C# console application with the required AppFabric assemblies added to its reference.

How to do it...

We will need to initialize the cache (from configuration or programmatically) first. Then we will create two instances of the `DataCache` class to simulate the pessimistic concurrency scenario.

1. Repeat steps 1 to 3 from the *Using optimistic concurrency* recipe. This will initialize two instances of `DataCache`, definitions of key value pairs, as well as add an item to the cache based on the key-value pair definition.

2. Declare an instance of `DataCacheLockHandle` and initialize it with a null value:

   ```
   DataCacheLockHandle lockHandleA = null;
   ```

3. Invoke the `GetAndLock` method on the `cacheA` instance as shown below:

   ```
   cacheA.GetAndLock(key, TimeSpan.FromSeconds(30), out lockHandleA);
   ```

    Notice the usage of `TimeSpan` in the `GetAndLock` call. Both `GetAndLock` and `PutAndLock` use the notion of timeouts based on the provided instance of a `TimeSpan` class. This ensures that the lock is removed (based on the configured timeout) even when the cache client does not explicitly remove it (via `Unlock`).

4. Invoke a `Get` method on the `cacheB` to retrieve and print the value of the cache item (that was locked in the previous step) as shown below:

   ```
   Console.WriteLine("Getting a cache item after the GetLock has been
   placed on it. Cache key={0}, value={1} ",
   key, cacheA.Get(key));
   ```

5. Subsequent `GetAndLock` will not succeed on the same cache item and it will raise an exception. So the following code will fail with the following error message: "`Err orCode<ERRCA0011>:SubStatus<ES0001>:Object being referred to is currently locked, and cannot be accessed until it is unlocked by the locking client. Please retry later.`"

   ```
   DataCacheLockHandle lockHandleB = null;
   cacheB.GetAndLock(key, TimeSpan.FromSeconds(30), out lockHandleB);
   ```

6. To update the value of the locked cache item, invoke `PutAndUnlock` on cacheA by passing in the same handle that was set up using the initial `GetAndLock` call:

   ```
   cacheA.PutAndUnlock(key, value2, lockHandleA);
   ```

How it works...

The pessimistic concurrency mode of the Windows Server AppFabric cache uses locks. Locks are implemented as the `DataCacheLockHandle` class.

```
[DataContract(Name = "DataCacheLockHandle", Namespace = "http://
schemas.microsoft.com/velocity/namespace")]
public class DataCacheLockHandle
{
    [DataMember]
    private DMLockHandle _handle;
    [DataMember]
    private InternalCacheItemVersion _version;
```

For each lock acquired, there is a timeout value associated with it. This is very useful for avoiding (or minimizing the span of) deadlock situations. Using this timeout, Windows Server AppFabric removes the lock on cache items implicitly.

As long as there is a lock on the cache item, it will never be evicted.

Transaction spanning operations are not supported in Windows Server AppFabric cache.

Setting up expiration

Cache items do not remain in the Windows Server AppFabric cache indefinitely. Either they are taken out from the cache explicitly (by invoking the `Remove` method) or they are removed implicitly via expiration or eviction.

Simply put, expiration allows you to control the lifespan of cache items in the cache. By setting up cache expiration values, we tell Windows Server AppFabric cache to remove the cache item from the cache as soon as its lifespan is completed.

It should be noted that cache items that have a lock handle active on them are not removed from the cache by Windows Server AppFabric. Cache items remain in the Windows Server AppFabric cache for as long as the lock handle is valid. However, cache items are removed from the Windows Server AppFabric cache as soon as the lock handle expires.

We have already seen how to explicitly remove cache items from the cache in *Chapter 2, Getting Started with AppFabric Caching*. In this recipe, we will focus on setting up an expiration of cache items. We will look at some of the code examples based on the API offered by `DataCache` clients that support expiration.

Windows Server AppFabric allows the setting up of timeout values for each cache item individually. This allows finer control over the item lifecycle so that a program can decide to keep some items for a longer time span in the cache.

The following is a list of methods available on the `DataCache` client that allow a timeout value to be passed for cache item expiration:

- `public DataCacheItemVersion Add(string key, object value, TimeSpan timeout, string region)`

- `public DataCacheItemVersion Add(string key, object value, TimeSpan timeout)`

- `public DataCacheItemVersion Add(string key, object value, TimeSpan timeout, IEnumerable<DataCacheTag> tags)`

- `public DataCacheItemVersion Add(string key, object value, TimeSpan timeout, IEnumerable<DataCacheTag> tags, string region)`

- `public DataCacheItemVersion Put(string key, object value, TimeSpan timeout)`

- `public DataCacheItemVersion Put(string key, object value, DataCacheItemVersion oldVersion, TimeSpan timeout)`

- `public DataCacheItemVersion Put(string key, object value, TimeSpan timeout, string region)`

- `public DataCacheItemVersion Put(string key, object value, TimeSpan timeout, IEnumerable<DataCacheTag> tags)`

- `public DataCacheItemVersion Put(string key, object value, DataCacheItemVersion oldVersion, TimeSpan timeout, string region)`

- `public DataCacheItemVersion Put(string key, object value, DataCacheItemVersion oldVersion, TimeSpan timeout, IEnumerable<DataCacheTag> tags)`

- `public DataCacheItemVersion Put(string key, object value, TimeSpan timeout, IEnumerable<DataCacheTag> tags, string region)`

- `public DataCacheItemVersion Put(string key, object value, DataCacheItemVersion oldVersion, TimeSpan timeout, IEnumerable<DataCacheTag> tags, string region)`

Expiration is also relevant for the local caching scenario. We have already seen how `Timeout` based invalidation is set up for Windows Server AppFabric's local caching in our recipe titled Using *AppFabric local cache* in *Chapter 2, Getting Started with AppFabric Caching*. Windows Server AppFabric's local client cache is different from a server-based cache when it comes to setting up expirations. The difference is mostly because of the granularity with which timeout values can be specified. In the local cache, Windows Server AppFabric only allows you to set up a timeout value for the entire local cache. However, for server-side caching it allows you to set up a timeout individually for each item that is being placed in the cache.

Getting ready

We will need the AppFabric cache to be up and running as well as a C# console application with the required AppFabric assemblies added to its reference.

How to do it...

We will add a cache item with a small timeout value. We will then retrieve a cache item after its timeout has elapsed.

1. Define a key-value pair to be used for the timeout example:

   ```
   var key = "keyForTimeOut";
   var value = "valueForTimeOut";
   ```

2. Use an overload for the `Add` method on the `DataCache` client with `TimeSpan` as a parameter on an instance of the `DataCache` class. Pass the `key`, `value`, `timespan`, as well as `region` to the `Add` method as shown in the following code:

   ```
   cache.Add(key, value, TimeSpan.FromSeconds(2),regionName);
   ```

    It should be noted that for a real-world application/service, the `TimeSpan` value should be read from a configuration.

3. Sleep for 10 seconds (that is longer than cache item's timeout value):

   ```
   SleepFor(TimeSpan.FromSeconds(10));
   ```

    `SleepFor` is a utility method that is available with the code samples for this book.

4. Invoke a `Get` on the instance of the `DataCache` class and assert that the value is `null` to validate that cache item is not available in the Windows Server AppFabric cache:

   ```
   Debug.Assert(cache.Get(key) == null);
   ```

How it works...

These four steps show that it is easy to attach a timeout to the cache item. It also validates that once the cache item has timed out, it is no longer available to the cache client.

Windows Server AppFabric passes the timeout value (along with other cache item related information) to the cache host via its `internal` method called `ExecuteAPI`.

`ExecuteAPI` takes in an object of type `RequestBody`. Some of the key attributes of `RequestBody` are shown as follows:

```
[DataContract(Name = "RequestBody", Namespace = "http://schemas.
microsoft.com/velocity/namespace")]
internal class RequestBody : MessageBody
{

    [DataMember]
    public InternalCacheItemVersion Version = new
    InternalCacheItemVersion();
    [DataMember]
    public TimeSpan TTL = TimeSpan.Zero;
    [DataMember]
    private DMLockHandle _DMLockHandle = new DMLockHandle();
    [DataMember]
    publicReqTypeReq;
    [DataMember]
    public string CacheName;
    [DataMember]
    public string RegionName;
    [DataMember]
    public Microsoft.ApplicationServer.Caching.Key Key;
    [DataMember]
    publicInternalCacheItemVersionEventVersion;
    // More code
```

The `TimeSpan` attribute of `RequestBody` gets initialized with the time span that is provided by the cache client. Otherwise it is defaulted to `TimeSpan.Zero`. Internally, Windows Server AppFabric cache uses this timeout value to manage the lifecycle of cache items.

 Similar logic applies to the Windows Server AppFabric's local cache client. It looks up the internal object cache and if the object has not outlived its time span, (or if there is no cache update notification on it) then it is served locally.

Another implicit mechanism for taking cache items off from the Windows Server AppFabric cache is based on the notion of eviction.

 If the timeout value is not provided via `DataCache` client overload methods, then the default timeout value from configuration is used.

There's more...

There are two additional methods available on the `DataCache` class that can be invoked to extend the lifetime of a cache item:

- `public void ResetObjectTimeout(string key, TimeSpannewTimeout, string region)`
- `public void ResetObjectTimeout(string key, TimeSpannewTimeout)`

 Both of these methods validate provided timespan and key. If the `TimeSpan` is`<= 0` or the `key` is invalid (that is not available in the cache) then an `ArgumentException` is thrown.

Setting up eviction

Windows Server AppFabric uses expiration and eviction to maintain the size of its cache and available memory on each cache host.

Eviction is usually dependent upon two levels of thresholds called Watermarks. When the memory usage of cache on a particular host reaches its Low Watermark (LWM) then the expired cache items are taken off from the cache. However, when the memory usage of the cache reaches High Watermark (HWM) then cache items are evicted based on LRU, regardless of their expiry status.

 The Windows Server AppFabric cache's eviction is based on a Least Recently Used, or LRU, policy.

This eviction continues until cache usage goes under the lower watermark levels. When cache usage is above watermark levels, subsequent caching requests are routed to other hosts in the cache cluster.

Eviction will also occur when the amount of available physical memory on the Windows Server AppFabric cache host is critically low.

 Eviction should not be treated as a problem or an issue; it is just a symptom. Eviction could be triggered by other aspects such as system configuration, memory load on the host server, or the application configuration for the Windows Server AppFabric cache.

The Windows Server AppFabric cache host enters into a throttling state if the amount of available physical memory gets too low. We will discuss throttling and how to solve it later in this chapter.

Getting ready

We will use the same C# console application that we used in the previous recipe.

How to do it...

Eviction is enabled by default on the Windows Server AppFabric cache host. To create a new cache without eviction, we will need to use a `New-Cache` command with `-eviction = None`:

1. Launch **Caching Administration Windows PowerShell** with administrative privileges.

2. Invoke `Use-CacheCluster` and `Start-CacheCluster` to set the context right and ensure that cache cluster is up and running.

3. Invoke a `New-Cache` command as shown below:

   ```
   PS C:\Windows\system32> New-Cache -cacheName cacheForEvictionTest
   -Eviction None
   ```

4. Invoke `Get-CacheConfig` command to check if the eviction is set to LRU or none:

   ```
   PS C:\Windows\system32> Get-CacheConfig cacheForEvictionTest
   ```

5. This should result in a configuration as shown below (with **EvictionType** set to **None**):

   ```
   CacheName            : cacheForEvictionTest
   TimeToLive           : 10 mins
   CacheType            : Partitioned
   Secondaries          : 0
   IsExpirable          : True
   EvictionType         : None
   NotificationsEnabled : False
   ```

Switching off eviction implies that Windows Server AppFabric will no longer remove the cache items from the cache. In the face of increasing memory pressure this will lead to *OutOfMemory* exceptions.

6. To switch eviction back on to LRU, simply execute `Remove-Cache` and `New-Cache` by passing the same cache name as shown below:

```
PS C:\Windows\system32> Remove-Cache cacheForEvictionTest
PS C:\Windows\system32> New-Cache cacheForEvictionTest
```

How it works...

Eviction at the cache host in Windows Server AppFabric is based on watermarks. LWM forces eviction of expired cache items. LWM should not have an impact on application performance as it only evicts the cache items that are already expired.

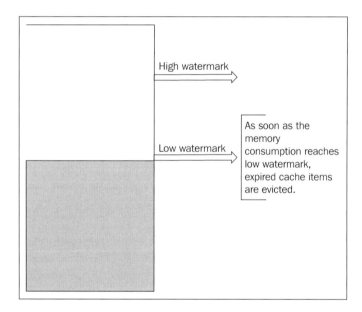

High watermark makes use of the LRU strategy to remove cache items. Once a high watermark is reached, the Windows Server AppFabric cache starts removing cache items from the cache so that memory is available for subsequent caching requests.

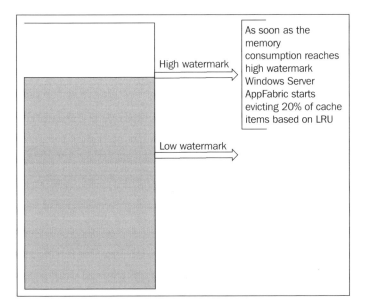

HWM, once reached, has performance implications associated with it. As the cache host is removing cache items, subsequent `Get`, `Put`, and `Add` requests will fail on this host.

 Windows Server AppFabric cache host enters a throttled state when it cannot write to the cache due to lack of available memory.

Setting up notifications

Windows Server AppFabric uses notifications to update cache clients about the changes that are made to the cache cluster. These notifications are sent asynchronously and can be subscribed at the level of granularity that suits the cache client's requirements. For local cache, these notifications serve as automatic means of cache invalidation.

The Windows Server AppFabric development team made a design choice that caches will have to opt in for notifications. This is so cache notifications are not switched on by default and also so the cache clients can subscribe for notifications at the level of granularity that is required.

Cache clusters can publish notifications for the following cache operations (defined at the region and cache level respectively):

1. Region level:
   - ❑ When a new region is created
   - ❑ When all the cache items in a region are cleared/removed
   - ❑ When the region is removed

2. Cache level:
   - ❑ When a new item is added to the cache
   - ❑ When an existing cache item is replaced
   - ❑ When a cache item is removed

 These operations are programmatically defined via `DataCacheOperation`.

A cache client may not be interested in every single change that happens on the cache. Windows Server AppFabric allows notification scopes that cover the changes either at the cache level, at the region level, or even at the individual cache item level.

Cache client can use the following methods to subscribe to the cache notification based on the relevant notification scope:

- ▸ `AddCacheLevelCallback`
- ▸ `AddRegionLevelCallback`
- ▸ `AddItemLevelCallback`

In this recipe, we will see how to define a cache that raises notifications. We will also see how to write cache clients that can subscribe to and leverage on these notifications at the cache, region, and item level.

Getting ready

We will need to launch the Caching Administration Windows PowerShell tool with elevated privileges so that PowerShell can access all the servers in the cache cluster with administrative rights.

We will also need a C# console application with the required AppFabric assemblies added to its reference.

How to do it...

We will start with creating a new cache with notifications enabled on it. We will follow it up with updating the configuration of an existing cache so that it supports notifications.

1. Launch **Caching Administration Windows PowerShell** with administrative privileges.

2. Execute the `New-Cache` command with `-NotificationsEnabled` set to `true`, as shown:

```
PS C:\Windows\system32> New-Cache -cacheName cacheWithNotification
-NotificationsEnabled true
```

Or, to update an existing cache, use the following three steps:

1. Stop the cache cluster using the `Stop-CacheCluster` command:

```
PS C:\Windows\system32> Stop-CacheCluster
```

2. Update the configuration using the following `set-CacheConfig` command:

```
PS C:\Windows\system32> set-CacheConfig ReferenceData
-NotificationsEnabled true
```

> You will receive the following message once the `set-CacheConfig` command is executed:
>
> **WARNING**: To reflect these changes, any clients currently referring to this cache must create a new `DataCacheFactory` instance and call `GetCache` on this cache.

3. Execute the `start-CacheCluster` command:

```
PS C:\Windows\system32> start-cacheCluster
```

> If the cache cluster is already running, then you will get the following exception: `ErrorCode<ERRCAdmin001>:SubStatus<ES0001>` `:Hosts are already running in the cluster`.

Now that notification has been enabled at the cache level, we can programmatically subscribe cache clients to receive notifications from the cache cluster. We will start with item level callback.

1. Define a method called `OnCacheChange` that takes exactly the same parameter as `DataCacheNotificationCallback`:

```
public static void OnCacheChange(string cacheName, string
region, string key, DataCacheItemVersion itemVersion,
DataCacheOperations operationId, DataCacheNotificationDescriptor
notificationDescriptor)
```

```
        {
                Console.WriteLine("A cache-level notification has been
                triggered. Following are the details:");
                Console.WriteLine("Cache: " + cacheName);
                Console.WriteLine("Region: " + region);
                Console.WriteLine("Key: " + key);
                Console.WriteLine("Operation: " +
                operationId.ToString());
                Console.WriteLine("Notification Description: " +
                notificationDescriptor.DelegateId);
                Console.WriteLine("Finished executing the cache
                notification callback.");
        }
```

2. Register `OnCacheChange` for item level callbacks using `DataCache`'s
    `AddItemLevelCallback` method. Provide the filter parameter by applying bitwise
    OR (defined as `|`- pipe operator - in C#) on `DataCacheOperations` (enumeration).
    This filter sets the scope of notification. `AddItemLevelCallback` returns an
    instance of `DataCacheNotificationDescriptor`, which must be stored in the
    program so that it can be used to remove this callback when needed.

    ```
    var notificationDescriptor = cache.AddItemLevelCallback("key",
    DataCacheOperations.AddItem |DataCacheOperations.ReplaceItem |
    DataCacheOperations.RemoveItem, OnCacheChange);
    ```

> In this example, Windows Server AppFabric will inform this
> cache client every time an item with key = "key" has been added,
> updated, or removed in this cache. This add/update/remove data
> cache operation becomes the filter for the notification.

Let's register a callback at the region level now:

3. Use the same `OnCacheChange` method for adding a region level callback. Use
    `DataCacheOperations` enumerations with bitwise operator as highlighted
    previously. For example, you can use: `DataCacheOperations.AddItem` and
    `DataCacheOperations.ClearRegion` as shown:

    ```
    var notificationDescriptor = cache.AddRegionLevelCallback(regionNa
    me, DataCacheOperations.AddItem | DataCacheOperations.ClearRegion,
    OnCacheChange);
    ```

Similarly, we can now register a callback at the cache level (that is covering regions and cache items):

4. Again, use `OnCacheChange` method for adding cache level callback and pass the `DataCacheOperations` enumerations as a filter:

    ```
    var notificationDescriptor = cache.AddCacheLevelCallback(Data
    CacheOperations.AddItem | DataCacheOperations.CreateRegion |
    DataCacheOperations.ClearRegion, OnCacheChange );
    ```

> For the sake of simplicity we have used the same function while registering a callback with `DataCache`. All these three callback registrations could have used different functions.

How it works...

Using Windows Server AppFabric cache notifications is fairly simple. Client API is easy to use and all we need to do is to register a callback with specific filter and we are all set to receive notifications.

However, under the surface there is a complex architecture involved to make notifications propagate seamlessly from cache cluster to the cache client. We should not forget that there are possibly hundreds of cache hosts that are holding cache items at any point in time across the cache cluster. Also the filter mechanism needs to be robust such that different cache clients can subscribe to different scopes of change and still receive all the relevant notifications.

Another thing that happens seamlessly, under the hood, is that the cache client polls for the notification updates. This is based on the specified polling interval. There are two ways to set the polling interval for the cache client:

► Via application configuration, use the `pollinterval` attribute of the `clientNotifications` element

► Use the `NotificationProperties` property of the `DataCacheFactoryConfiguration` class before passing it to `DataCacheFactory` to create `DataCache` client

It is possible for a `DataCache` client to miss out notifications from the Windows Server AppFabric cache. By design, Windows Server AppFabric notifications are not built on reliable messaging. This is an important architectural choice made in favor of performance.

Just imagine what would happen if a `DataCache` client registered a callback for all the items and region level changes on the cache, which is very frequently updated. How many messages would the Windows Server AppFabric cache hold until the client hit its notification interval and pulled the messages? Where would these messages be stored? And most importantly, what if the cache host keeping the messages went down?

As shown in the following diagram, notifications are saved in queues on the host level. These queues are not durable (not backed by a persistent storage) and only have limited capacity to hold messages. Due to this limitation, once the queue is full, messages will get truncated. Also because these queues are not durable, if the cache host goes down, all the notifications are lost.

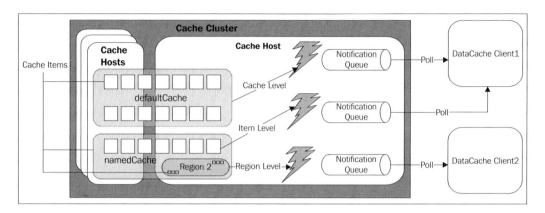

Windows Server AppFabric is smart enough to notify its clients when messages are truncated. This is possible only when the client has subscribed for failure notifications via the `AddFailureNotification` method on the `DataCache` client class.

 There is no way that the Windows Server AppFabric cache can notify the cache client that a particular host went down and all the notifications were lost. This is because we have notifications on the cache, region, and the item level, but not on the cluster level.

There's more...

Failure notifications offer another useful level of error communication between the cache host and the cache client. Failure notifications can be attached using a callback to the `DataCache` client via the `AddFailureNotification` method:

```
public DataCacheNotificationDescriptor
AddFailureNotificationCallback(DataCacheFailureNotificationCallback
failureCallback)
```

The `DataCacheFailureNotification` delegate is defined as follows:

```
public delegate void DataCacheFailureNotificationCallback
(string cacheName, DataCacheNotificationDescriptor nd);
```

Once the notification has been added, it is possible to remove it via the `RemoveCallback` method on the `DataCache` class. `RemoveCallback` takes in the notification descriptor to uniquely identify which callback to remove:

```
void RemoveCallback(DataCacheNotificationDescriptor nd)
```

There is also a bulk change notification method called `AddCacheLevelBulkCallback` available on the `DataCache` client. This method should be used only if the cache client is interested in being notified on all the operations on all the regions and items:

```
public DataCacheNotificationDescriptor AddCacheLevelBulkCallback(DataC
acheBulkNotificationCallback clientCallback);
```

The `DataCacheBulkNotificationCallback` delegate is defined as follows:

```
public delegate void DataCacheBulkNotificationCallback(string
cacheName, IEnumerable<DataCacheOperationDescriptor> operations,
DataCacheNotificationDescriptor nd);
```

Using performance counters

Performance gain is a key driver for distributed in-memory caching. However, if Windows Server AppFabric cache is not configured properly, it may lead to a number of issues including performance degradation.

Windows Server AppFabric caching provides a number of performance counters out of the box. These performance counters are installed along with Windows Server AppFabric and help with monitoring and troubleshooting scenarios, especially pertaining to the (lack of) cache performance.

Windows Server AppFabric's caching related performance counters are divided into three categories:

- **Cache related** (called `AppFabric Caching:Cache`): Covers cache (that span across different hosts) level statistics.

- **Host related** (called `AppFabric Caching:Host`): Covers host level statistics.

- **Secondary host related** (called `AppFabric Caching:Secondary Host`): Covers secondary host related statistics. This is only applicable for High Availability configurations.

The following screenshot (taken via `perfmon.exe` – more on this later in the recipe) shows these three categories:

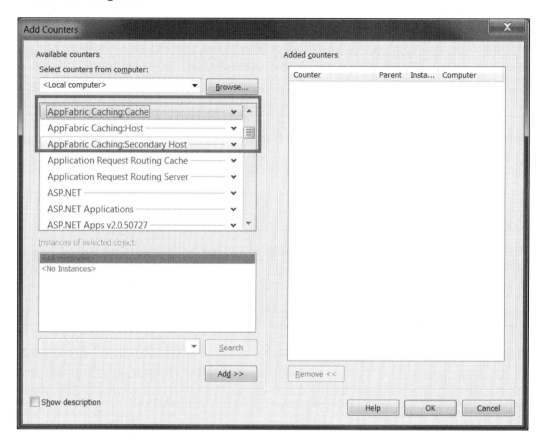

In this recipe, we will see how Windows Server AppFabric's cache related performance counters can be used to monitor and troubleshoot caching.

The Windows Server AppFabric cache offers around 60 performance counters. Instead of adding individual counters to monitor and troubleshoot a cache it is better to use an existing Data CollectorSet. For more details on Data Collector Sets, visit: `http://technet.microsoft.com/en-us/library/cc749337.aspx`.

In this recipe we will use a pre-defined collector template to measure the performance of Windows Server AppFabric cache.

Getting ready

Make sure the data collector set template is accessible (available with the source code of this chapter) and you have access to `perfmon.exe`.

How to do it...

We will launch a `perfmon` utility and use an existing template to define a Data Collector Set:

1. Click on **Start**, click on the Start Search box, type **perfmon**, and press *Enter*. This will launch a performance monitor as shown:

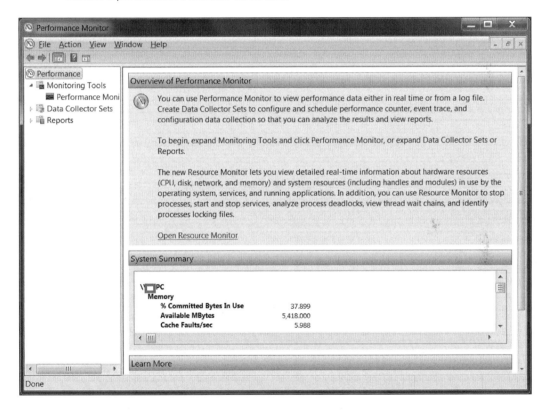

2. Under **Data Collector Sets**, right-click on **User Defined**. Under the **New** context menu, select **Data Collector Set** as shown in the following screenshot:

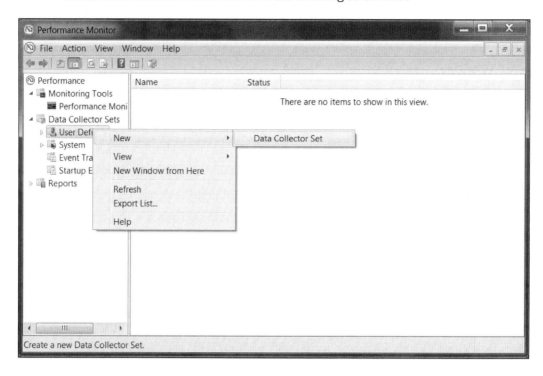

3. Select **Create from a template (Recommended)** and type **AppFabricPerf** under the **Name**:

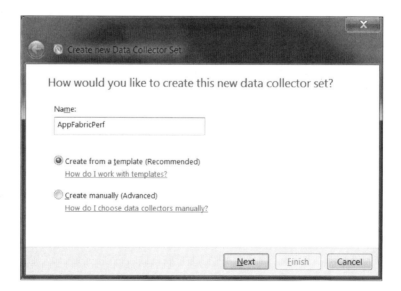

4. Click on **Next** and it will show a **Create new Data Collector Set** screen:

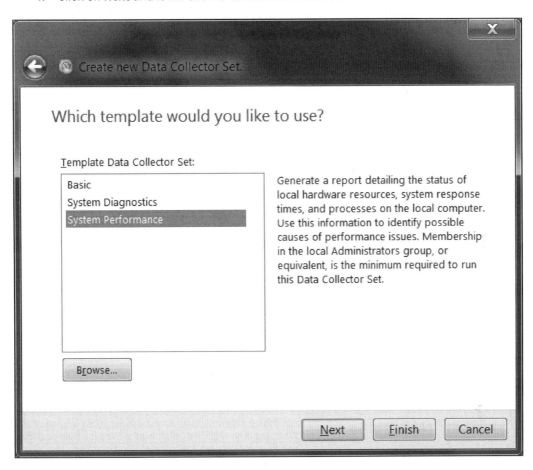

5. Click on **Browse...** and select the **Data Collector** template file (named `AFCache-PerfCounters.xml`) from the code samples directory.

6. You should see a **test** entry under the **Template Data Collector** list as shown in the following screenshot. Click on **Next** to continue:

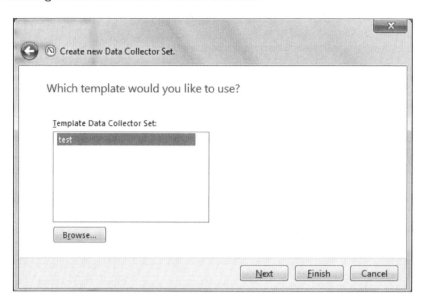

7. Select the **Root Directory** and click on **Next** (make sure that this directory is not being used by another counter otherwise it will not work):

8. Click on **Next**, select **Save and close**, and click on the **Finish** button.

9. Select the newly defined Data Collector Set and you should see a performance data collector called **DataCollector01**, as shown in the following screenshot:

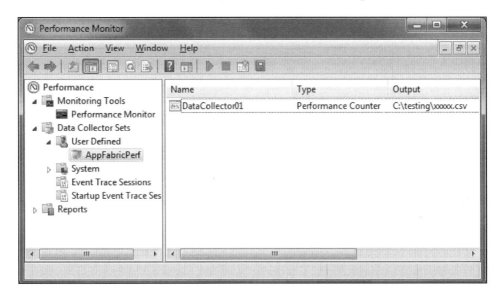

10. Right-click on this newly created data collector set and select **Start** from the context menu:

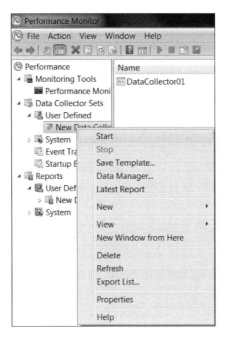

Assuming that the cache application is already running, the Data Collector Set will start getting the data.

11. Once the data is captured, right-click on your data collector set and select **Stop**:

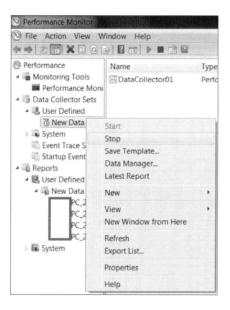

12. Right-click on your user defined data collector set and select **Latest Report**:

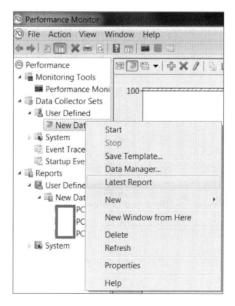

13. You should be able to see a performance report that looks as follows:

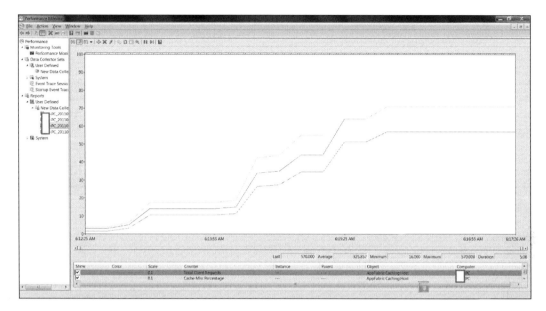

How it works...

Windows Performance Monitor uses performance counters, as well as event trace data and configuration to provide useful analysis on the state of the system or application. Performance monitoring can be done in real time as well as through data (captured via logs) for on demand analysis.

Data Collector Sets simplify collection of relevant distinct data points by aggregating different types of collectors. Currently, Data Collectors support three types of data collectors:

- ▶ Performance counters
- ▶ Event trace data
- ▶ System configuration (such as registry values)

Windows Server AppFabric cache provides a number of useful performance counters that can be monitored to identify the state of the cache at any point in time. These performance counters provide information on the state of the system or any particular aspect of it.

Performance monitor can also be used to view performance counters in real time. This is done by launching `perfmon.exe` and adding relevant performance counters.

There's more...

To better understand what is happening with the Windows Server AppFabric cache at any point in time, we will need to look at logs and Windows events as well.

See also

We will cover Monitoring for Windows Server AppFabric in *Chapter 7, Monitoring Windows Server AppFabric Deployments*.

Troubleshooting throttling

We learned about throttling in the *Setting up eviction* recipe earlier in this chapter. In this recipe we will identify the root causes of throttling and learn how to fix them.

In the Windows Server AppFabric cache, a cache host may enter a throttled state when the available physical memory becomes so low that it can no longer write data to the cache. A cache host remains in throttled state until more memory is made available.

Whenever a cache host enters a throttled state, cache clients will start receiving `DataCacheException` errors with `ErrorCode = RetryLater` and `SubStatus = Throttled`. To validate that a cache host has entered a throttled state, the following steps should be executed:

1. Use `Get-CacheClusterHealth` and see if any cache (host) has entered into a `Throttled` state.

2. Use performance counters (as highlighted in the previous recipe) and check for `AvailableMBytes` (under the `Memory` group of counters in `perfmon.exe`) on each cache host and validate if its value is less than 15%.

3. Look for `Event 116` with description = `Service is in throttled state` in the Operations log under the event viewer.

 In Version 1.1 of Windows Server AppFabric this log is available under **Microsoft-Windows-Application Server-Applications/Operational**.

The following diagram shows the location of the **Operational** log in Windows **Event Viewer**:

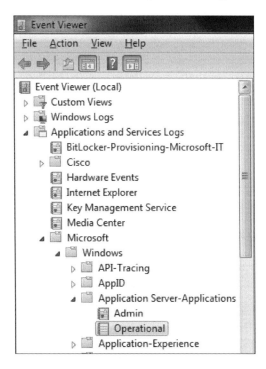

There is no single silver bullet to resolve throttling-related issues on the Windows Server AppFabric cache. In this recipe we will learn a number of things that can be done to ensure that there is enough memory available on a cache host to bring it out of the throttled state.

How to do it...

The following is a list of simple scenarios to help bring the cache host out of the throttling state:

1. Check if processes other than the Windows Server AppFabric cache are consuming too much memory on the cache host:

   ❏ If yes, then increase the amount of memory reserved for the AppFabric cache.

    You can use `Set-CacheHostConfig` AppFabric to set the size of available memory on the cache host.

   ❏ Or, increase the amount of available memory on the host

   ❏ Or, move the other processes (that are consuming too much memory) to another host

2. If the caching service is consuming too much memory:

    ❑   Check expiration and eviction settings to make sure that objects are being expired and evicted from the cache

    ❑   Or, increase the amount of available physical memory to meet the load on AppFabric caching service

    ❑   Or, run `Invoke-CacheGC` on the throttled cache host to force the execution of Garbage Collector (GC)

3. Check for custom regions as they always store cache data on a particular host:

    ❑   If there are region(s) on a cache host with a large amount of data then refactor your application to avoid placing large amounts of data in cache

    ❑   Or, add more available physical memory to the cache host

How it works...

The following diagram shows a basic flowchart of how to resolve throttling related issues on a cache host:

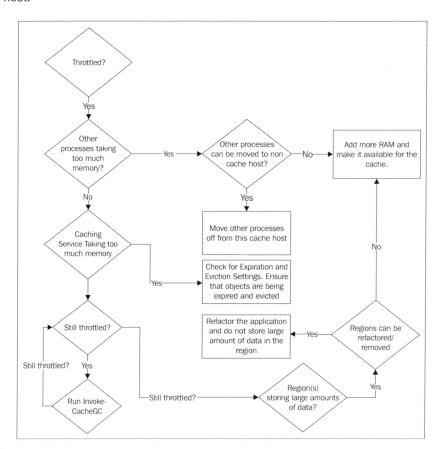

Bringing Windows Server AppFabric cache host out of throttled state requires a multi-dimensional approach. Going through the steps of this recipe (as highlighted in the preceding diagram) will help us fix the cache host. As soon as the throttling issue is resolved, the cache host will be available for regular caching scenarios.

Troubleshooting eviction

The Windows Server AppFabric cache uses an eviction policy to regulate the amount of memory used by cached data. We have seen earlier in this chapter that eviction occurs when the cache host is running low on memory and memory consumption goes beyond High Watermark (HWM). In this recipe, we will see how to identify if the cache host is continuously running in eviction state.

How to do it...

We will start with evaluating performance counters to identify the state of the cache host:

1. Use the following performance counters (using `perfmon.exe`) available under `AppFabric Caching:Host` to check the increase in the number of eviction runs:

    - `Total Eviction Runs`
    - `Total Data Size Bytes`
    - `Total Evicted Objects`
    - `Total Memory Evicted`

     The eviction counters mentioned previously are cumulative and the increase in these numbers should be noted over a period of time.

2. Look for `Event Id 118` and `115` in Windows Server AppFabric's Operational log using Windows **Event Viewer**.

3. Once the eviction is confirmed on the cache host, use `Get-CacheHostConfig` to check the cache size.

4. If the cache size can be increased, then increase the size of the cache using the `Set-CacheHostConfig` command.

5. If the cache host is also in throttled state, then follow the steps highlighted in the previous recipe, *Troubleshooting throttling*.

How it works...

Although eviction is enabled by default, it can be switched off. For caches with disabled eviction, the eviction run will not have any effect on easing memory pressure.

Keep in mind that eviction doesn't point to a problem or an issue, it is a symptom that highlights memory pressure on the cache host. This recipe should help resolve any eviction related errors.

Setting up read through – write behind

Windows Server AppFabric version 1.0 only supported "cache-aside" programming pattern. As we have seen in *Chapter 2, Getting Started with AppFabric Caching* (under the recipe called *Programming AppFabric Cache Client*), with a cache-aside pattern, developers are responsible for doing custom implementations to ensure cache item availability as well as backend consistency in the face of cache updates.

The good news is that with version 1.1, Windows Server AppFabric has added support for Read Through as well as the Write Behind scenarios:

▶ **Read Through**: If the client calls a `Get` on `DataCache` object with the `key` that does not exist in the cache, it gets a `null` reference. In a cache-aside pattern it is the responsibility of the calling client to then load the item in the cache so that it is available for the subsequent calls. However, with the new Read Through implementation for cache-miss scenarios the AppFabric cache transparently loads the missing item into the cache.

▶ **Write Behind**: In version 1 of the Windows Server AppFabric cache it was the responsibility of the client to update the backend every time a new cache item was added or updated. With version 1.1, the AppFabric cache provides new write behind capability that allows means for periodic and asynchronous updates to the backend.

We need to do the following three things to implement the Read Through and Write Behind capabilities in Windows Server AppFabric:

1. Implement Windows Server AppFabric cache's `DataCacheStoreProvider` class in a separate assembly.
2. Sign this assembly with a strong name and register it with the AppFabric cache.

3. Xcopy this assembly (along with the assemblies that contain the implementation of types that are stored in the cache) across the cache hosts in Windows Server AppFabric's cache cluster.

 Our `DataCacheStoreProvider` implementation is a skeleton code that shows how this scenario can be done. In a real-world case you will have an access to underlying data provider such that you can:

> ► Read the missing items from the database
>
> ► Write the new additions to the database
>
> ► Remove the deleted items from the database

Getting ready

We will need to access Visual Studio 2010 with administrative privileges. We will be launching a Visual Studio command prompt as well as a AppFabric PowerShell console.

We will also require access to AppFabric 1.1 binaries.

How to do it...

We will start with implementation of `DataCacheStoreProvider` and then follow it up with the strong signing and registering with the cache hosts in the AppFabric cache cluster:

1. Create a C# class library and name it `ReadThroughWriteBehindProvider`.

2. Add a reference to `Microsoft.ApplicationServer.Caching.Core`.

 `Microsoft.ApplicationServer.Caching.Core`, along with the rest of the binaries for Windows Server AppFabric, is available under `\Program Files\AppFabric 1.1`.

3. Add the following using statement:

```
using Microsoft.ApplicationServer.Caching;
```

4. Rename the `class1` to `CustomDataCacheStoreProvider` and inherit from `DataCacheStoreProvider`:

```
public class CustomDataCacheStoreProvider : DataCacheStoreProvider
```

5. Add the following two variables to the `CustomDataCacheStoreProvider` class:

```
private readonly string cacheName;
private readonly Dictionary<string, string> config;
```

6. Implement the constructor with the following signature:

```
public CustomDataCacheStoreProvider(string cacheName,
Dictionary<string, string> config)
{
            this.cacheName = cacheName;
            this.config = config;
}
```

 The custom provider must implement this constructor as it gets invoked each time the cache host is restarted as well when the cache first enables the read through or the write behind on a particular cache host.

7. Depending on the backend store, implement the following `Read`, `Write`, `Delete`, and `Dispose` methods:

```
public override void Delete(Collection<DataCacheItemKey> keys)

public override void Delete(DataCacheItemKey key)

protected override void Dispose(bool disposing)

public override void Read(ReadOnlyCollection<DataCacheItemKey>
keys, IDictionary<DataCacheItemKey, DataCacheItem> items)

public override DataCacheItem Read(DataCacheItemKey key)

public override void Write(IDictionary<DataCacheItemKey,
DataCacheItem> items)

public override void Write(DataCacheItem item)
```

 Note that `Read`, `Write`, and `Delete` methods have multiple overloads, one each for the individual cache item and another for a collection of cache items.

8. The `Read` method returns `DataCacheItem` and it can be created by using `DataCacheItemFactory` as shown:

```
object returnValue = DbProvider.Read(key.Key); //your underlying
db provider

if(returnValue != null)
      return DataCacheItemFactory.GetCacheItem(key, cacheName,
      returnValue, null);
else
      return null;
```

9. Similarly, the overload of Read with the collection of keys can be implemented as shown in the following code:

```
public override void Read(ReadOnlyCollection<DataCacheItemKey>
keys, IDictionary<DataCacheItemKey, DataCacheItem> items)
{
    foreach(DataCacheItemKey key in keys)
    {
        items[key] = Read(key);
    }
}
```

 Note that you may want to consider increasing the cache client's timeout value for `DataCache.Get` operation. This is important as the time spent in the Read methods of the provider adds to the total request time for the `DataCache.Get` method.

10. Write method implementation should update the underlying data provider. Cache items successfully written to the underlying provider must be removed from the items collection. Or, conversely if all the items are successfully written to the underlying provider then a clear method can be invoked:

```
public override void Write(DataCacheItem item)
{
    DbProvider.Write(item);
}

public override void Write(IDictionary<DataCacheItemKey,
DataCacheItem> items)
{
    foreach (var item in items)
    {
        Write(item.Value);
    }

    items.Clear();
}
```

 It is very important to remove the items from the list if they are written successfully to the underlying provider. If items are not removed from the list, AppFabric will retry to write them again.

Likewise, the `Delete` method can be implemented to synchronize the changes with the backend. Now we will sign the assembly, install it to GAC, and then register it with the AppFabric cache:

1. Sign the assembly using the Visual Studio properties tab.

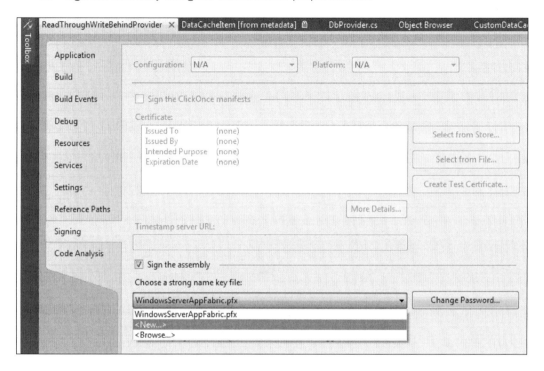

2. Install this signed assembly to Global Assembly Cache (GAC) by using the following command on the Visual Studio 2010 command prompt:

   `C:\Windows\system32>gacutil /i "<YourFilePath>\ \`
   `ReadThroughWriteBehindProvider.dll"`

   `Microsoft (R) .NET Global Assembly Cache Utility.  Version`
   `4.0.30319.1`

   `Copyright (c) Microsoft Corporation.  All rights reserved.`

   `Assembly successfully added to the cache`

3. Query the GAC for the versioning information on `ReadThroughWriteBehingProvider.dll` using the following command on the Visual Studio 2010 command prompt:

   `C:\Windows\system32>gacutil /l ReadThroughWriteBehindProvider`

   `Microsoft (R) .NET Global Assembly Cache Utility.  Version`
   `4.0.30319.1`

   `Copyright (c) Microsoft Corporation.  All rights reserved.`

The Global Assembly Cache contains the following assemblies:

```
  ReadThroughWriteBehindProvider, Version=1.0.0.0,
Culture=neutral, PublicKeyTok

en=75be72d7adb73ac7, processorArchitecture=MSIL


Number of items = 1
```

4. Register your provider with AppFabric cache using the following command on Cache Administration PowerShell:

```
PS C:\Windows\system32> Set-CacheConfig CacheWithReadWrite
-ReadThroughEnabled t

rue -WriteBehindEnabled true -WriteBehindInterval 60 -ProviderType
"ReadThroughW

riteBehindProvider, Version=1.0.0.0, Culture=neutral,
PublicKeyToken=75be72d7adb

73ac7, processorArchitecture=MSIL" -ProviderSettings @
{"DbConnection"="<your con

nection string>";}
```

```
CacheName                : CacheWithReadWrite
TimeToLive               : 10 mins
CacheType                : Partitioned
Secondaries              : 0
MinSecondaries           : 0
IsExpirable              : True
EvictionType             : LRU
NotificationsEnabled     : False
WriteBehindEnabled       : True
WriteBehindInterval      : 60
WriteBehindRetryInterval : 60
WriteBehindRetryCount    : -1
ReadThroughEnabled       : True
ProviderType             : ReadThroughWriteBehindProvider,
Version=1.0.0.0, Cul
                           ture=neutral, PublicKeyToken=75be72d7ad
b73ac7, proce
                           ssorArchitecture=MSIL
ProviderSettings         : {"DbConnection"="<your connection
string>"}
```

You have registered your custom `DataCacheStoreProvider` with Windows Server AppFabric successfully. Now you can easily code against this cache and your changes will trickle down for Write Behind scenarios and you will get the cache items loaded atomically via Read Through implementation.

How it works...

`DataCacheStoreProvider` is available as an abstract type in the `Microsoft.ApplicationServer.Caching.Core` assembly:

```
public abstract class DataCacheStoreProvider : IDisposable
{
protected DataCacheStoreProvider()
{    }

public abstract void Delete(DataCacheItemKey key);

public abstract void Delete(Collection<DataCacheItemKey> keys);

public void Dispose()
{
    this.Dispose(true);
    GC.SuppressFinalize(this);
}

protected abstract void Dispose(bool disposing);

public abstract DataCacheItem Read(DataCacheItemKey key);

public abstract void Read(ReadOnlyCollection<DataCacheItemKey> keys,
IDictionary<DataCacheItemKey, DataCacheItem> items);

public abstract void Write(DataCacheItem item);

public abstract void Write(IDictionary<DataCacheItemKey,
DataCacheItem> items);}
```

When the Read Through and/or Write Behind are enabled on an existing cache, AppFabric initializes the registered implementation of `DataCacheStoreProvider`. Once the custom implementation is initialized, Windows Server AppFabric invokes the `Read`, `Write`, and `Delete` methods seamlessly. These calls happen under the hood and the calling client is oblivious of these details. On initialization, the AppFabric cache provides the cache name and other information, such as connection settings, to the custom provider so that it can initialize the underlying store and work as expected.

For the cluster scenarios, the assembly implementing the custom `DataCacheStoreProvider` must be copied across the cache hosts in the cluster. If there are user defined types being persisted, then the assemblies containing these types should also be copied over to all the hosts in the cache cluster.

> It should be noted that `DataCacheItem` objects are stored in the cache cluster in a serialized form. If these `DataCacheItem` objects are required to be deserialized before being persisted in to the underlying store, then the assemblies associated with those serialized objects must also be in the GAC across all the cache hosts.

There's more...

In case of errors `DataCacheStoreException` can be thrown to the calling client. `DataCacheStoreException` is implemented as following:

```
[Serializable]
public class DataCacheStoreException : Exception
{
public DataCacheStoreException()
{   }
public DataCacheStoreException(string message, Exception
innerException) : base(message, innerException)
{   }

public DataCachcStoreException(string message) : base(message)
{   }

protected DataCacheStoreException(SerializationInfo info,
StreamingContext context) : base(info, context)
{   }

}
```

If there is an exception during the Read method then the calling client will get `DataCacheException` with the `ErrorCode = DataCacheErrorCode.ReadThroughProviderFailure`.

If the `Write` operation fails for the first time AppFabric will retry based on the configuration policy.

> You can also try using a GUI based interface to register a custom implementation of `DataCacheStoreProvide` by using the tool available at CodePlex:
> `http://appfabricadmin.codeplex.com/`

4
Windows Server AppFabric Hosting Fundamentals

In this chapter, we will cover:

- ▶ Installing the Web Deployment tool (Web Deploy)
- ▶ Packaging services for deployment with Web Deploy
- ▶ Hosting WCF services
- ▶ Hosting WCF REST services
- ▶ Hosting basic workflow services

Introduction

Built on top of IIS7 and Windows Process Activation Services (WAS), Windows Server AppFabric provides a premier hosting environment for WCF 4 and WF 4 services. As an extension of IIS 7, Windows Server AppFabric provides key hosting capabilities that are useful to developers who create these services and IT Pros who are tasked with hosting them.

By leveraging a familiar management model while reducing the amount of XML and complex configuration that developers and IT Pros often contend with, Windows Server AppFabric makes deploying and configuring WCF and WF services much simpler than with IIS alone.

By using Windows Server AppFabric, you will immediately benefit from a consistent deployment, hosting, and management experience provided by a graphical administrative user interface that is immediately familiar to developers and IT Pros that are accustomed to working within MMC style tools.

In this chapter, we will explore how to get your WCF and WF services up and running quickly and easily with recipes for deploying, hosting, and configuring WCF and WF services.

You will learn how to install and configure the Microsoft Web Deployment tool for standardizing the deployment of your WCF and WF service applications, get hands-on guidance for deploying basic WCF SOAP services, get REST services up and running in a URI-friendly manner, as well as learn the basic steps for configuring simple WF services.

Additional hosting features such as configuring persistence for supporting long-running workflows, leveraging auto-start, and using common hosting commandlets are covered in the recipes in the next chapter.

 Unless otherwise noted, all of the recipes in this chapter are based on Windows Server AppFabric and Microsoft AppFabric 1.1 for Windows Server running on a Windows 7 PC.

Installing the Web Deployment tool (Web Deploy)

The Web Deployment tool (Web Deploy) is an extension of IIS 7 that simplifies the packaging and deployment of Windows Server AppFabric applications and services.

While there is no reason that you can't use your own deployment framework (including XCOPY deployment, which is certainly supported), Web Deploy is useful for providing a consistent, yet extensible way to streamline the deployment of WCF and WF service-based applications to IIS and Windows Server AppFabric. Web Deploy facilitates a seamless transition from Visual Studio to Windows Server AppFabric whether you are targeting one or multiple instances of Windows Server AppFabric, which is useful for single server, modestly sized, or larger enterprise deployments.

In this recipe, we will follow a step-by-step process for installing, configuring, and testing Web Deploy on Windows Server AppFabric.

Getting ready

Please ensure that you have installed and configured Windows Server AppFabric before proceeding (see *Chapter 1, Installing Windows Server AppFabric*).

You will also want to ensure you have an Internet connection if you have not previously downloaded the Web Deployment tool (please note the latest version of the tool as of this writing is 2.1).

Web Deploy is supported on Windows 7, Windows Server 2003, Windows Server 2003 R2, Windows Server 2008, Windows Server 2008 R2, Windows Vista, and Windows XP; however, not all features are available on machines not running IIS7/Windows Server AppFabric.

How to do it...

The Microsoft Web Platform Installer (WPI) offers a highly streamlined package/software download installation experience. You can get the WPI from Microsoft's website at: `http://www.microsoft.com/web/downloads/platform.aspx`. After downloading and installing WPI, you can use the following steps to launch the Windows Server AppFabric Installer:

1. Go to **All Programs**, under the **Start** menu. If using Windows 7, type `Web Platform Installer` in the search box, find the **Web Platform Installer**, and launch it.

2. Accept the **User Account Control** (UAC) warning. This will allow WPI to make changes to your computer.

3. Type `Web Deploy` in the search box (in the top right-hand corner of the screen) and press the *Enter* key.

4. Look for an entry called **Web Deployment Tool 2.1** and click on the **Add** button.

5. Next, click on the **Install** button to begin the installation:

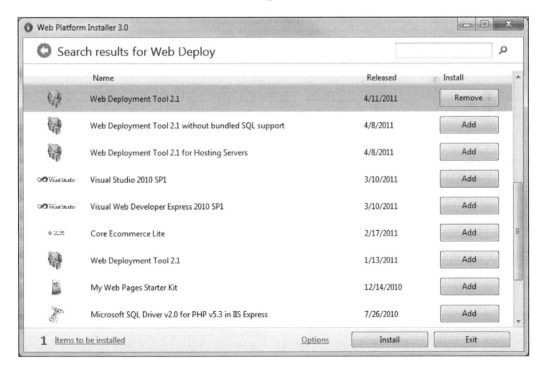

6. Now the WPI will ask for a review of the download and installation of all the required software components. Select **I Accept** to continue.

 The list of components, third-party application software, and Microsoft products will vary from machine to machine. Web Platform Installer will determine any missing components and will list them on this screen.

7. Once you select **I Accept,** WPI will download and install all the required software components.

8. Once the installation process is complete, click on **Finish** on the **Web Platform Installation** screen and click on **Exit** to exit from Windows Platform Installer.

How it works...

The Web Platform Installer installs the **Web Deployment Framework**, including the following components:

- ▶ IIS Manager UI Module
- ▶ IIS 7 Deployment Handler
- ▶ Configure for Non-Administrator deployments
- ▶ Management Service Delegation UI
- ▶ Remote Agent Service

In addition, depending on what components are available on the target machine, the following SQL Server components may have also been installed:

- ▶ SQL Server System CLR types
- ▶ SQL Server Native client
- ▶ SQL Server Management objects

The tool is installed in the `IIS\Microsoft Web Deploy V2` path of the `Program Files` directory (on my machine this is `C:\Program Files\IIS\Microsoft Web Deploy V2`) and cannot be moved. The directory includes the `msdeploy.exe` application as well as supporting documentation and assemblies that make up the deployment framework.

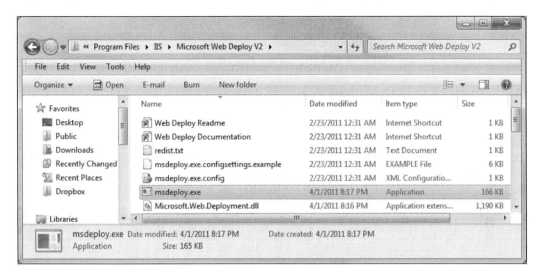

Additionally, the Remote Agent Service is installed as a new service called **Web Deployment Agent Service** and is started, and set to start automatically. The Remote Agent Service is configured to run on HTTP Port 80 with a URI such as `http://localhost/MsDeployAgentService`.

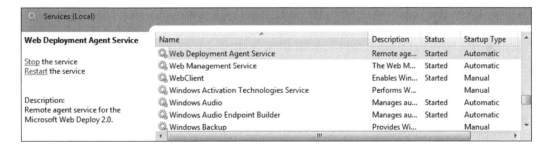

Lastly, you can verify if the IIS Manager UI Module was successfully installed by starting IIS and confirming that the **Deploy** group in the **Actions** pane is present and includes the options to import (deploy) and export an application:

There's more...

By targeting Windows Server AppFabric (which by definition is built on IIS 7 or later) you'll be able to take advantage of the IIS Manager UI Module that provides a graphical user experience for deploying and exporting applications and the IIS 7 Deployment Handler that allows both administrators and non-administrators to remotely manage deployments to IIS7/Windows Server AppFabric.

At its core, only the Web Deployment Framework and IIS Manager UI Module are necessary to take advantage of the most basic deployment options. However, the remaining features enable common scenarios including delegating deployment to non-administrators and support for remote deployments which is very useful in most environments, particularly when deploying to more than one machine across environments or in a farm.

Further, support for SQL Server DDL and DML objects are also supported, which is very useful because many WCF and WF services will rely on SQL Server or some other backing store for persisting its model.

If you would prefer to disable or remove any of these features, please refer to the following TechNet article, which provides more details around each feature and supported configurations: `http://technet.microsoft.com/en-us/library/dd569059(WS.10).aspx`.

See also

For a step-by-step guide for installing Windows Server AppFabric, refer to the *Installing Windows Server AppFabric* recipe in *Chapter 1, Installing Windows Server AppFabric*.

Packaging services for deployment with Web Deploy

One of the many benefits of using the Web Deployment tool (Web Deploy) is that it allows you to standardize your applications and services in a consistent package that is compatible with developer tools such as Visual Studio and tools suited to both administrators and developers such as command line scripts and the graphical user interface provided by IIS 7.x and Windows Server AppFabric.

In addition, deployment to remote machines is firewall friendly, as the deployment endpoint is exposed over HTTP on Port 80. This eliminates the need to install other proprietary agents or create file shares to move deployment packages around, supporting a centralized deployment model for your applications and services.

In this recipe, we will use Visual Studio to package a WCF service application and deploy it by importing the standardized package into IIS/Windows Server AppFabric so that it can be prepared for hosting.

 Note that the Web Deployment tool can be used to deploy multiple project types that support hosting in IIS. For example, the same approach could equally be applied to ASP.NET, WCF, and WF service projects as well as SQL Server Database Projects.

Getting ready

Before proceeding with this recipe, ensure you have installed the Microsoft Web Deployment tool (Web Deploy) on the development and target machine (see the preceding recipe). You may dual purpose your machine as a development and IIS/Windows Server AppFabric target; however, if you have set up a remote target server, ensure that the **Remote Agent Service** has been installed on the target machine according to the recipe previously referenced.

How to do it...

Visual Studio 2010 provides a feature that allows you, as a developer, to package your project directly from within Visual Studio. From there, you can move the package to a location accessible from the target server and import the package to Windows Server AppFabric. Let's get started.

1. In Visual Studio, right-click the project that you want to deploy and select **Build Deployment Package** from the context menu.

2. Note the status of the packaging process in the lower left-hand corner of Visual Studio. You will see a message indicating that publishing has started as soon as the project is compiled, followed by a message indicating that the publishing succeeded. Although somewhat misleading, the same messages are displayed whether you are simply packaging the project for deployment or publishing it to the target server.

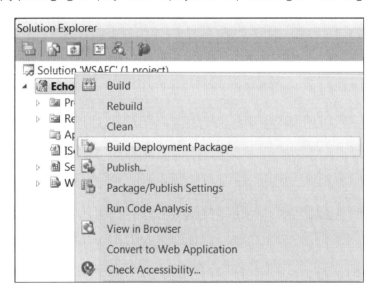

3. When the package has been prepared, it will be placed in a folder called `Package` in the following path directly under the root folder of the project: `obj\Debug\Package`.

4. Browse to the package location and you will notice a file with a `.zip` extension named after the project name. Copy the full path to your clipboard by selecting the path from **Windows Explorer**, right-clicking and choosing **Copy**, or by pressing *Ctrl+C* on your keyboard to copy the path contents to your clipboard.

5. Open IIS 7, expand the **Sites** node to enumerate the websites that have been configured, and right-click on the website to which you would like to deploy the package. Select **Deploy**, and then select **Import Application...** to start the import wizard:

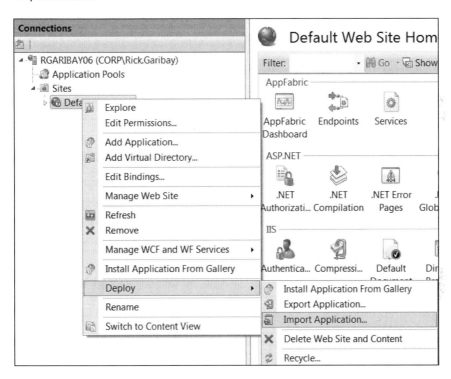

6. Paste the path to the package that you saved in your clipboard in the **Package path** text box followed by the name of the package and click on **Next**:

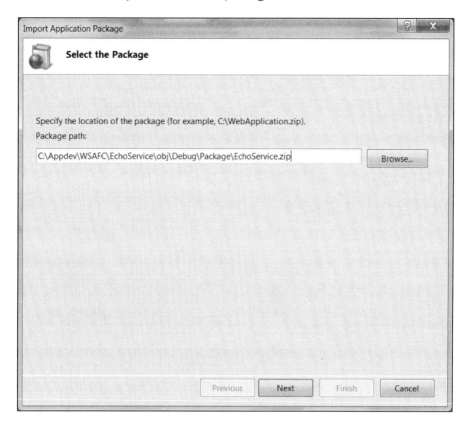

7. Click on **Next** again in the following screen to accept the default package contents selections.

8. Provide a name for the application and click on **Next**.

9. The application is deployed and a summary screen is displayed. Click on **Finish** to complete the deployment:

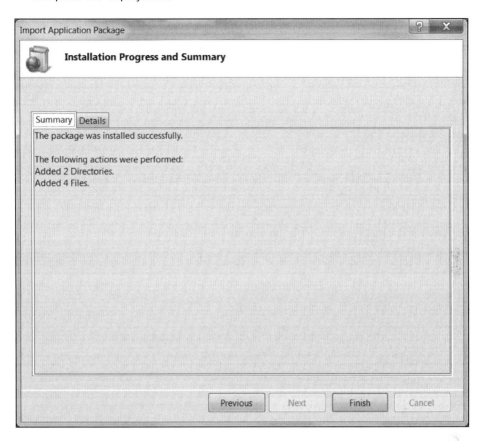

How it works...

The **Import Application Package** wizard unpacks the package and provides you with an opportunity to customize the deployment as required. From there, it deploys the necessary artifacts to IIS/Windows Server AppFabric by copying the necessary files to the website directory.

At this point, the application is ready to be configured to take advantage of the hosting, monitoring, and persistence features of Windows Server AppFabric.

There's more...

It is possible to publish the package directly from within Visual Studio. Depending on your organization's approach to application lifecycle management, unless you are targeting your development machine, it is unlikely that you will use this approach for deployment. Having said that, the publish feature in Visual Studio does provide a graphical user experience that gives you some insight into how the command line tool works, so feel free to experiment.

In addition, you can control a number of aspects of how the project is packaged by managing the Package/Publish settings for each project. To do so, right-click on the project and select **Package/Publish Settings**. From there, you can determine what artifacts you want included in the package, what the package should be called, the path in which you would like the package created (if you prefer a different path than the default) and, if you choose to publish from Visual Studio, what name you would like the application to be created with in IIS/Windows Server AppFabric.

Deploying a package from the command line

Depending on your role and the application lifecycle management policies in place in your organization, scripting deployments to Windows Server AppFabric may be preferable if not practical, particularly for multi-server deployments or moving an application across development, integration, testing, and production environments.

If you take a look at the `C:\Program Files\IIS\Microsoft Web Deploy V2` folder in which Web Deploy is installed, you will notice an executable called `msdeploy.exe`. This executable contains everything that you need to package and deploy MS Deploy packages to your target IIS/Windows Server AppFabric servers, whether they are local or remote.

To learn more about the options available in the command-line interface, simply open a command prompt that points to the location of the executable and type `msdeploy` at the command prompt. You will see a comprehensive list of commands and an explanation of what each command does:

Including SQL artifacts in your deployment

If you followed the first recipe of this chapter, you will have noticed that a number of SQL Server components are installed when you install Web Deploy (unless you explicitly choose to omit them). These components support another interesting feature of Web Deploy, which allows you to create a composite deployment package that includes the application artifacts as well as databases you create in the `App_Data` folder of your Visual Studio project.

To specify settings for optionally deploying a SQL database, right-click on the project, select **Package/Publish Settings**, and click on the **Package/Publish SQL** tab. From there you can define target connection strings as well as specify additional automation steps such as pulling a schema and/or data from a different source database and executing custom scripts against the target database.

See also

For a step-by-step guide for installing Windows Server AppFabric, refer to the *Installing Windows Server AppFabric* recipe in *Chapter 1, Installing Windows Server AppFabric*.

For a step-by-step guide for installing the Microsoft Web Deployment tool, see the *Installing the Web Deployment tool (Web Deploy)* recipe in this chapter.

Hosting WCF services

Windows Server AppFabric provides a premier hosting environment for hosting your WCF services. As Windows Server AppFabric is built on top of/extends IIS 7 and Windows Process Activation Services (WAS), you get all the benefits of this proven hosting platform plus a number of features designed specifically for working with WCF (and WF) services.

Windows Server AppFabric provides an intuitive user experience that allows you to set common WCF knobs without having to resort to complex XML configuration. For example, once you've deployed an application consisting of one or more WCF services, you can configure common settings such as whether to expose metadata, set up monitoring and tracing, enable the service(s) to start automatically, and configure throttling to ensure that demand can keep pace with available resources.

Also, as working with WCF services is very different than a typical website or ASP.NET application, Windows Server AppFabric recognizes these differences and allows you to manage your WCF service(s) in an intuitive manner at the service and endpoint level.

In this recipe, we will deploy and configure an application consisting of two WCF services. We will then examine and manage each service separately, even though they are part of the same application.

Getting ready

This recipe assumes that you have installed Windows Server AppFabric. If this isn't the case, please refer to the recipes referenced in the *See also* section at the end of this recipe.

> While this recipe will show you how to host an application consisting of two services, the process for hosting an application consisting of one service is identical.
>
> You can find the sample project used for this recipe in the source code download that is available with this book.

You will want to be familiar with techniques for deploying applications to IIS/Windows Server AppFabric, and there are some recipes that cover this topic referenced at the end of this recipe. Of course, XCOPY deployment is a perfectly valid approach for deploying your applications to IIS/Windows Server AppFabric as well.

How to do it...

In this recipe, we'll use a simple WCF 4.0 service that is created for you when you use the WCF Service Application template that ships with Visual Studio 2010.

Follow these steps to take advantage of the hosting capabilities available to you when deploying your WCF services to an IIS Server configured with Windows Server AppFabric:

1. Deploy your WCF application to IIS/Windows Server AppFabric using your preferred method of deployment. You can use XCOPY deployment or follow the recipes in this chapter for leveraging the Microsoft Web Deployment tool.

> At a minimum, you will need to deploy the `.svc` and `web.config` files as well as the assemblies located in the `bin` directory of your application root. If you use Web Deploy, this will happen automatically for you (see the *How it works...* section of the previous recipe).

2. Ensure that the virtual directory that hosts your deployment is configured as an application and that the application is bound to a .NET 4.0 application pool. While Web Deploy will do this for you automatically, if you are using a different approach such as XCOPY, you will want to right-click on the virtual directory and click on **Convert to Virtual Application**.

3. Next, right-click on the application and select **Manage WCF and WF Services** followed by **Configure**. Also, notice that there is an option to **Start Application** (which is currently grayed out) and **Stop Application**. We'll revisit these settings shortly.

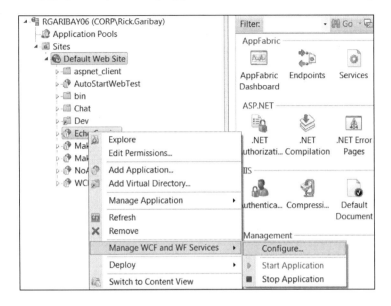

4. The **General** tab provides the opportunity to toggle whether metadata will be exposed. Select the checkbox to enable sharing of metadata and click on **Apply**:

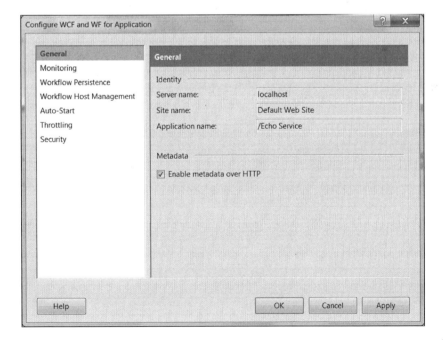

5. Next, click on the **Auto-Start** tab. As you can see, you have three options for determining start up behavior. Leave it with the default value, **Disabled** for now.

6. Now, click on the **Throttling** section to review the defaults provided for WCF throttling. You can change these values as per your requirements and more information on this topic is provided later. For now, click on **Apply** to close the configuration dialog.

7. Ensure you are in **Features View**, and under the **AppFabric** group, double-click on the **Services** icon:

 The application hiearchy in which you are working is relevant to the level that you want to manage. For example, if you were to select **Default Web Site** as the root node, then the **Services**, **Endpoints**, and **Dashboard** would include all services within that context.

8. After clicking on the **Services** icon, notice that the services that are part of your application are enumerated and that clicking on one of them results in additional useful details about the service being displayed:

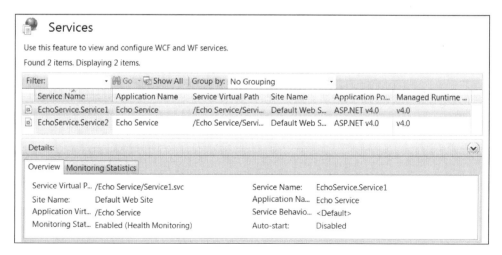

You can also view monitoring information about each service by clicking on the **Monitoring Statistics** tab, which is covered in *Chapter 7, Monitoring Windows Server AppFabric Deployment.*

9. Hit the back button in the upper left-hand corner of your screen to return to **Features View**, and click on the **Endpoints** icon. You can review the attributes of each endpoint such as the address, binding, and contract:

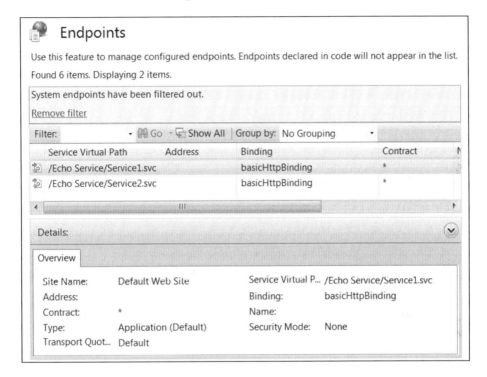

10. Hit the back button once again and click on the **Content View** tab. Locate the `.svc` file for the service you are hosting, right-click the file, and click on **Browse** to launch the service page and verify that the service is hosted and ready.

11. When the page loads, you should see a service page come up that provides you with the ability to browse the WSDL, confirming that your services have been hosted and are ready to be consumed:

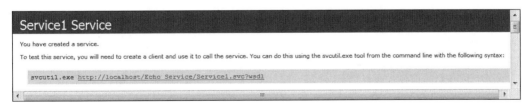

How it works...

There are a number of options for hosting WCF and WF services on the Microsoft Platform and choosing the right host will vary according to the scenario at hand.

For example, if you want to take advantage of self-hosting for quick prototyping, or implementing duplex services that support call-backs, you can choose any CLR host (Windows Forms, WPF, Console, and so on). You can gain immediate benefits from using Windows services (think "NT Services") as a host by adding additional reliability and useful management capabilities such as automatic start-up on reboot, and the ability to pause and stop a service.

However, Microsoft has worked hard to make IIS a premier hosting environment for WCF and WF services, adding support for multiple protocols including HTTP, TCP, MSQM, and IPC via Windows Process Activation Services (WAS). Since Windows Server AppFabric is an extension to IIS, when the WCF service is hosted in Windows Server AppFabric, it automatically takes advantage of all of the features of IIS 7.x and WAS. Windows Server AppFabric extends these capabilities by adding support for graphical configuration of service and endpoint behaviors as well as the ability to automatically start the service(s) before the first message is received.

> Note that Auto-Start is covered in detail in the corresponding recipe in *Chapter 5, More Windows Server AppFabric Hosting Features*.

While Windows Server AppFabric certainly makes your configuration experience a whole lot easier, there's nothing magical happening here. When you enabled metadata on your application, the corresponding `<serviceMetadata>` service behavior in your `Web.config` file was modified to set the `httpGetEnabled` attribute to `true`, just as you would do manually:

```
<serviceBehaviors>
    <behavior>
    <serviceMetadata httpGetEnabled="true"/>
    </behavior>
</serviceBehaviors>
```

There's more...

While we did not modify any of the throttling settings, if you had, you would have noticed that the corresponding `<serviceThrottling>` service behavior would have been configured with whatever values you specified in Windows Server AppFabric.

In addition, the setting for whether Auto-Start is enabled is persisted to a special file called the `ApplicationHost.config` file, which is scoped to hosting configuration settings. The file can be found in `C:\Windows\System32\inetsrv\config` with values for your application resembling something similar to the following:

```
<application path="/Echo Service" applicationPool="ASP.NET v4.0"
enabledProtocols="http,tcp" serviceAutoStartEnabled="false" serviceAut
oStartProvider="Service">

<virtualDirectory path="/" physicalPath="%SystemDrive%\inetpub\
wwwroot\Echo Service" />
```

See also

For a step-by-step guide for installing Windows Server AppFabric, refer to the *Installing Windows Server AppFabric* recipe in *Chapter 1, Installing Windows Server AppFabric.*

For a step-by-step guide for installing the Microsoft Web Deployment tool, see the *Installing the Web Deployment tool (Web Deploy)* recipe in this chapter.

Hosting WCF REST services

Windows Server AppFabric provides a premier environment for hosting your WCF services whether you are developing traditional SOAP services or REST services. As Windows Server AppFabric is built on top of IIS 7 and Windows Process Activation Services (WAS), you get all of the benefits of this hosting platform plus a number of features specific to working with WCF services.

As with working with traditional SOAP WCF services, Windows Server AppFabric provides an intuitive user experience that allows you to manage common settings such as certificate-based security, monitoring and tracing configuration, enabling your REST service to start automatically, as well as the ability to configure throttling to ensure that demand can keep pace with available resources.

In addition, depending on the manner in which you choose to configure your WCF REST service with regard to URIs, it is possible to manage your RESTful WCF service(s) in a manner that is very close to what you would expect from hosting traditional SOAP WCF services.

Some common considerations when working with REST services as opposed to SOAP include:

- ▶ Exercising control over URI paths so that they are intuitive and easy to understand
- ▶ Leveraging sophisticated routing techniques for mapping URIs to service methods
- ▶ Working without the .svc extension, which while common with traditional WCF SOAP services, is not desirable in the REST world
- ▶ Taking advantage of the caching benefits which are inherent to working with HTTP

In this recipe, we will configure a WCF REST service to adhere to common URI path styles as well as take advantage of routing and extension-less (svc-less) activation. In addition, we will configure the service to take advantage of HTTP output caching and demonstrate all of these features working together on Windows Server AppFabric.

Getting ready

WCF 4 supports building REST-focused HTTP services with the WebHttpBinding, including support for dynamic routes, XML and JSON encoding formats as well as automatic help page generation.

You can start working on a WebHttpBinding based service by adding a WCF project to your solution like any other WCF project template; however, there is nothing about the default templates that make it obvious that you are working with REST. Therefore, I recommend downloading the WCF 4.0 REST Services Template from the Visual Studio Gallery. While this template isn't necessary for building and hosting WCF REST services for Windows Server AppFabric, it does simplify things significantly, and is the approach we'll take as we walk through this recipe for getting the best out of hosting WCF 4 REST services in Windows Server AppFabric.

How to do it...

Follow these steps to get up and running with that WCF REST on Windows Server AppFabric in no time:

1. In Visual Studio 2010, click on **Tools** and select **Extension Manager...**.

2. In the search dialogue, type WCF REST and look for the template called **WCF REST Service Template 40 (CS)** or **(VB)** (for this recipe, I've chosen the C# template) and click on **Close**:

3. Now, select your solution, right-click on it, and choose **Add New Project...**. From there, type WCF REST in the search dialog and you will see the new service template you just downloaded called "WCF REST Service Application C#" appear. Select it, provide a name for the new project, and click on **OK**.

4. Once the template is created, reviewing it will reveal that it is a familiar WCF template, but has been optimized for REST style web service programming.

5. Now that you are familiar with the default template, download the SingleTrackService solution that is provided in the download area for this book. The project is based on the WCF REST Service Application template you just downloaded and includes some minor refactoring to make the domain of the service more intuitive as well as some additional configuration I've added to simplify this recipe, which we will review next.

The sample project consists of a simple read-only (GET) REST service which provides information about mountain bike trails (single tracks) which get their name due to the width of the trail approximating that of a vehicle with a single axle, typical of a bicycle.

As with the files that the project template generates by default, you will notice that the template consists of four files:

- ▶ The SingleTrackService.cs file includes the definition and implementation of the service

- ▶ The SingleTrack.cs file includes the Data Contract that models a single track trail

- ▶ The Global.asax file defines some key events that we'll hook into to enable dynamic routing

- ▶ The Web.config file will include some key configuration for enabling dynamic routing and supporting extension-less (svc-less) URIs among other things

I won't review the project exhaustively as it consists of standard WCF REST conventions; however, I will highlight some key changes that I've made to enable key features for hosting and managing the service in Windows Server AppFabric.

6. Note that the `Global.asax.cs` file includes an implementation for the
    `Application_Start` method which ensures that any requests to the service,
    regardless of URI or VERB, get routed to the `SingelTrackService` service:

```
public class Global : HttpApplication
{
    void Application_Start(object sender, EventArgs e)
    {
        RegisterRoutes();
    }

    private void RegisterRoutes()
    {
        RouteTable.Routes.Add(new ServiceRoute("", new
        WebServiceHostFactory(), typeof(SingleTrackService)));
    }
}
```

7. Open the `Web.config` and review the configuration within the
    `<system.webServer>` element:

```
<system.webServer>
    <modules runAllManagedModulesForAllRequests="true">
        <removename="UrlRoutingModule"/>
        <addname="UrlRoutingModule"
        type="System.Web.Routing.UrlRoutingModule, System.Web,
        Version=4.0.0.0, Culture=neutral,
        PublicKeyToken=b03f5f7f11d50a3a" />
    </modules>
</system.webServer>
```

8. Next, note the use of the `<webHttpEndpoint>` **Standard Endpoint**, which enables a
    useful help page and the ability to support requests for multiple formats such as XML
    and JSON:

```
<standardEndpoints>
    <webHttpEndpoint>
        <standardEndpointname=""helpEnabled=
        "true"automaticFormatSelectionEnabled="true"/>
    </webHttpEndpoint>
</standardEndpoints>
```

9. The last configuration item to orient you to before we deploy is the `<caching>` element, which supports the ability to cache HTTP GET requests:

```
<caching>
    <outputCacheSettings>
        <outputCacheProfiles>
            <addname="CacheProfile"duration="10"varyByParam=
            "format" />
        </outputCacheProfiles>
    </outputCacheSettings>
</caching>
```

10. Next, deploy the `SingleTrackService` to IIS/Windows Server AppFabric using whichever method you prefer (including Web Deploy as outlined in the first and second recipes in this chapter). Once deployed, the **Content View** should, at a minimum, include the `bin` folder with the compiled assemblies, the `Global.asax` and `Web.config` files, and a folder containing some images:

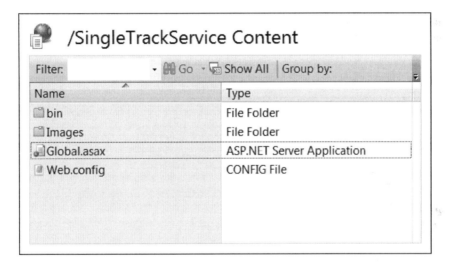

Notice there is no `.svc` file! That is because we are leveraging dynamic routing provided by the `UrlRoutingModule` and `UrlRoutingHandler` in concert with the RouteTable in the `Global.asax` file , which results in a friendly and intuitive URI that is desirable to REST style developers.

11. To test the service, navigate to it by pointing your favorite browser to `http://localhost/SingleTrackService` (assuming the application name is `SingleTrackService`):

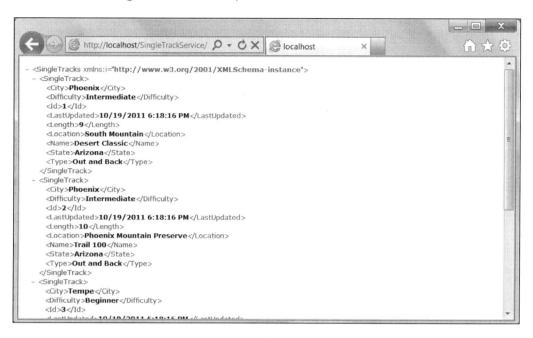

12. Note the timestamp in the `LastUpdated` element. Hit refresh a few times within a 10 second period. Notice the timestamp on each `SingleTrack` element remains the same until 10 seconds has elapsed.

13. Now, add the string `help` at the end of the URI so that it reads `http://localhost/SingleTrackService/help`. You are greeted by a web page that provides documentation on how to work with the service:

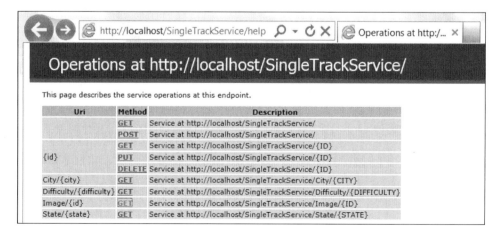

How it works...

There are some differences when working with REST services that require some special attention. While you didn't have to do much to take the `SingleTrackService` and host it in IIS/Windows Server AppFabric, there is some code and configuration we reviewed which is key to making this all work.

First, in addition to some useful scaffolding for getting going with building a WCF REST service, the WCF REST Service Application template includes some fundamental code and configuration necessary for working with and hosting WCF REST service in IIS/Windows Server AppFabric.

The first thing you probably noticed is the absence of a `.svc` file. This is because for most REST developers, having extensions in the URI is not desirable because it takes away from the natural and intuitive structure of a well-designed URI scheme. While everything "just worked" as shown in the previous screenshot depicting the resource catalog, there are some important things you should be familiar with to get the most out of working with WCF REST services in Windows Server AppFabric.

The `runAllManagedModulesForAllRequests` attribute shown in step 7 in the `modules` element is required to be set to true to ensure that any requests that come into the request pipeline that are not mapped to an extension are resolved by the **RouteTable**. We added an entry to the table in the `Global.asax` file in step 6. The `Add` method takes a `ServiceRoute` instance for which we provide three parameters:

```
RouteTable.Routes.Add(new ServiceRoute("", new
WebServiceHostFactory(), typeof(SingleTrackService)));
```

The first parameter is known as a route prefix and signals the root path that will be mapped to a given WCF service type. In this case, anything following the host name will route to the `SingleTrackService` class. The second parameter is also interesting. Unlike traditional SOAP services that use a `ServiceHost`, the `WebServiceHostFactory` was designed to deal with HTTP-based services exclusively.

Next, the `UrlRoutingModule` module is required to enable dynamic routing for hosting in Windows Server AppFabric, and the configuration shown in step 7 registers the module and ensures that it, along with all other registered modules, is executed for requests that do not include extensions (such as `.svc`, which we want to avoid). Without this configuration, Windows Server AppFabric/IIS (rightfully) assumes that you are asking to browse the contents of the `SingleTrackService` directory, which is fortunately forbidden unless explicitly allowed.

All of this also requires that ASP.NET compatibility is enabled declaratively in the
`Web.config` by setting the `aspNetCompatibilityEnabled` attribute to true in
the `serviceHostingEnvironment` element and adding the
`AspnetCompatabilityRequirements` attribute to the `SingleTrackService` class:

```
[ServiceContract]
[AspNetCompatibilityRequirements(RequirementsMode =
    AspNetCompatibilityRequirementsMode.Allowed)]
[ServiceBehavior(InstanceContextMode = InstanceContextMode.PerCall)]
public class SingleTrackService
{
}
```

You probably also noticed the lack of some of the configuration elements you would typically
see in a traditional WCF service. To simplify the approach for hosting services in WCF 4,
there is the concept of default endpoints which automate the creation of common endpoint
configurations for getting your WCF services up and running quickly and easily. Standard
Endpoints build on this simplicity by providing common configurations packaged into an
element and exercising convention over configuration. By using the `WebHttpEndpoint`, all of
the common configurations for hosting a WebHttpBinding based service are taken care of and
you are provided with some common configuration knobs such as enabling support for the
help page we saw in step 13.

Finally, one of the biggest benefits of designing REST services, or services that leverage the
HTTP protocol exclusively, is that you get all of the features inherent to the HTTP protocol
including support for caching GET requests. The configuration in step 9 allows us to use a
named cache profile on the methods for various mapped routes. For example, on the catch-all
method in the `SingleTrackService` class called `GetCollection`, I've added an attribute
called `AspNetCacheProfile` and mapped the profile I defined in step 9, which enables the
caching of identical results for 10 seconds:

```
[WebGet(UriTemplate = "")]
[AspNetCacheProfile("CacheProfile")]
public SingleTracks GetCollection()
{
    return GetSingleTracks();
}
```

There's more...

Some developers and administrators may be concerned about the potential performance
implications that enabling the `runAllManagedModulesForAllRequests` attribute
introduces for static requests such as HTML pages, image files, and so on, as each of
these requests must run through all of the configured modules unnecessarily. Fortunately,
Microsoft introduced an alternative to this approach in a QFE Hotfix which enables dynamic
routing without impacting static requests. You can download and install Hotfix from
`http://support.microsoft.com/kb/980368`.

After installing the hotfix, three new handlers with a name prefix of `ExtensionlessUrlHandler` are installed in IIS, which correspond to 32, 64 bit, and integrated hosting modes and are applied to all applications accordingly.

With these handlers installed, you can remove or disable the `runAllManagedModulesForAllRequests` attribute and all routing will continue to function as expected.

Where's my XML?

Depending on the browser you are using, you may or may not see XML when you issue a GET request to the `SingleTrackService` service. This is because browser vendors treat raw XML differently.

The first thing to do is to disable special treatment of XML or ATOM feeds. If that doesn't do the trick, there are some other options available.

For example, in Internet Explorer 9, when issuing a root GET request on the `SingleTrackService`, the results are formatted and rendered as follows:

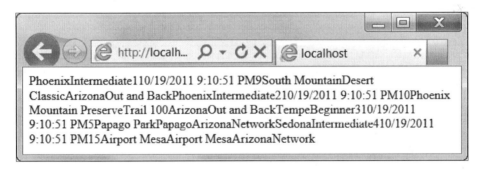

If you are like me, you must have your XML! You can use the **F12 Developer Tools** feature to enable targeting of older browser versions which treat the response as plain old XML, such as Internet Explorer 8, which is what I used in step 11.

Extension-less caveats

While the majority of hosting management features in Windows Server AppFabric are available to WCF 4 services regardless of whether they are SOAP or REST based, one thing that you will notice is that the ability to work with the Services and Endpoints feature of Windows Server AppFabric is not available when you use extension-less URIs.

You can still manage the service at the application level, but the ability to view monitoring statistics at the service level as well as configure specific services individually and toggling back and forth between views is definitely a nice feature provided by Windows Server AppFabric.

Fortunately, there is a good solution to this problem.

There is a feature in WCF 4 known as service activation which allows you to eliminate the `.svc` file for traditional services. Although we are using dynamic routing to avoid extensions as well as support cleaner and more elegant URI templates, we can add service activations as a trick to keep these capabilities while not losing the nice management features in Windows Server AppFabric as follows:

```
<serviceActivations>
    <addrelativeAddress="SingleTrackService/Foo.svc"
        service="Services.SingleTrackService"
        factory="System.ServiceModel.Activation.
                WebServiceHostFactory"/>
</serviceActivations>
```

After adding the configuration above and redeploying the service, the ability to work with this extension-less REST service in Windows Server AppFabric is fully restored as with traditional WCF services:

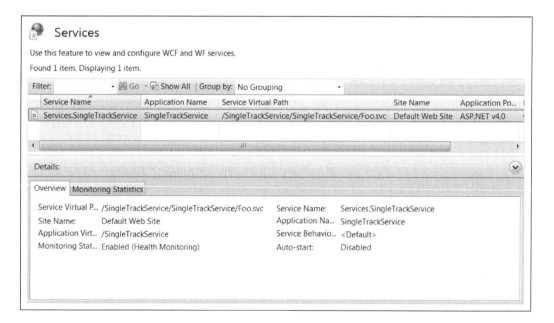

Advanced conditional HTTP GET caching support

In addition to the output caching capabilities I demonstrated in this recipe, WCF and IIS/Windows Server AppFabric also support the ability to leverage conditional HTTP GET caching by leveraging ETag and the If-None-Match HTTP request header.

The basic idea is that an ETag provides a unique identifier (such as a GUID perhaps) that is issued by the service when a resource is requested that essentially represents a resource version. The ETag is stored on the client and then subsequent requests are sent to the service with the latest ETag value in the If-None-Match HTTP request header. If the resource has changed, the latest version of the resource is returned in response to the GET request. Otherwise, a benign HTTP status code 304 (Not Modified) is returned with an empty body.

Of course, for trivial payloads, this may be overkill, but for larger resource payloads, or very high density scenarios, leveraging conditional HTTP GET caching can have a significant impact on bandwidth requirements and application performance.

You can learn more about conditional HTTP GET caching in WCF 4 here: `http://blogs.msdn.com/b/endpoint/archive/2010/02/25/conditional-get-and-etag-support-in-wcf-webhttp-services.aspx`.

See also

For a step-by-step guide for installing Windows Server AppFabric, refer to the *Installing Windows Server AppFabric* recipe in *Chapter 1, Installing Windows Server AppFabric*.

For a step-by-step guide for installing the Microsoft Web Deployment tool, please see the *Installing the Web Deployment tool (Web Deploy)* recipe in this chapter.

Hosting basic workflow services

Windows Server AppFabric provides a premier hosting environment for hosting your WCF and WF services. Built on IIS 7.x and Windows Process Activation Services (WAS), your WCF and WF Services will instantly benefit from the hosting, monitoring, and caching capabilities provided by Windows Server AppFabric, including a number of features that were specifically designed to allow you to get the most out of hosting WF Services.

WF Services combine the declarative, model-oriented approach to designing the logic flow of your services with the robust messaging capabilities of WCF. Together, WCF and WF provide some pretty powerful capabilities for designing and hosting long-running services that maximize resources while providing your users with a very responsive user experience.

There are extensive configuration options available for both WCF and WF. When working with WCF or WF services, you have the option of configuring your service either imperatively, in code, or declaratively within the `Web.config` file. It is recommended to always prefer the declarative approach so that runtime configuration can be managed after the application has been deployed, but this has not always been a trivial task.

While the *Hosting long-running workflow services* recipe in *Chapter 5, More Windows Server AppFabric Hosting Features* goes into detail to show you how to get the most out of hosting long-running WF 4 workflow services in Windows Server AppFabric, in this recipe, we'll explore how to get a simple workflow service up and running quickly and easily by taking advantage of the simplified configuration experience introduced with WCF 4.0, often referred to as "tag-less" configuration.

> The XML elements that make up the declarative configuration experience within the `Web.config` file are often referred to as configuration "tags", which is where the term "tag-less" comes from.

Getting ready

This recipe assumes that you've already installed and configured Windows Server AppFabric. If you haven't, please follow the recipes in *Chapter 1, Installing Windows Server AppFabric*.

We'll use the Reservation Service sample WF application that is available for download as part of the resources available for this book.

While not required, we'll also leverage the Microsoft Web Deployment tool for seamlessly deploying the WF service to IIS/Windows Server AppFabric, so if you are not familiar with it, please refer to the first two recipes in this chapter.

How to do it...

In this recipe, we'll deploy the Reservation Service WF Service application (that is available for download with this book) without applying any manual configuration whatsoever:

1. In Visual Studio, create a new WF Service project by creating a new project using the **WCF Workflow Service Application** template and providing a name for the project.

> The WCF Workflow Service Application template provides a simple project including the basic artifacts and configuration for getting up and running with a WF 4 Workflow Service and includes:
>
> ▸ A declarative XAML service file called `Service1.xamlx` which contains the implementation of the workflow service
>
> ▸ A `Web.config` file for declaratively configuring the WF Service using elements or tags

2. Once the project has been created, open `Service1.xamlx` and orient yourself to the workflow which is rendered in the designer:

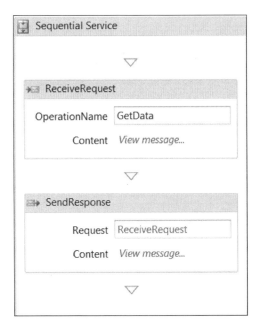

 The workflow consists of a composite sequence activity consisting of a Receive and Send messaging activity that models the requirements for providing a classic request-reply service (which in this case just happens to be implemented with WF 4 instead of imperative code).

3. Open the `Web.config` file and you will notice that the typical service and endpoint elements are absent. Delete everything between the configuration tags so that the `Web.config` file is effectively empty:

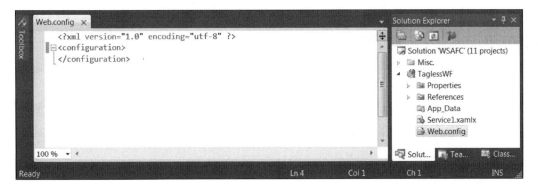

4. Deploy the WF Services application to Windows Server AppFabric using your preferred method of deployment. You can use XCOPY deployment or follow the recipes in this chapter for leveraging the Microsoft Web Deployment Tool.

 At a minimum, you will need to deploy the `.xamlx` and `web.config` files as well as the assemblies located in the `bin` directory of your application root. If you use Web Deploy, this will happen automatically.

5. Ensure that the virtual directory that hosts your deployment is configured as an application and that the application is bound to a .NET 4.0 application pool. While Web Deploy will do this for you automatically, if you are using a different approach such as XCOPY, you will want to right-click on the virtual directory and click on **Convert to Virtual Application**.

6. Next, right-click on the application and select **Manage WCF and WF Services** followed by **Configure**:

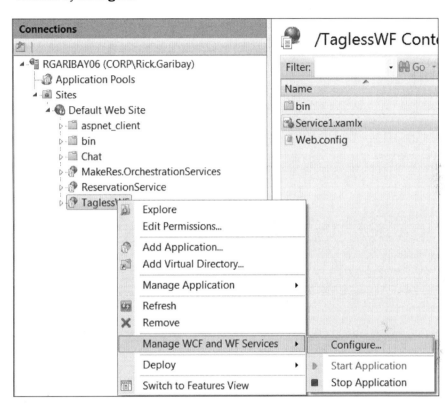

7. The **General** section provides the opportunity to toggle whether metadata will be exposed. If it is not already checked, select the checkbox to enable sharing of metadata and click on **Apply**:

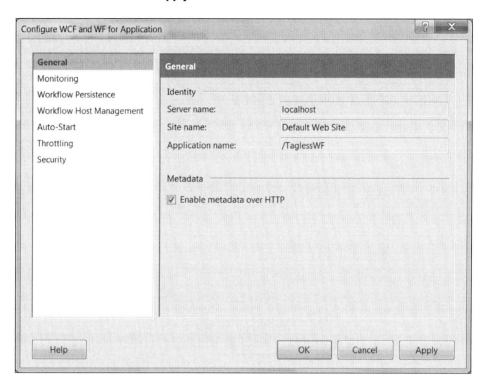

8. Next, click on the application you just deployed, select **Content View**, right-click on the `Service1.xamlx` file, and click on **Browse.**

9. The service page appears indicating that the service is hosted, exposing metadata and ready to begin serving requests. Click on the hyperlink to request the WSDL:

How it works...

Since a workflow service is really a WF application exposed as a WCF service, you get all of the benefits of WF and WCF when designing your workflow services, which is really the best of both worlds.

Despite clearing all configuration from the `Web.config` file, by simply deploying the project to IIS/Windows Server AppFabric as an application, and enabling metadata exchange via the application configuration, the service is hosted and metadata exchange is enabled with no configuration whatsoever.

This is certainly a simpler approach than configuring WCF or WF services manually, but let's take some time to understand how all of this worked so effortlessly.

The most significant improvement to the configuration experience in WCF 4 is the automatic application of **default endpoints**. To quickly review, an **endpoint** consists of an **address**, a **binding**, and a **contract**. While every WCF service comprises one or more endpoints, default endpoints take care of this boilerplate configuration for you.

The following is a very simple yet common example of the boilerplate configuration that is typical for configuring a simple WCF service. The service and endpoint is explicitly defined as is the binding configuration and behavior configuration:

```xml
<configuration>
    <system.serviceModel>
        <services>
            <service name="Demo1.Service1"
                    behaviorConfiguration="Service1Behavior">
                <endpoint name="Basic"
                        address=""
                        binding="basicHttpBinding"
                        bindingConfiguration="BasicConfig"
                contract="Demo1.IService1"/>
            </service>
        </services>
        <bindings>
            <basicHttpBinding>
                <binding name="BasicConfig" openTimeout="00:02:00"/>
            </basicHttpBinding>
        </bindings>
        <behaviors>
            <serviceBehaviors>
                <behavior name="Service1Behavior">
                    <serviceMetadata httpGetEnabled="true"/>
                    <serviceDebug
                    includeExceptionDetailInFaults="true"/>
```

```
                 </behavior>
              </serviceBehaviors>
           </behaviors>
        </system.serviceModel>
     </configuration>
```

For this particular service, when the host is opened, the WCF service model will create a service named Service1, with one endpoint listening on the HTTP protocol/scheme that is compatible with the WS-I Basic Profile 1 standard. When a message arrives at the endpoint, the service model will dispatch the message to the matching method that has been implemented per the configured contract. In addition, I have specified (via a service behavior) that I would like the service to provide a WSDL file over HTTP if requested, and in the event of an exception, the service should serialize low-level .NET exception details and return them in SOAP faults.

As Windows Server AppFabric is designed for WCF 4 and WF 4 services, the endpoint(s) is automatically created for every combination of protocol/schemes provided by the base address(es) in IIS/Windows Server AppFabric, as you can see in the WSDL from step 9.

There's more...

If you want to take advantage of default endpoints, use a WS-* binding such as WsHttpBinding or a REST binding such as WebHttpBindin, instead of using BasicHttpBinding as the default binding for HTTP. You can accomplish this very easily by simply adding a `protocolMapping` element to your configuration as shown:

```
<protocolMapping>
    <add scheme="http" binding="wsHttpBinding"/>
</protocolMapping>
```

If you were to add the element above to the otherwise empty `Web.config` that we deployed to IIS/Windows Server AppFabric, the default endpoint for the HTTP protocol will be configured with the `wsHttpBinding` binding. Try it!

See also

For a step-by-step guide for installing Windows Server AppFabric, refer to the *Installing Windows Server AppFabric* recipe in *Chapter 1, Installing Windows Server AppFabric*.

For a step-by-step guide for installing the Microsoft Web Deployment Tool, please see the *Installing the Web Deployment tool (Web Deploy)* recipe in this chapter.

For a more detailed recipe that covers more advanced aspects of hosting WF 4 workflow services including persistence, correlation, basic monitoring please see the *Hosting long-running workflow services* recipe in *Chapter 5, More Windows Server AppFabric Hosting Features*.

5
More Windows Server AppFabric Hosting Features

In this chapter, we will cover:

- ► Hosting long-running workflow services
- ► Taking advantage of WAS and Auto-Start
- ► Hosting Windows Azure Relay services
- ► Using common Server AppFabric hosting commandlets

Introduction

This chapter picks up where the last chapter left off as we move beyond the basic hosting capabilities of Windows Server AppFabric.

Recipes for configuring persistence for supporting long-running workflows, how to configure your WCF and WF services to start without waiting for a message to arrive, and step-by-step guidance for enabling Azure Service Bus Relay bindings for supporting hybrid composite scenarios will enable you to reach beyond the basics and get the most of what Windows Server AppFabric's hosting capabilities have to offer.

While much of this book is focused on the graphical user experience that is one of the extension's key benefits for simplifying hosting and management, this chapter concludes with a recipe that will show you the most common PowerShell commands that allow administrators to interact with Windows Server AppFabric from a console as well as enabling automated scripting for things such as obtaining the configuration information of your WCF and WF services at the application and service level, configuring an application to take advantage of the Auto-Start feature, reviewing and modify monitoring settings, and starting and stopping a Windows Server AppFabric application.

 Unless otherwise noted, all of the recipes in this chapter are based on Windows Server AppFabric and Microsoft AppFabric 1.1 for Windows Server running on a Windows 7 PC.

Hosting long-running workflow services

Windows Server AppFabric provides a premier hosting environment for hosting your WCF and WF services. Built on IIS 7.x and Windows Process Activation Services (WAS), your WCF and WF Services will instantly benefit from the hosting, monitoring, and caching capabilities provided by Windows Server AppFabric, including a number of features that were designed to allow you to get the most out of WF Services specifically.

WF Services combine a declarative, model-oriented approach to designing the logic flow of your services with the messaging capabilities of WCF. Together, WCF and WF provide some pretty powerful capabilities for designing and hosting long-running services that maximize resources while providing your users with a very responsive user experience.

Unlike WCF services, however, which simply require a host, and take advantage of the hosting and monitoring capabilities of Window Server AppFabric, WF services require additional capabilities that Windows Server AppFabric provides out of the box, including a preconfigured persistence store, the ability to configure how a workflow instance behaves with regards to memory management, and sophisticated support for persisting instances of workflows (not to mention robust monitoring capabilities, which are covered in *Chapter 7, Monitoring Windows Server AppFabric Deployment*).

Getting ready

This recipe assumes that you've already installed and configured Windows Server AppFabric. If you haven't, please follow the recipes in *Chapter 1, Installing Windows Server AppFabric*.

We'll use the sample WF application called "Reservation Service" that is available for download as part of the resources available for this book.

As the name of the application suggests, the Reservation Service simulates a restaurant reservation workflow service wherein a patron requests a reservation (perhaps from a web frontend or via an inbound automated call center agent) that is managed by the workflow service. The workflow service accepts the reservation and sends the would-be patron an e-mail confirming the receipt of the reservation (but not the reservation itself). The service then awaits approval from the director of reservations (common in the hospitality space where stellar customer experience is a top priority) or maître d to ensure that the requested accommodations and patron preferences can be met. If so, a second e-mail is sent to the patron welcoming them to the restaurant at the requested time, or notifying them that their request could not be accommodated.

Please note that the sample workflow service used in this recipe contains a custom activity that is implemented in the SendEmail.cs class, which simulates a confirmation e-mail to a local directory (C:\AppDev\Demos\Mail). Please make sure that you create a directory in C:\AppDev\Demos\Mail, or change the path in the SendEmail activity to a path of your choice: smtpClient.PickupDirectoryLocation = @"C:\AppDev\Demos\Mail";.

While not required, we'll also leverage the Microsoft Web Deployment tool for seamlessly deploying the WF service to Windows Server AppFabric, so if you are not familiar with it, refer to the first two recipes in *Chapter 4, Windows Server AppFabric Hosting Fundamentals*.

How to do it...

In this recipe, we'll deploy the Reservation Service WF service application that is available in the download area for this chapter and take advantage of the hosting capabilities available to you when deploying your long-running WF services to Windows Server AppFabric:

1. Deploy the Reservation Service application to Windows Server AppFabric using your preferred method of deployment. You can use XCOPY deployment or follow the recipes in *Chapter 4, Windows Server AppFabric Hosting Fundamentals* for leveraging the Microsoft Web Deployment tool.

    At a minimum, you will need to deploy the .xamlx and web.config files as well as the assemblies located in the bin directory of your application root. If you use Web Deploy, this will happen automatically.

2. Ensure that the virtual directory that hosts your deployment is configured as an application and that the application is bound to a .NET 4.0 application pool. While Web Deploy will do this for you automatically, if you are using a different approach like XCOPY deployment, you will want to right-click on the virtual directory you created and click on **Convert to Virtual Application** to ensure that the virtual directory is treated as an IIS application.

3. Next, right-click on the application and select **Manage WCF and WF Services**, followed by **Configure**:

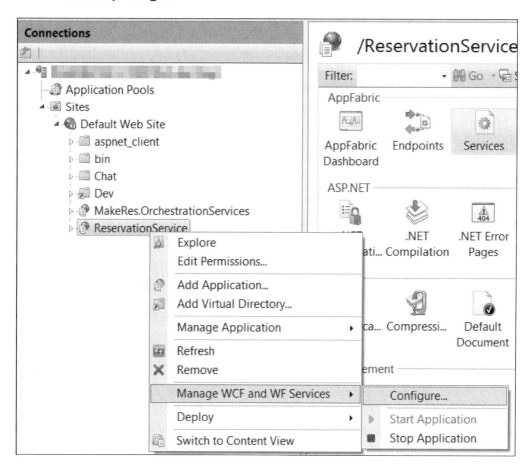

4. The **General** section provides the opportunity to toggle whether metadata will be exposed. If it is not already checked, click on the checkbox to enable sharing of metadata and click on **Apply**.

5. Click on the **Monitoring** tab. Notice that monitoring is enabled at the **Health Monitoring** level and that monitoring events will be written to the Windows Server AppFabric monitoring store.

6. Next, click on the **Workflow Persistence** tab. Turn on support for persistence by selecting the radio button next to **SQL Server Workflow Persistence** and selecting the persistence store that was configured when Windows Server AppFabric was installed, and then click on **Apply**:

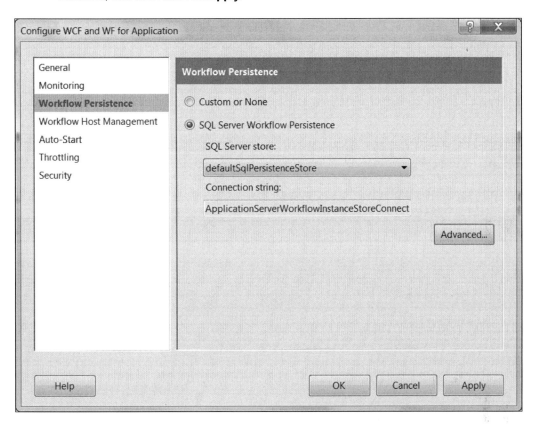

 Note that if the drop-down list under **SQL Server store** is empty, you'll need to configure persistence for Windows Server AppFabric. *Chapter 1, Installing Windows Server AppFabric* provides a recipe that will walk you through each step of the process.

7. Now, click on the **Workflow Host Management** tab and ensure that the **Enable instance control** and **Unload instances when idle** checkboxes are checked.

8. Select the **Persist instances when idle** checkbox, set the **Persist timeout** and **Unload timeout** to 5 seconds, and click on **Apply**:

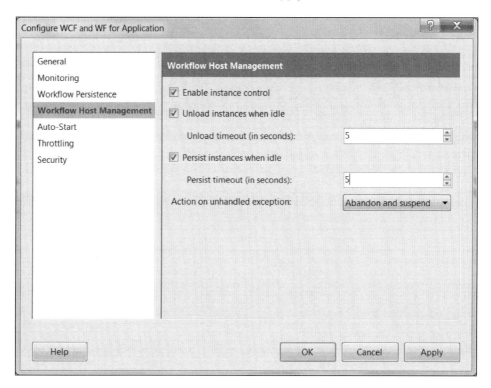

 In a production environment, you will very likely set the unload and persist timeouts to a higher number (default is 60 seconds for each); however, starting with a lower setting will allow you to better understand the effects of these settings on persistence as you learn by using the Windows Server AppFabric Dashboard to monitor the workflow as it transitions from various states.

9. Accept the warning indicating that the services in the hosted application may be recycled as a result of Windows Server AppFabric modifying the `web.config` for the workflow service.

10. Ensure you are in **Features View**, and under the **AppFabric** group, double-click on the **Services** icon:

 The application hierarchy in which you are working is relevant to the level that you want to manage. For example, if you were to select **Default Web Site** as the root node, then the **Services**, **Endpoints**, and **Dashboard** would include all services within that context.

11. After clicking on the **Services** icon, notice that the **Reservation Service** is listed and clicking on it results in additional useful details about the service being displayed:

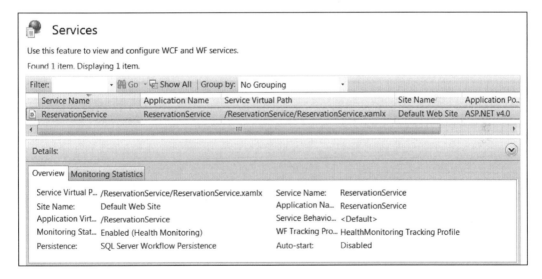

 You can also view more detailed monitoring information about the service by clicking on the **Monitoring Statistics** tab, which will show the number of calls received versus completed, along with a count of any exceptions. *Chapter 7, Monitoring Windows Server AppFabric Deployment* is dedicated to monitoring Windows Server AppFabric applications.

12. Hit the back button in the upper left-hand corner of your screen to return to Features View, and click on the **Endpoints** icon. You can review the attributes of each endpoint including the **Address**, **Binding**, and **Contract**, among other things:

13. Finally, hit the back button once again and click on the **Content View** tab. Find the `.xamlx` file for the service you are hosting, right-click it, and click on **Browse** to launch the service page and verify that the service is hosted and ready.

14. If all is well, you should see a service page come up that provides you with the ability to browse the WSDL:

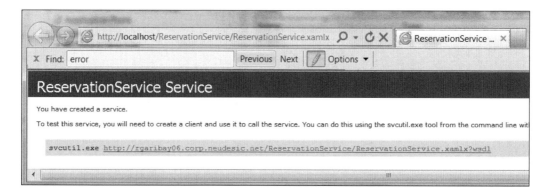

15. Copy the URL in the address bar of your browser to your clipboard and launch the Visual Studio Command Prompt.

16. At the prompt, type `wcftestclient`, hit space, and paste the URL:

 This will launch the WCF Test Client, a lightweight test harness that ships with the framework SDK that is useful for exercising SOAP-based WCF and WF Services.

17. Expand the endpoint exposed over `BasicHttpBinding` and double-click the **SubmitReservation** operation. Enter some test values for the reservation request and click on **Invoke**. Note the **Confirmation Number** that is returned (3155 in the following example):

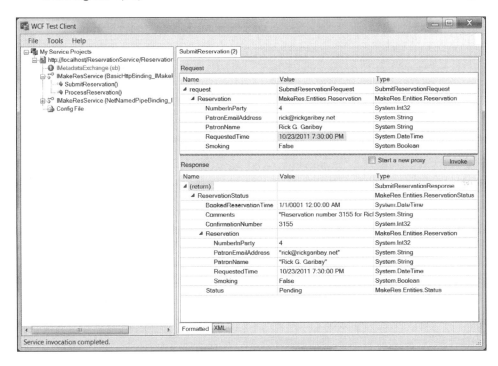

 Minimize, but do not close the WCF Test Client window. We'll come back to it shortly.

18. In IIS, double-click on the **AppFabric Dashboard** to get a birds-eye view of what's happening with the Reservation Service:

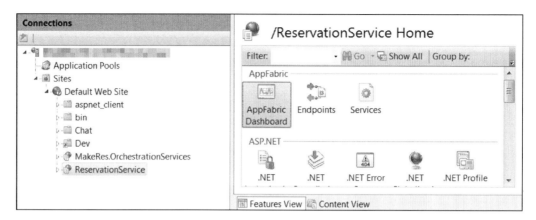

19. Notice that there is a single WF instance that is idle. Before clicking on the **Idle** link/icon, make a note of the number of WF Instance completions at the bottom of the dashboard:

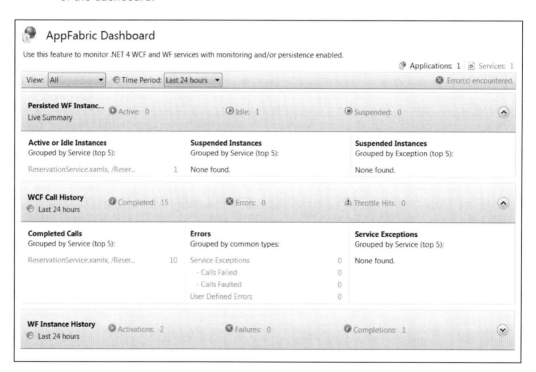

20. As you can see, that's our instance of the Reservation Service workflow, waiting for the approval message:

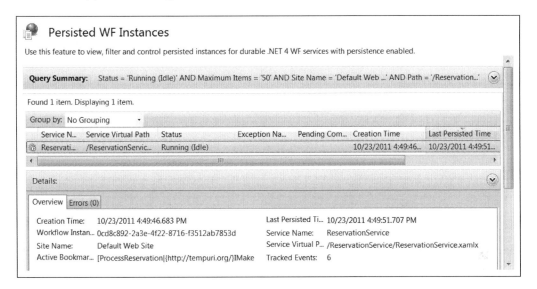

21. Now, get back to the WCF Test Client and double-click on the **ProcessReservation** operation. Paste in the confirmation number (3155 in this case) and set the status field to **Confirmed**. Click on **Invoke**. Click **OK** on the one-way message delivery confirmation's pop-up window:

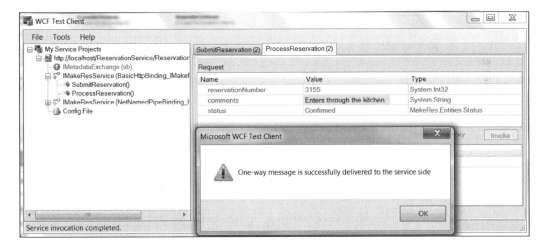

 The confirmation message is sent to the Reservation Service and no response is expected.

22. Finally, go back to the AppFabric Dashboard and refresh it by pressing *F5*. Notice that there are no longer any idle workflow instances, but the **Completions** count under **WF Instance History** has been incremented (on my machine, there was one completion prior to this one):

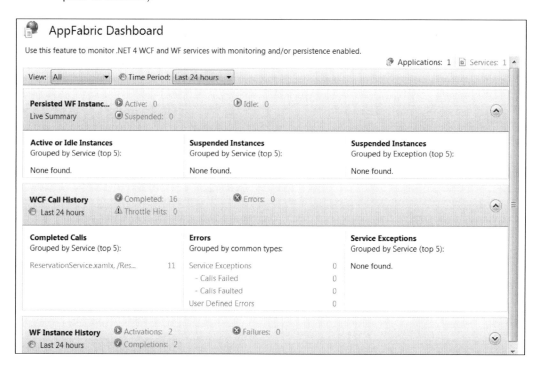

How it works...

By enabling metadata exchange over HTTP, we added a service behavior to the web.config (`<serviceMetadata httpGetEnabled="true" />`) for the Reservation Service application, just as we would manually.

While we did not make any changes to the **Monitoring** tab, it is worth noting that by default, the **Health Monitoring** setting is configured for you automatically. Unless you increase, decrease, or disable monitoring completely, you might not find an entry in your web.config file; however, the default configuration resembles something very close to the following:

```
<microsoft.applicationServer>
    <monitoring>
        <default enabled="true"
                 connectionStringName=
                 "ApplicationServerMonitoringConnectionString"
                 monitoringLevel="HealthMonitoring" />
    </monitoring>
</microsoft.applicationServer>
```

You can play with the monitoring slider, click on **Save**, and inspect the contents of the `Web.config` file to see the impact of these changes on the monitoring element shown previously.

You can probably already appreciate some of the benefits of Windows Server AppFabric hosting and management, as we haven't had to write any XML at all!

On that note, one of the things that is not very trivial to configure at all is persistence. While we are able to wire up the persistence provider with just a couple of clicks, peeking under the hood reveals some heavy lifting being done in the `web.config` file by Windows Server AppFabric, which writes out a comprehensive entry for the `sqlWorkflowInstance store` behavior:

```
<sqlWorkflowInstanceStore instanceCompletionAction="DeleteAll"
instanceEncodingOption="None"
instanceLockedExceptionAction="NoRetry"
connectionStringName="ConnectionString"
hostLockRenewalPeriod="00:00:30"
runnableInstancesDetectionPeriod="00:00:05" />
```

The `SQLWorkflowInstanceStore` behavior defines a number of key aspects of persistence, including whether the instance should be retained in the store once it completes, if you want to compress the instance data, and what to do if the instance is locked by another process when attempting to persist the instance. In addition, the connection string for the persistence store itself is also stored here. Lastly, some attributes we did not configure, but are written to the `web.config` nonetheless due to the defaults being applied include the `hostLockRenewalPeriod`, which determines how long the persistence provider should wait before unlocking the instance making it available for another host, and the `runnableInstancesDetectionPeriod`, which configures the interval at which the host checks to see if there are any instances or activities available for execution so that they can be loaded and executed accordingly.

Lastly, the persist and unload settings are configured via the `workflowIdle` behavior, and are also written in the `serviceBehaviors` element:

```
<workflowIdle timeToPersist="00:00:05" timeToUnload="00:00:05" />
```

The distinction between the unload and persist timeout is that when the former fires, the workflow instance is unloaded from memory, whereas the latter results in the persistence of the current state to the persistent store.

When enabled, monitoring events are written to the monitoring store that is configured when you complete Windows Server AppFabric configuration, and the Windows Server AppFabric Dashboard reads its metrics from this store.

There's more...

When we first submitted the initial reservation request by exercising the `SubmitReservation` operation in step 17, the Reservation Service workflow service executed a Sequence activity consisting of a number of nested activities that execute in sequential order:

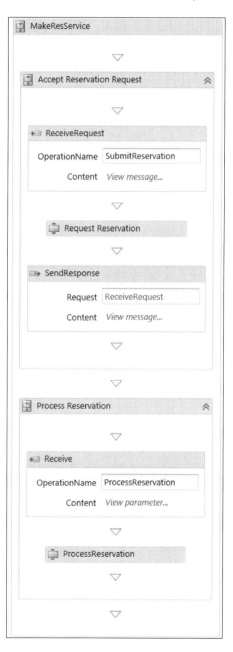

The activity labeled **ReceiveRequest** is a messaging activity that is capable of receiving a WCF message. In this case, I configured it to expose an operation called `SubmitReservation` over the `BasicHttpBinding`, which was activated by the initial message. From there, it executed a custom `CodeActivity` that simply generates a confirmation number and passes control back to the sequence activity. Next, a Send activity labeled **SendResponse** is executed which returns the confirmation payload to the caller (in our case the WCF Test Client that we used to invoke the operation).

Since we configured the workflow to unload and persist in 5 seconds, it did so, which is what we verified when we opened the AppFabric Dashboard in step 19.

From there, calling the **ProcessReservation** operation from the WCF Test Client resulted in a one-way message to flow to the service, which was then correlated to the persisted instance of the workflow and Windows Server AppFabric activated the instance, re-hydrating it and allowing the workflow instance to complete as we verified when we went back to the AppFabric Dashboard and hit refresh in step 22.

WCF and WF Services support both request-response and one-way message exchange patterns.

If you are familiar with web services development, you've likely used the request-response pattern, which is similar to invoking a method and waiting; however briefly for the method to return. This is typically regarded as a "synchronous" or "blocking" call.

When asynchrony is desired, such that the client blocks as briefly as possible, or the service operation is not designed to provide a response, a one-way message exchange is appropriate, also commonly referred to as fire-and-forget. However, note that contrary to popular belief, a WCF one-way operation call does indeed block, albeit briefly; until the message is dispatched to the method mapped to the service operation.

More on persistence

There are a number of conditions which will cause a workflow instance to persist, including the unload (and persist) threshold that we configured being reached.

As per MSDN, these conditions are as follows:

- When a Persist activity executes
- When a workflow instance is terminated or finishes
- When a `TransactionScope` activity completes or a `TransactedReceiveScope` activity completes
- When using messaging activities or a Delay activity, the workflow instance becomes idle and the `WorkflowIdleBehavior` is set

▶ When a `WorkflowApplication` becomes idle and the `PersistableIdle` property of the application is set to `PersistableIdleAction.Persist`

▶ When a host application is instructed to persist or unload a workflow instance

You can find more details on WF 4 persistence on MSDN by following this URL: `http://msdn.microsoft.com/en-us/site/dd489420`

Understanding correlation

Correlation is a feature of WF 4 that allows more than one disparate message to be routed to the same workflow instance, even when that workflow instance is no longer in memory. It works hand-in-hand with persistence, which is the mechanism by which a workflow instance can be unloaded from memory and serialized to disk, freeing up valuable resources and supporting long-running workflows such as the two-step reservation scenario in this recipe.

WF 4 supports a number of different correlation types which are designed to support a number of different scenarios.

For example, **Request-Response Correlation** provides correlation between messaging activities such as the `SendAndReceiveReply` activity, which is really a composite activity that allows you to send a one-way message to a service from which you eventually expect a callback of some sort.

Context Correlation is used in accordance with the .NET Context Exchange Protocol Specification, which standardizes the use of cookies and headers for the purpose of instance identification and is supported when using bindings such as the `BasicHttpContextBinding`, `WSHttpContextBinding`, or `NetTcpContextBinding`.

Content Correlation, which is the approach that we used in this recipe, is simply the means by which you can use a shared, known identifier, (such as the confirmation ID) to correlate subsequent messages such as the approval message back to the workflow instance.

There are a number of features such as **Correlation Handle**, which stores the key value pair of the correlation identifier, and **Correlation Initializer**, which provides a mechanism for grabbing the identifier and storing it in a correlation handle that you will want to become familiar with when working with correlation in your workflow services (`CorrrelationScope` and `InitiailizeCorrelation` activities can serve to automate some of this and can definitely come in handy as well).

Understanding the Workflow Management Service

The Workflow Management Service (WMS) is a key service provided by Windows Server AppFabric that is responsible for activating workflow instances that have been stored in a persistence store. When a workflow instance becomes a candidate for activation, the WMS is responsible for activating the instance so that processing can be resumed.

In this recipe, when the correlating approval message was received by Windows Server AppFabric, the WMS was responsible for activating the instance that had been persisted so that the workflow instance could be resumed.

The WMS also provides the ability to restart instances of a workflow that have been orphaned due to a lock expiring on the instance but the instance still being locked by a host. This can happen if the host that had ownership of the workflow instance is hung or has become otherwise unresponsive, which while uncommon, can be problematic. In addition, when a lock from a host has expired, but the instance is still locked, the WMS supports the ability to retry handing the instance to another capable host within a given configured threshold, using a feature known as instance lock retry.

You can configure these settings in the **Advanced Persistence Settings** of the **Workflow Persistence** tab.

See also

For a step-by-step guide for installing Windows Server AppFabric, refer to the *Installing Windows Server AppFabric* recipe in *Chapter 1, Installing Windows Server AppFabric*.

For a step-by-step guide for installing the Microsoft Web Deployment Tool, refer to the *Installing the Web Deployment tool (Web Deploy)* recipe in *Chapter 4, Windows Server AppFabric Hosting Fundamentals*.

For a simpler recipe that covers how to host a simple WF 4 workflow service in Windows Server AppFabric without the need for any additional configuration, refer to the *Hosting basic workflow services* recipe in *Chapter 4, Windows Server AppFabric Hosting Fundamentals*.

Taking advantage of WAS and Auto-Start

Windows Process Activation Service (WAS) was first introduced in Windows Vista and Windows Server 2008 as an application environment that extends IIS 7 and later to provide first-class support for hosting WCF and WF services.

Built on top of IIS, WAS provides additional capabilities such as:

- Message-based activation, which ensures that processes and applications are only activated when there are requests arriving at the service
- Support for both HTTP and non-HTTP protocols such as NetTcp, NetMSMQ, and NetPipes
- Support for Auto-Start, which allows for expensive initialization work for a service to take place when the application is started as opposed to waiting for the first message to arrive

▶ Intelligent application recycling to provide automatic health management of problematic applications by recycling the worker process based on number of requests, memory thresholds, or at a scheduled time

Windows Server AppFabric builds on and extends these capabilities by providing management and configuration tools that take advantage of WAS-hosted application capabilities via the IIS Manager and Windows PowerShell, increasing the granularity of the Auto-Start capability so that it can be applied to specific service endpoints.

In this recipe, we will configure a WCF service to take advantage of WAS and Windows Server AppFabric including support for non-HTTP protocols and the Auto-Start feature.

Getting ready

This recipe assumes that you've already installed and configured Windows Server AppFabric. If you haven't, please follow the recipes in *Chapter 1, Installing Windows Server AppFabric*.

The first thing you want to do is ensure you have WAS enabled. To do so, in Windows 7, go to **Control Panel | Programs, Programs and Features** and click on **Turn Windows Features On or Off** and make sure that all of the checkboxes under **Windows Process Activation Service** are selected:

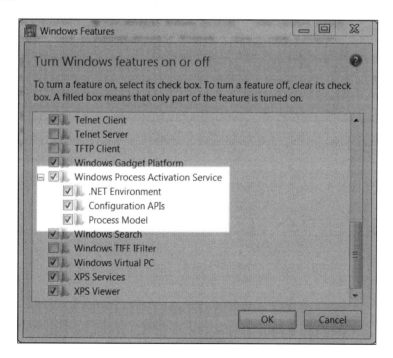

Next, scroll up and find the entry called **Microsoft .NET Framework 3.5.1** and ensure all entries are checked. This will ensure that Windows Server AppFabric is configured for both HTTP and non-HTTP protocols such as NetTcp, NetPipes, NetMSMQ, and so on:

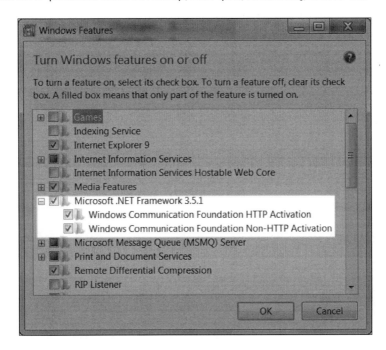

In addition, for this recipe, we will use a WCF service application that is available for download with this book called "WCFAutoStart". Please ensure that you have downloaded Visual Studio 2010 solution and opened it with Visual Studio in Administrator mode.

How to do it...

We'll start by reviewing the WCFAutoStart project and deploy it to Windows Server AppFabric. From there, we will configure the application to leverage the NetTcp and NetNamedPipe protocols in addition to HTTP. Finally, we will explore the impact of enabling Auto-Start on the application.

1. Expand the WCFAutoStart project to reveal the IService1.cs, Service1.cs, and Web.config files. In the Service1.cs file, notice that there is a Service Factory called AutoStartServiceFactory and that it includes a call to System. Threading.Thread.Sleep and passes in a value of 5000 (or 5 seconds):

    ```
    public class AutoStartServiceFactory : ServiceHostFactoryBase
    {
        public override ServiceHostBase
        CreateServiceHost(string constructorString, Uri[]
            baseAddresses)
    ```

```
        {
            System.Threading.Thread.Sleep(5000);
            return new ServiceHost(typeof(Service1), baseAddresses);
        }
    }
}
```

2. Next, right-click on the `Service1.svc` file, select **View Markup**, and notice that I have included a reference to the `AutoStartServiceFactory` in addition to the common attributes shown as follows:

```
<%@ ServiceHost Language="C#"
Debug="true"
Service="WCFAutoStart.Service1"
CodeBehind="Service1.svc.cs"
Factory="WCFAutoStart.AutoStartServiceFactory"%>
```

> The `AutoStartServiceFactory` class will be used to demonstrate how the Auto-Start feature works shortly.

3. Next, inspect the `Web.config` file and notice that there is no explicit configuration of services or endpoints.

4. Right-click on the **WCFAutoStart** service project and click on **Publish**. You can choose any method with which you'd like to publish this service to Windows Server AppFabric. In this case, I have used Web Deploy to deploy to the **Default Web Site** on my local machine and specified an application name of **WCFAutoStart**.

5. With the WCFAutoStart application deployed to IIS/Windows Server AppFabric, open **IIS**, expand **Default Web Site**, right-click the **WCFAutoStart** application, select **Manage Application**, and click on **Advanced Settings...**.

6. In the **Enabled Protocols** field, add a comma after HTTP followed by **net.tcp** and **net. pipe** to enable the NetTcp and Net Named Pipe protocols for the application:

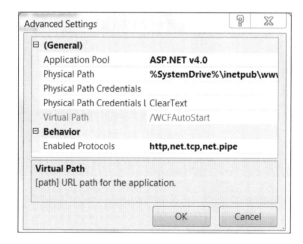

7. Browse to the **WSDL** endpoint for the application (in my case it is `http://localhost/WCFAutoStart/Service1.svc?wsdl`) and notice that a binding has been created for each of the protocols we just enabled:

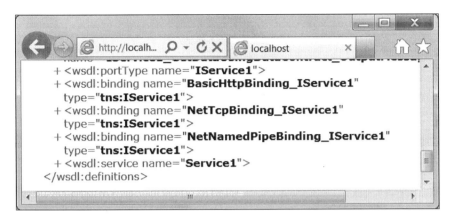

 The WCFAutoStart service is now configured to support the NetTcp and Net Named Pipe protocols in addition to HTTP.

8. Now, let's enable the use of the Auto-Start feature. In IIS, right-click on the **WCFAutoStart** application, click on **Manage WCF and WF Services**, and select **Configure...** to launch the Windows Server AppFabric configuration UI:

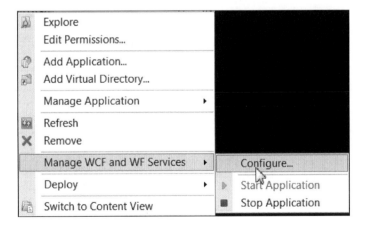

9. Next, click on the **Auto-Start** tab and enable the use of the Auto-Start feature by selecting the radio button next to **Custom (services that opt-in will auto-start)** and clicking on **Apply**:

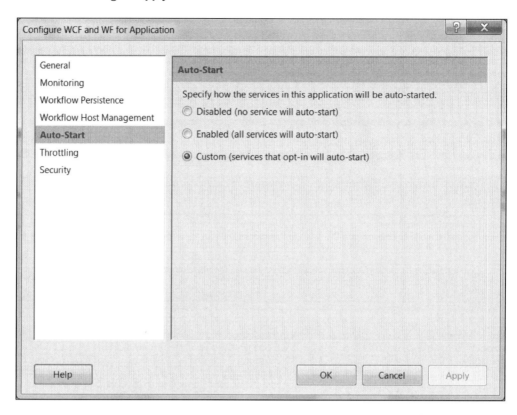

10. Now, let's enable Auto-Start for the service. In IIS, click on **Features View** and click on the **Services** icon in Windows Server AppFabric:

11. Right-click on the **Service** entry in the grid and click on **Configure**. On the configuration UI, click on the **Auto-Start** tab. Check **Enable** and click on **Apply**:

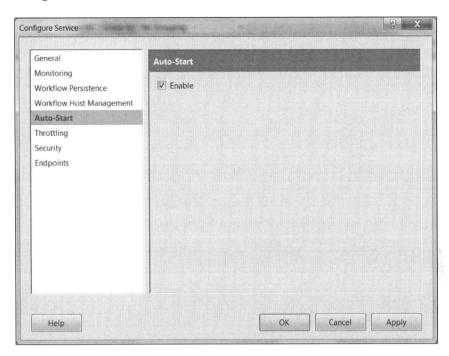

 Auto-Start is enabled for the service only, not the entire application.

12. In Visual Studio, right-click the **WCFAutoStart** service once again and select **Publish**, but this time, modify the name of the application to be created to **WCFNoAutoStart** and click on **Publish**.

13. Finally, right-click the **Client** project and click on **Debug** to run it. Notice that the call to the **WCFAutoStart** application executed much faster than the call to the **WCFNoAutoStart** application:

How it works...

WCF 4 includes a new feature called **Default Endpoints** that takes a conventional approach to endpoint configuration by inspecting the base address(es) for a service and automatically creating the endpoints that would otherwise require boilerplate configuration. When we added the net.tcp and net.pipe protocols to the WCFAutoStart application in step 6, we exposed two new base URIs for the application. A URI is the combination of a base URI prefix (which is based on the protocol bindings we enabled in step 6) and the application URI (in our case `/WCFAutoStart/Service1.svc`).

For example, the following URIs are each valid endpoint URIs for the WCFAutoStart service:

- ▶ `http://localhost/WCFAutoStart/Service1.svc`
- ▶ `net.tcp://localhost/WCFAutoStart/Service1.svc`
- ▶ `net.pipe//localhost/WCFAutoStart/Service1.svc`

When we browsed the `http://localhost/WCFAutoStart/Service1.svc?wsdl` URI, the WSDL was generated based on the endpoints that WCF created for us, which were based on the base URIs that we configured.

The Auto-Start feature is useful for services that have some initialization work to do, such as loading a list into memory or establishing a connection to a socket. As these types of initialization chores can be costly, the first client to consume the service may have to wait for an inordinate period of time before the service is ready to handle its request.

Windows Server AppFabric enhances WAS support for Auto-Start by allowing you to configure Auto-Start at the service level in addition to the application/application pool level. This allows you to have multiple services hosted by the same application/application pool with different Auto-Start behaviors.

To take advantage of Auto-Start at the service level, you first make the feature available for use at the application level as we did in step 9. From there, you can configure each service you want to opt-in to Auto-Start by configuring the service through the Services view, as we did in steps 10 and 11.

To take advantage of Auto-Start, you must hook your initialization work within a custom factory which will be invoked when the **Opening** event on the **ServiceHost** fires. Steps 1 and 2 provided a walkthrough of the code both in the factory itself, and the necessary modification required to the `.svc` file in ServiceHost directive.

By deploying a copy of the **WCFAutoStart** application, and calling it **WCFNoAutoStart**, the application was deployed with the default settings that leave Auto-Start disabled. The client included as part of the solution download, exercises both endpoints sequentially and reports back on the execution time of each. As you can see from the results in step 13, the call to the **WCFAutoStart** application is significantly faster than the **WCFNoAutoStart** application because the call to `System.Threading.Thread.Sleep(5000)` took place as soon as the IIS/Windows Server AppFabric application hosting the service was started as opposed to waiting for the first message to arrive as is the case with the identical service deployed without Auto-Start enabled in the WCFNoAutoStart application.

There's more...

Windows Server AppFabric relies on, and extends IIS and WAS hosting to provide additional features and capabilities. It is worth understanding how hosting in IIS and WAS works.

Applications are organized into websites in IIS, and each application maps to one or more application pool. An application pool is configured for a specific runtime version (for Windows Server AppFabric-hosted applications, only CLR 4 is supported) and process identity and can host one or many applications. Each application pool represents an instance of the `w3wp.exe` worker process, and the process separates each application into its own private `.NET` app domain.

Each application or website is configured with one or more protocol bindings. If the only protocol configured is HTTP, then it is the role of `HTTP.sys` to route the message to the w3svc listener process, which will then route incoming HTTP messages to WAS. For non-HTTP protocols, such as NetTcp and so on, a protocol adapter for each is responsible for listening to incoming messages on the socket, port, or queue and dispatching them to WAS. WAS is then responsible for resolving the worker process in which the application lives and, if the worker process has not been started, doing so upon the receipt of a message. If the worker process is already started, WAS dispatches the message to the appropriate application within the worker process.

Windows Server AppFabric extends the capabilities of WAS by introducing the Workflow Management Service (WMS), which uses the Service Management Service (SMS) to provide additional hosting and management capabilities for WF services. Support for remote instance management, advanced persistence scenarios, and workflow instance activation are all provided by these services.

Avoiding application pool recycling

Application pools managed by WAS benefit from automatic process recycling, which improves the health of an application by monitoring for message receive thresholds, memory usage, or based on a configured schedule and recycling the entire process or application domain when one of the configured conditions are met. In addition, by default, an application pool managed by WAS will recycle every 29 hours to maintain optimal health of an application.

Often, this behavior is a good thing, but there are certainly times when you don't want your application or the application pool restarted. While there is nothing that can be done to prevent an application domain from recycling as a result of modifying the `machine.config`, `web.config`, or `applicationHost.config` files or deploying a new version of an assembly, you can configure the application pool to not automatically recycle every 29 hours and relax other thresholds by modifying the advanced settings through IIS. The following article provides some good information on what setting options are recommended for eliminating application pool recycling: `http://msdn.microsoft.com/en-us/library/ee677371.aspx`.

See also

For a step-by-step guide for installing Windows Server AppFabric, refer to the *Installing Windows Server AppFabric* recipe in *Chapter 1, Installing Windows Server AppFabric*.

For a step-by-step guide for installing the Microsoft Web Deployment Tool, refer to the *Installing the Web Deployment Tool (Web Deploy)* recipe in *Chapter 4, Windows Server AppFabric Hosting Fundamentals*.

The technique for demonstrating the improvements in call performance provided by Auto-Start is based on a sample provided by the WCF team, which is available at `http://archive.msdn.microsoft.com/WCFAfAutoStart`.

Hosting Windows Azure Relay services

Windows Azure Service Bus provides a highly robust messaging fabric hosted by Windows Azure that provides both relayed and brokered messaging. You can use the capabilities provided by Azure Service Bus to enable hybrid messaging scenarios between applications and services deployed both on-premise and in the cloud. For example, it is common in modern distributed systems to have clients on-premise and services hosted on a cloud provider or a partner data center, or the inverse: clients on a cloud provider or partner network with services hosted on-premise, and any combination thereof.

As services hosted on-premise are often hosted on NAT networks behind both hardware and software firewalls, it is not easy to consume services without investing in a hosting provider or standing up a DMZ, both of which can be expensive.

Azure Service Bus significantly reduces this friction by providing a relay between the client and service allowing you to host services and consume them from pretty much anywhere in the world.

What makes Azure Service Bus so practical is that the relay capabilities are modeled on WCF and as such, services exposed on the Azure Service Bus are first-class citizens on Windows Server AppFabric.

To on-ramp Azure Service Bus, you just need to choose the binding corresponding to the channel shape and protocols of interest. Support for REST and SOAP over HTTP as well as SOAP over TCP is provided by the following relay bindings:

> ▶ **BasicHttpRelayBinding**: Complements BasicHttpBinding for WS-I Basic Profile Request-Response MEP over HTTP/S

> ▶ **WebHttpRelayBinding**: Complements WebHttpBinding for REST Request-Response MEP over HTTP/S

> ▶ **WS2007HttpRelayBinding**: Complements WsHttpBinding for WS-* Request-Response MEP over HTTP/S

> ▶ **NetTcpRelayBinding**: Complements NetTcpBinding for Request-Response MEP over TCP

> ▶ **NetOneWayRelayBinding**: Smart, optimized datagram messaging over bi-directional TCP

> ▶ **NetEventRelayBinding**: Smart, optimized multicast messaging over bi-directional TCP

In this recipe, we will start with a simple WCF service and deploy it to Windows Server AppFabric with the NetTcpRelayBinding, which offers the best mix of capabilities and is also the most performant. From there, we will call the service over the Azure Service Bus messaging fabric to verify that the service was deployed and configured correctly.

Microsoft recommends the NetTcpRelayBinding whenever your scenario allows because it takes advantage of the performance benefits inherent to TCP sockets and in addition, will attempt to establish a direct connection between two connections and if possible, upgrade the connection.

In addition, Version 1.6 and later of the Azure SDK includes support for high availability, allowing you to host multiple instances of a relay service while ensuring that the message is always only routed to one.

Getting ready

You'll need an active Azure account with an Azure Service Bus Namespace configured to proceed with this recipe. If you are new to Azure Service Bus, please visit `http://azure.com` to get started.

In addition, you will need the latest Windows Azure SDK, which can be obtained from the Platform Installer or directly from Microsoft. To obtain the latest Azure SDK, please visit `http://www.windowsazure.com/en-us/develop/net/`.

This recipe assumes that you've already installed and configured Windows Server AppFabric. If you haven't, please follow the recipes in *Chapter 1, Installing Windows Server AppFabric*.

While not required, we'll also leverage the Microsoft Web Deployment tool for seamlessly deploying the WF service to Windows Server AppFabric, so if you are not familiar with it, please refer to the first two recipes in *Chapter 4, Windows Server AppFabric Hosting Fundamentals*.

How to do it...

We'll begin by creating a regular WCF service using the WCF Service Application template. From there, we'll add some Azure Service Bus specific configuration, deploy to Windows Server AppFabric, and wrap up with some final configuration before writing some code to test the service:

1. Start by opening Visual Studio 2010 and creating a new WCF Service Application project called `WCFRelayService`. Take a moment to orient yourself to the `IService1.cs` and `Service1.cs` files, noting that this is a very simple request/response WCF service that will echo back whatever value is sent to it from the client.

2. Open the `IService1.cs` file and add the following interface declaration anywhere inside the `Namespace` or following the IService1 interface declaration:

    ```
    public interface IService1Channel : IService1, IClientChannel { }
    ```

3. Now, add a reference to the `Microsoft.ServiceBus.dll` assembly, which is available in the `C:\Program Files\Windows Azure AppFabric SDK\V1.5\Assemblies\NET4.0` folder that is created after installing the Windows Azure SDK 1.5.

    > Alternatively, you can use the NuGet package installer to obtain the required assembly.

4. Open the `Web.config` file and add the following tags, which define a service endpoint that will use the NetTcpRelayBinding:

    ```
    <system.serviceModel>
        <services>
            <service name="WCFRelayService.Service1">
                <endpoint address=""
                            binding="netTcpRelayBinding"
                            contract-"WCFRelayService.IService1" />
            </service>
        </services>
    </system.serviceModel>
    ```

5. Next, add a binding configuration for the NetTcpRelayBinding that disables WCF security:

    ```
    <bindings>
        <netTcpRelayBinding>
            <binding>
    ```

```
                <security mode="None" />
            </binding>
        </netTcpRelayBinding>
    </bindings>
```

6. Now, add an endpoint behavior that defines the security scheme required by Azure Access Control Service:

```
<behaviors>
    <endpointBehaviors>
        <behavior>
            <transportClientEndpointBehavior
            credentialType="SharedSecret">
                <clientCredentials>
                    <sharedSecret issuerName="owner"
                                  issuerSecret="SECRET" />
                </clientCredentials>
            </transportClientEndpointBehavior>
        </behavior>
    </endpointBehaviors>
</behaviors>
```

7. Save the `Web.config`. At this point, the `Web.config` should resemble the following:

```
Web.config
    <?xml version="1.0" encoding="utf-8"?>
    <configuration>
      <runtime>
        <dependentAssembly>
          <assemblyIdentity name="Microsoft.ServiceBus" publicKeyToken="31bf3856ad364e35" culture="neutral" />
          <bindingRedirect oldVersion="1.0.0.0" newVersion="1.5.0.0"/>
        </dependentAssembly>
      </runtime>
      <system.web>
        <compilation debug="true" targetFramework="4.0" />
      </system.web>
      <system.serviceModel>
        <services>
          <service name="RelayService.Service1">
            <endpoint address="" binding="netTcpRelayBinding" contract="RelayService.IService1" />
          </service>
        </services>
        <bindings>
          <netTcpRelayBinding>
            <binding >
              <security mode="None" />
            </binding>
          </netTcpRelayBinding>
        </bindings>
        <behaviors>
          <endpointBehaviors>
            <behavior>
              <transportClientEndpointBehavior credentialType="SharedSecret">
                <clientCredentials>
                  <sharedSecret issuerName="owner" issuerSecret="SECRET" />
                </clientCredentials>
              </transportClientEndpointBehavior>
            </behavior>
          </endpointBehaviors>
        </behaviors>
        <serviceHostingEnvironment multipleSiteBindingsEnabled="true" />
      </system.serviceModel>
    </configuration>
```

8. Now, deploy the project to Windows Server AppFabric using your preferred method of deployment. You can use XCOPY deployment or follow the recipes in *Chapter 4, Windows Server AppFabric Hosting Fundamentals* for leveraging the Microsoft Web Deployment Tool.

 At a minimum, you will need to deploy the `.xamlx` and `web.config` files as well as the assemblies located in the `bin` directory of your application root. If you use Web Deploy, this will happen automatically

9. Ensure that the virtual directory that hosts your deployment is configured as an application and that the application is bound to a .NET 4.0 application pool. While Web Deploy will do this for you automatically, if you are using a different approach like XCOPY, you will want to right-click on the virtual directory and click on **Convert to Virtual Application**.

10. Next, right-click on the application and select **Manage WCF and WF Services** followed by **Configure**:

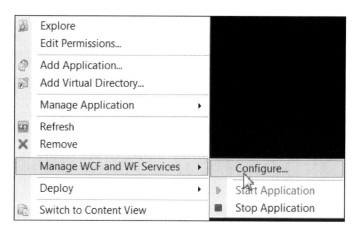

11. Next, click on the **Auto-Start** tab and enable the use of the Auto-Start feature by selecting the radio button next to **Custom (services that opt-in will auto-start)** and clicking on **Apply**:

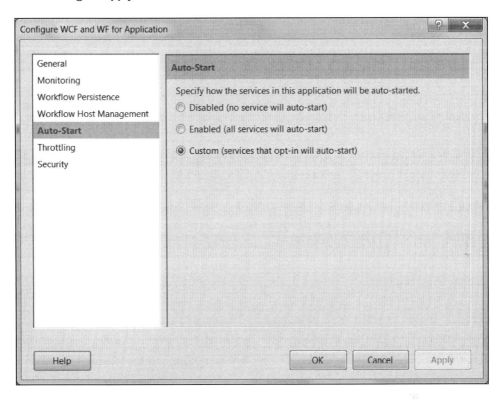

12. Now, let's enable Auto-Start for the service. In IIS, click on **Features View** and click on the **Services** icon in Windows Server AppFabric.

13. Right-click on the **Service** entry in the grid and click on **Configure**. On the configuration UI, click on the **Auto-Start** tab. Click on **Enable** and then on **Apply**:

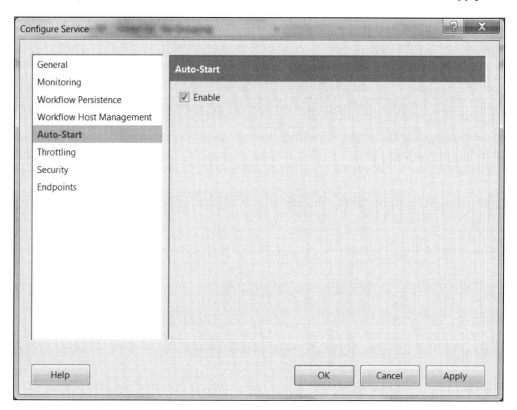

 Auto-Start is enabled for the service only, not the entire application.

14. Now, click on the Endpoints icon next to the Services icon you just clicked and find the entry for the NetTcpRelay endpoint. Right-click the endpoint and click on **Configure**:

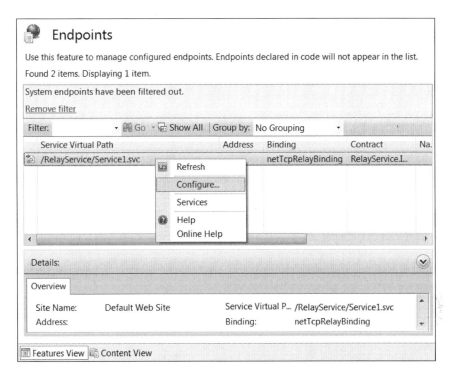

15. Notice that the endpoint address setting is empty. Enter your **Service Gateway URL** followed by **RelayService** to reserve this endpoint on the Service Bus messaging fabric. For example, my full URI would be `sb://rickgaribay.servicebus.windows.net/RelayService`:

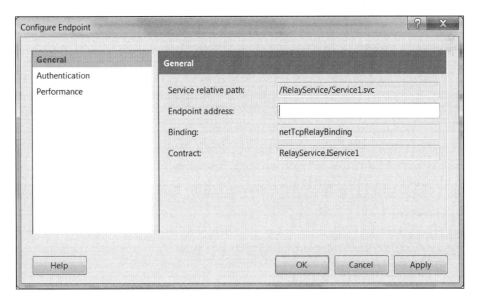

16. Now it's time to test our service over the Azure Service Bus. Create a Console Application project called **RelayClient** and ensure that you set the **Target Framework** to **.NET Framework 4**.

17. Add a reference to the `Microsoft.ServiceBus.dll` assembly, which is available in the `C:\Program Files\Windows Azure AppFabric SDK\ V1.5\Assemblies\NET4.0` folder that is created after installing the Windows Azure SDK 1.5.

 Alternatively, you can use the NuGet package installer to obtain the required assembly.

18. Next, copy the `IService1.cs` file that you modified in step 2 to the RelayClient project. Either change the namespace to match the client's namespace or add a namespace reference to it in the `Program.cs` file of the RelayClient.

19. Add the following code to the `Main` method, which creates the service behavior for requesting an access token for calling the RelayService:

```
TokenProvider provider =
TokenProvider.CreateSharedSecretTokenProvider("owner","SECRET");
TransportClientEndpointBehavior transportClientBehavior = new
TransportClientEndpointBehavior(provider);
```

20. Next, create an instance of the `NetTcpRelayBinding` and set the security mode to `None`:

```
var binding = new NetTcpRelayBinding();
binding.Security.Mode = EndToEndSecurityMode.None;
```

21. Now, create a `ChannelFactory`, templating it with the IService1Channel contract we created in step 2, and passing in the binding and an EndpointAddress instance with the URI to our RelayService:

```
Uri serviceUri = new
Uri("sb://YourNamespace.servicebus.windows.net/RelayService");
ServiceBusEnvironment.CreateServiceUri("sb", serviceNamespace,
"Service1");

ChannelFactory<IService1Channel> channelFactory = new
ChannelFactory<IService1Channel>(binding, new
EndpointAddress(serviceUri));
```

22. Now, add the service behavior we created in step 6 to the instance of the Channel Factory:

```
channelFactory.Endpoint.Behaviors.Add(transportClientBehavior);
```

23. Lastly, create a channel that implements the IService1Channel from the Channel Factory instance, open the channel, and call the GetData operation, writing the result of the service call to the Console:

```
IService1Channel channel = channelFactory.CreateChannel();
channel.Open();
Console.WriteLine(String.Format("Result:{0}", channel.
GetData(42)));
```

24. The full client implementation should resemble the following:

```
static void Main(string[] args)
{
    TokenProvider provider =
    TokenProvider.CreateSharedSecretTokenProvider
    ("owner","SECRET");
    TransportClientEndpointBehavior transportClientBehavior = new
    TransportClientEndpointBehavior(provider);

    var binding = new NetTcpRelayBinding();
    binding.Security.Mode = EndToEndSecurityMode.None;

    Uri serviceUri = new
    Uri("sb://YourNamespace.servicebus.windows.net/
    RelayService");
    ServiceBusEnvironment.CreateServiceUri
    ("sb", serviceNamespace,
    "Service1");

    ChannelFactory<IService1Channel> channelFactory = new
    ChannelFactory<IService1Channel>(binding, new
    EndpointAddress(serviceUri));
    channelFactory.Endpoint.Behaviors.
    Add(transportClientBehavior);

    IService1Channel channel = channelFactory.CreateChannel();
    channel.Open();

    Console.WriteLine(String.Format("Result:{0}",
    channel.GetData(42)));

    Console.ReadLine();

}
```

25. Finally, run the client. You should see the response from the service as shown in the following screenshot:

How it works...

Azure Service Bus relayed messaging works by acting as a relay between two (or more) endpoints. A client and service (or services) establish an outbound, bi-directional socket connection over either TCP or HTTP on the relay and thus, messages from the client tunnel their way through the relay to the service.

In this way, both the client and service are really peers on the same messaging fabric. The service receives messages from the relay on behalf of the client and as such the roles can easily be reversed. This pattern enables true hybrid enterprise composition and allows clients to communicate with services and vice-a-versa beyond the enterprise, and literally from anywhere in the world, provided an Internet connection exists.

To take advantage of Azure Service Bus relay capabilities, you simply create a WCF service or client and reference the `Microsoft.ServiceBus` assembly and configure the service and client accordingly.

For the service, we added a declarative endpoint that defined the binding and contract for the endpoint. We left the address blank because when hosting WCF services in IIS, IIS determines the address based on the configure protocol (base address) and application path.

We also added an endpoint behavior that is required for obtaining a WRAP token from the Azure Access Control Service (ACS). This happens transparently in the background; however, the `issuerName` and `issuerSecret` are required to ensure that your application is authorized to obtain a token.

When we deployed the service to IIS/Windows Server AppFabric, we enabled the Auto-Start feature which is required for Azure Service Bus because it requires the establishment of the bi-directional outbound socket connection a priori to the first message being received, which is an excellent application of the Auto-Start feature. Once we enabled the use of the feature, we constrained Auto-Start to only apply to the RelayService, which is a feature only available in Windows Server AppFabric.

We also provided an interesting service address for the endpoint which started with `sb://`. This URI prefix is proprietary to Azure Service Bus and is required when using non-HTTP bindings to expose a service over the relay.

The last thing we did was write a simple client that uses a `ChannelFactory` to consume the service. In step 2, we added an interface declaration called `IService1Channel` that inherits from `IService1`, the service contract we copied over from the service project and `IClientChannel`, which defines a request response client interface. This is required for the `ChannelFactory` to know the channel shape and contract that it should build the channel stack for.

When consuming WCF and WF Services, you can use a proxy class, which can be hand-crafted, but is often generated using tools such as `svcutil.exe` or **Add Service Reference** in Visual Studio. With a proxy, artifacts such as the service contract and data contract are generated by inspecting the WSDL/metadata for the service you wish to consume and the client code executes the methods as if they were local to the application.

An alternate approach is to write your own `ChannelFactory`, which is useful when you have already obtained the service and data contract(s) out of band, or just don't want to fuss with proxies. Azure Service Bus Relay messaging supports both approaches. I have chosen a Channel Factory purely for the sake of simplicity.

When we ran the client, it created an outbound socket connection over TCP port 818 and sent the message to the Azure Service Bus, which in turn relayed the message to the RelayService hosted on IIS/Windows Server AppFabric. The listener was listening on TCP port 828. From there the message was dispatched to the GetData operation, which responded with the original request appended to the response payload.

There's more...

Azure Service Bus also supports a pull-based publish-subscribe model, commonly referred to as brokered messaging. Brokered messaging extends the capabilities of Azure Service Bus by adding support for durable messaging via queues, topics, and subscriptions. There are three APIs that are supported: a .NET Client API, a REST API, and a WCF API via the new `NetMessagingBinding`.

You can host a WCF service powered by the `NetMessagingBinding` just as you would the rest of the bindings and use the familiar WCF programming mode to consume it, however this binding is specific to brokered messaging and does not apply to relayed messaging.

See also

For a step-by-step guide for installing Windows Server AppFabric, refer to the *Installing Windows Server AppFabric* recipe in *Chapter 1, Installing Windows Server AppFabric*.

For a step-by-step guide for installing the Microsoft Web Deployment Tool, please see the *Installing the Web Deployment tool (Web Deploy)* recipe in this chapter.

To obtain the latest Azure SDK, please visit `http://www.windowsazure.com/en-us/develop/net/`.

To learn more about Windows Azure Service Bus, please visit `http://azure.com`.

If you are interested in learning more about Windows Azure Service Bus Brokered Messaging, please see the article "Introducing Queues and Topics in Azure Service Bus" written by the author in CODE Magazine: `http://www.code-magazine.com/Article.aspx?quickid=1112041`.

Using common Server AppFabric hosting commandlets

Windows Server AppFabric provides a simplified management experience for working with WCF and WF services. Whether you are a developer or IT Pro, you stand to benefit from the varied management capabilities that Windows Server AppFabric offers.

Most of the recipes in this book showcase the UI-based management techniques, as those are most common, but Windows Server AppFabric also offers the ability to manage applications using PowerShell cmdlets, both interactively and in an automated, scripted manner.

In this recipe, we'll prepare our workstation to use the **ApplicationServer** Powershell module, which contains a number of control and instance cmdlets that allow you to manage applications and services deployed to Windows Server AppFabric.

From there, we'll explore some common commands for obtaining configuration information at the application and service level, configuring an application to take advantage of the Auto-Start feature, reviewing and modifying monitoring settings, and starting and stopping a Windows Server AppFabric application.

Getting ready

This recipe assumes that you've already installed and configured Windows Server AppFabric. If you haven't, please follow the recipes in *Chapter 1, Installing Windows Server AppFabric.*

We'll use the Reservation Service sample WF application that is available for download as part of the resources available with this book.

> As the name of the application suggests, the Reservation Service simulates a restaurant reservation workflow service wherein a patron requests a reservation (perhaps from a web frontend or via an inbound automated call center agent) that is managed by the workflow service. The workflow service accepts the reservation and sends the would-be patron an e-mail confirming the receipt of the reservation (but not the reservation itself). The service then awaits approval from the director of reservations (common in the hospitality space) or maître d to ensure that the requested accommodations can be met. If so, a second e-mail is sent to the patron welcoming them to the restaurant at the requested time, or notifying them that their request could not be accommodated.

While not required, we'll also leverage the Microsoft Web Deployment Tool for seamlessly deploying the WF service to Windows Server AppFabric so if you are not familiar with it, please refer to the first two recipes in this chapter.

You will also need to ensure you have Windows PowerShell installed on your machine.

How to do it...

The first thing we need to do is import the ApplicationServer module so that it is accessible from the Windows PowerShell console. From there, we'll walk through some common cmdlets to orient you to managing Windows Server AppFabric applications interactively with PowerShell, and get a feel for some common commands.

1. Start Windows PowerShell in Administrator mode, and at the prompt enter `Import-Module ApplicationServer` to import the **ApplicationServer** module so that we can begin working with it.

2. Issue the following command to get acquainted with the different commands that are available in the ApplicationServer module: `Get-Command –module ApplicationServer`.

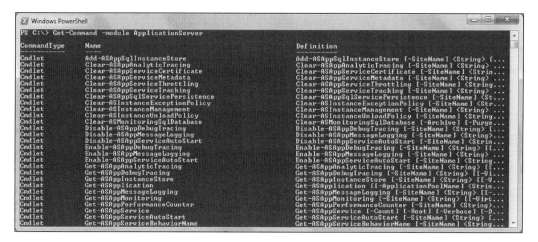

The **Get, Set, Add, Clear, Enable, Disable,** and other such prefixes for each command are referred to as verbs and the noun is the physical or logical entity that the command will operate on. Not all names are intuitive, and most have several parameters so feel free to use the following command to get more information on the purpose and intended use of each command of interest: `cmdlet: Get-Help [ModuleName]`.

Alternatively, you can refer to the MSDN documentation at the end of this recipe for more web-based navigation.

3. To view general configuration for the ReservationService application, use the `Get-AsApplication` cmdlet with the following command:

```
Get-AsApplication -SiteName "Default Web Site" -VirtualPath "/
ReservationService"
```

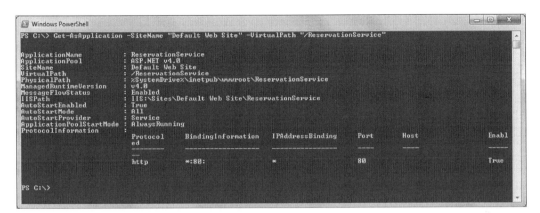

 Notice that the details provided are at the application-level and that the ReservationService application is not currently configured for Auto-Start as indicated by the **AutoStartEnabled** property being set to **False**.

4. Now, issue the `Get-ASAppService` command to view information about the ReservationService service that is part of the ReservationService application:

```
Get-ASAppService -SiteName "Default Web Site" -VirtualPath "/
ReservationService"
```

The details provided now are at a finer grain, focusing on the ReservationService.

5. Toggle the Auto-Start capability by using the `Set-ASApplication` cmdlet with the following parameters:

```
Set-ASApplication -SiteName "Default Web Site" -VirtualPath "/
ReservationService/ReservationService.xamlx" -AutoStartMode
"All" -EnableApplicationPool
```

 There is no response when issuing this command, provided that it executes successfully.

6. Now if you re-run the `Get-ASAppService` cmdlet with the same parameters in step 4, you should see that the `AutoStartEnabled` property is set to `True`. In fact, if you go to Windows Server AppFabric, right-click the ReservationService application, select **Manage WCF** and **Workflow Services**, click on **Configure**, and select the **Auto-Start** tab, you will see that the feature has been enabled.

7. By default, the monitoring level of the Windows Server AppFabric application is set to **Health Monitoring**. To raise the monitoring level of the ReservationService application to the maximum supported using the ApplicationServer module, use the `Set-ASAppMonitoring` command to increase the monitoring level to Troubleshooting:

```
Set-ASAppMonitoring -SiteName "Default Web Site" -VirtualPath "/
ReservationService" -MonitoringLevel "Troubleshooting"
```

8. Go to Windows Server AppFabric, right-click the ReservationService application, select **Manage WCF** and **Workflow Services**, click on **Configure**, and select the **Monitoring** tab to verify the change:

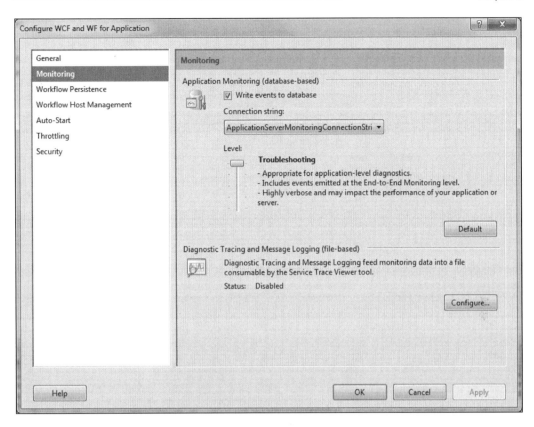

9. To verify the monitoring setting change using the PowerShell cmdlet, use the **Get-ASAppMonitoring** command:

```
Get-ASAppMonitoring -SiteName "Default Web Site" -VirtualPath "/
ReservationService"
```

10. Sometimes it is necessary to stop an application so that it no longer accepts messages, perhaps to remediate a hardware or software condition that is causing a fault. To do so using the ApplicationServer PowerShell module, use the **Stop-ASApplication** cmdlet to stop the application:

```
Stop-ASApplication -SiteName "Default Web Site" -VirtualPath
"/ReservationService"
```

 If you try to call the ReservationService after issuing this command, you will receive an HTTP Error 503 message, indicating that the service is unavailable.

11. To start the application, use the **Start-ASApplication** command as follows:

```
Start-ASApplication -SiteName "Default Web Site" -VirtualPath
"/ReservationService"
```

How it works...

Windows Server AppFabric packages the management cmdlets into a Windows PowerShell module called ApplicationServer, which is installed in the following path when Windows Server AppFabric is installed: `C:\Windows\System32\WindowsPowerShell\v1.0\Modules\ApplicationServer`.

Each cmdlet serves a distinct function, given a verb and noun. For example, cmdlets with a Get verb are known as query cmdlets and may traverse configuration files and configured database stores to return information about the application or service.

Cmdlets such as the `Set-ASApplication` and `Set-ASAppService` commands act on configuration stores such as `web.config`, `machine.config`, or `applicationhost.config`, depending on the level (application/service) or feature you are managing. These cmdlets use the Microsoft Web Administration (MWA) API, which provides a wrapper for working with configuration files. For example, the `Set-ASApplication` cmdlet we used in step 5 to enable the Auto-Start feature at the application level modified the `applicationhost.config` file that stores hosting settings such as whether the Auto-Start feature is enabled, while the `Set-ASAppMonitoring` cmdlet writes to the `web.config` file for the application.

In Step 5, the `Set-ASApplication` cmdlet requires the-`EnableApplicationPool` parameter to ensure that the corresponding application pool is configured for Auto-Start in addition to the application and service because Windows Server AppFabric extends the Auto-Start capabilities in IIS 7.x by allowing granular configuration at the service level in addition to the pool.

There's more...

In addition to starting, stopping, and managing hosting and monitoring capabilities, there are some very powerful cmdlets that support operations for managing instances of workflows.

For example, if an instance is idle for a long period of time, or you suspect that the instance may be corrupted, you can use the `Get-ASAppServiceInstance` cmdlet to obtain information about the instance(s) using the following command:

```
Get-ASAppServiceInstance -SiteName "Default Web Site" -VirtualPath
"/ReservationService"
```

From there, you can use the same cmdlet with the `-InstanceId` parameter:

```
Get-ASAppServiceInstance -InstanceId 947538cc-31b9-42f6-a82c-
367c15662718
```

To inspect only that particular instance, and you can combine it with the `Suspend-ASAppServiceInstance` by piping it as follows to issue a suspend request:

```
Get-ASAppServiceInstance -InstanceId 947538cc-31b9-42f6-a82c-
367c15662718| Suspend-ASAppServiceInstance
```

The command will then be queued and picked up by the Workflow Management Service, which will issue the command over the Instance Control Endpoint (ICE) that is exposed via the net.pipe protocol:

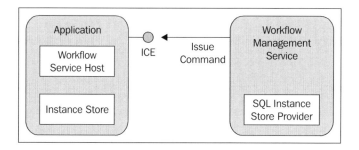

Note that the net.pipe protocol must be enabled for the application for instance control cmdlets such as `Suspend-ASAppServiceInstance`, `Stop-ASAppServiceInstance`, and `Resume-ASAppServiceInstance` to function. If you do not have the net.pipe protocol enabled, the above commands will fail silently and although you will see errors in the AppFabric Dashboard indicating that the `ServiceManagement.svc` service is not configured correctly, the workflow instance will remain in the idle state. For additional tips for managing your workflow services, please see *Chapter 7, Monitoring Windows Server AppFabric Deployment*.

Remote management

As you can see, the ApplicationServer module is pretty powerful on its own, and the ability to use these cmdlets to manage multiple servers makes it an even more worthwhile tool for managing your Windows Server AppFabric applications. As all of these operations are implemented in Windows PowerShell, the ability to manage remote machines is simply a matter of enabling the remote capabilities of Windows PowerShell on each server you want to manage. You accomplish this by installing PowerShell on all machines you want to manage, enabling the remoting feature on each server, and configuring a listener known as the WinRM service, which is a Windows Service that listens for requests from remote clients.

You can learn more about enabling remoting for PowerShell by visiting the link provided at the end of this recipe.

See also

For a step-by-step guide for installing Windows Server AppFabric, refer to the *Installing Windows Server AppFabric* recipe in *Chapter 1, Installing Windows Server AppFabric*.

For a step-by-step guide for installing the Microsoft Web Deployment Tool, please see the *Installing the Web Deployment tool (Web Deploy)* recipe in this chapter.

The MSDN documentation for all of the commands in the ApplicationServer cmdlets is a great reference for browsing the commands more quickly than via the get-help facilities in PowerShell: `http://msdn.microsoft.com/en-us/library/ee767662 (v=WS.10).aspx`.

Follow this guidance for enabling PowerShell remoting, which will allow you to manage multiple Windows Server AppFabric instances: `http://msdn.microsoft.com/en-us/library/ee677232.aspx`.

6
Utilizing AppFabric Persistence

In this chapter, we will cover:

- ▸ Using Windows Server AppFabric workflow persistence
- ▸ Programmatically querying persisted workflow instances
- ▸ Programmatically controlling persisted workflow instances
- ▸ Developing an Instance Store provider
- ▸ Developing an Instance Query provider
- ▸ Developing an Instance Control provider
- ▸ Registering and configuring custom store, query, and control providers

Introduction

Windows Server AppFabric builds on top of .NET Framework's Windows Communication Foundation and Windows Workflow Foundation (WF) and simplifies the scenario of hosting, managing, and monitoring long-running and durable workflows. Windows Server AppFabric's persistence enables two key use cases, which we'll look at now.

Durable application scale out

Windows Server AppFabric is a middleware platform and for most of the deployments, it will run on a distributed server farm. Windows Server AppFabric's Hosting subsystem uses its persistence capabilities to allow WF-based workflows to become scalable and durable. Windows Server AppFabric's provides its default SQL Server based persistence provider (also known as Instance Store), which allows these workflows to become durable.

Computational resources

Instead of keeping long running workflows sitting idle in memory (while they wait for human interaction or an external system impetus) and letting them consume memory/computational resources, it makes sense to suspend and persist them for as long as they are not needed and then resume them when they become activatable. Along with the Persistence Provider, Windows Server AppFabric uses a Workflow Management Service (WMS) that allows workflows to transition between an in-memory and persistent storage.

The following diagram shows how Windows Server AppFabric's Persistence Architecture allows it to save persistence data from services running on multiple AppFabric Nodes:

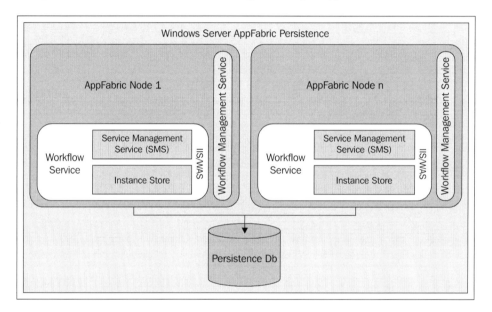

 Windows Server AppFabric is not a hosting environment like IIS or WAS. Rather, it provides an additional set of capabilities while running on top of IIS or WAS.

In this chapter, we will focus solely on the persistence capabilities of Windows Server AppFabric.

Using Windows Server AppFabric workflow persistence

Once the Windows Server AppFabric is installed successfully on the host machine, workflow services can start leveraging the underlying hosting, monitoring, and persistence features.

In this recipe, we will learn how persistence is enabled for workflow instances running on IIS/WAS. We will specifically focus on the following three related tasks:

▶ Workflow persistence configuration using AppFabric Dashboard

▶ Invoking a workflow service using WCF Test Client

▶ Viewing workflow instances using AppFabric Dashboard

Services built with `WCF Service Application`, `WCF Workflow Application`, and `WCF Service-Based Website` project templates in Visual Studio are managed by Window Server AppFabric by default.

For the sake of simplicity, we will use a sample workflow service available for download at MSDN via Windows Server AppFabric Samples (at `http://www.microsoft.com/download/en/confirmation.aspx?id=19603`).

We are using an existing sample so that we can focus solely on Windows Server AppFabric's platform hosting and persistence capabilities. This sample workflow that we are using is part of Windows Server AppFabric Samples and is available in the `yoursamplesDirectory\Hosting\InstanceQueryAndControl` folder. Discussing Windows Workflow Foundation is beyond the scope of this book.

Getting ready

We will need to launch Visual Studio 2010 (with administrative privileges) and open the `TestWorkflow` project, available under `yourSamplesDirectory$\Hosting\InstanceQueryAndControl`. While opening the `TestWorkflow` project **Microsoft Visual Studio** will prompt you for the creation of a virtual directory in IIS (as shown in the following screenshot). Click on **Yes** and Visual Studio will create a virtual directory for your workflow service:

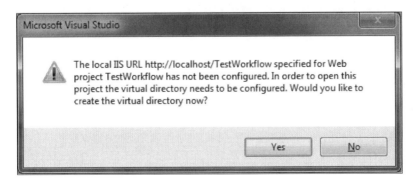

We will then proceed with invoking some of the methods available on this service and validate its impact on Windows Server AppFabric Persistence via IIS dashboard.

How to do it...

We will start this recipe by building the workflow and ensuring that it compiles successfully. We will then follow up with its persistence configuration using the IIS AppFabric dashboard. Then we will simply invoke the workflow using WCF Test Client and validate the workflow instances via the IIS AppFabric dashboard.

1. In the **Solution Explorer**, select the **TestWorkflow** project and **Build** it. It should compile successfully:

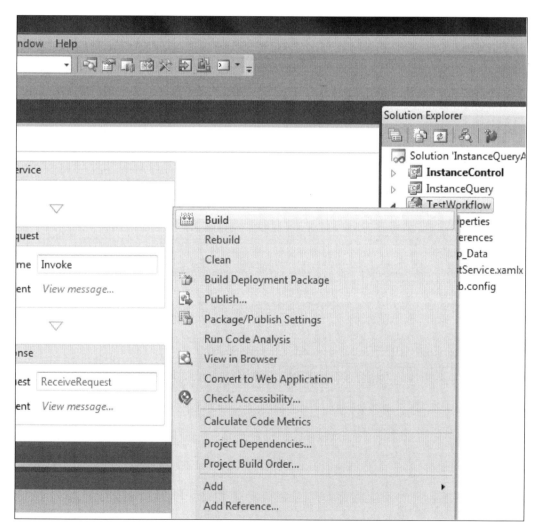

2. Launch IIS Manager (you can do this by typing `inetmgr` in your Windows 7 search box or by invoking the `run` command).

3. Select **TestWorkflow** and right-click on it to select **Manage WCF and WF Services**, and then select **Configure**:

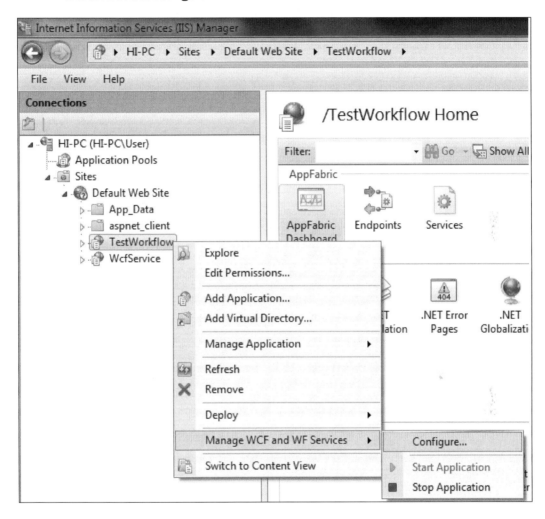

4. Select **Workflow Persistence** and ensure that **SQL Server Workflow Persistence** is selected:

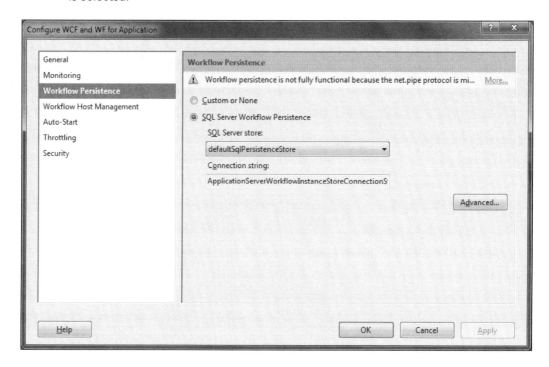

 If you have not enabled `net.pipe` protocol binding, workflow persistence will not be functional. To enable `net.pipe` protocol binding, add `net.pipe` in **Site Bindings**. Also make sure that `net.pipe` is available as a behavior under **Advanced Settings** for your workflow service.

5. Select **Advanced** and **Advanced Persistence Settings Dialog** will be shown. It should look like the following screen capture. Click on **OK** to continue:

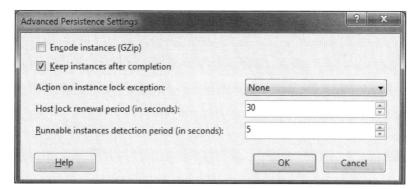

The **Advanced Persistence Settings** screen allows the user to configure the persistence behavior. For example, by selecting **Encode instances (GZip)** we tell Windows Server AppFabric to compress the instances. Likewise, with the **Keep instances after completion** option users can decide to remove the instance once the workflow has completed. More details can be found on MSDN at `http://msdn.microsoft.com/en-us/library/ee790926.aspx`.

6. Now select **Workflow Host Management** and check if we have instance level controls in place:

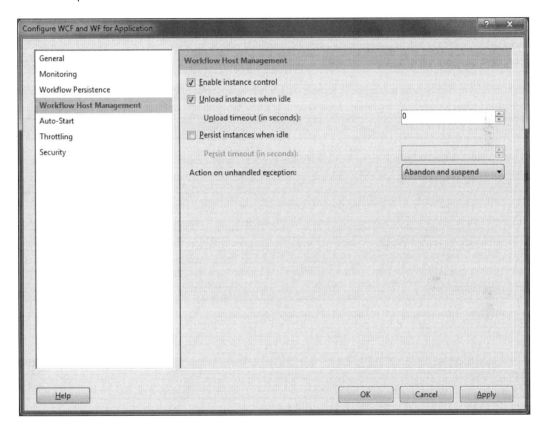

 These persistence and workflow host settings are stored in the workflow service configuration file via `sqlWorkflowInstanceStore`, `workflowInstanceManagement`, `workflowUnhandledException`, and `workflowIdle` `elements` under the `serviceBehaviors` tag.

7. Now that we have persistence and workflow host management controls in place, invoke the `TestWorkflow` service using **WCF Test Client** (available under `InstallDir:\Program Files (x86)\Microsoft Visual Studio 10.0\Common7\IDE`).

8. Add the `TestWorkflow` service URL (in my case it is `http://localhost/TestWorkflow/TestService.xamlx`) to the **WCF Test Client** and invoke the service:

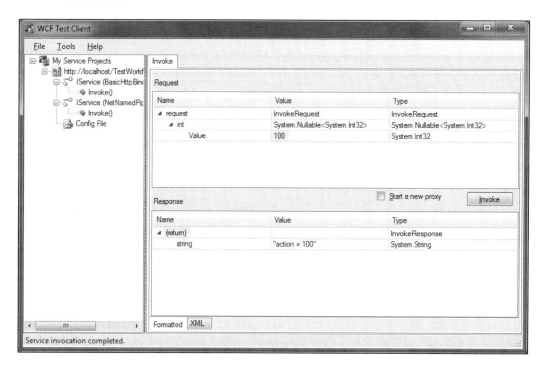

We are assuming that you are familiar with the concepts of WCF service hosting and the usage of WCF Test client. To learn more about WCF, please visit `http://msdn.microsoft.com/en-us/netframework/aa663324.aspx`.

9. Now we will check if the newly created workflow instance has been persisted or not. To do this, launch AppFabric Dashboard, available under IIS:

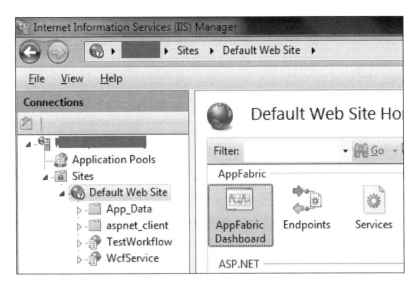

10. On the AppFabric Dashboard screen select **Persisted Workflow Instances**:

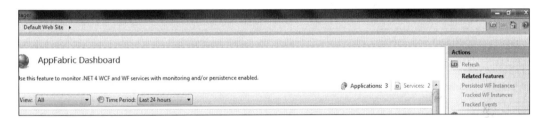

 Our workflow sample, based on the input value, will either complete immediately, throw an exception, or run for 10 minutes.

11. On the **Persisted WF Instance** screen, you will see a number of persisted workflow instances based on the default search criteria. **Persisted WF Instance** should look something like this:

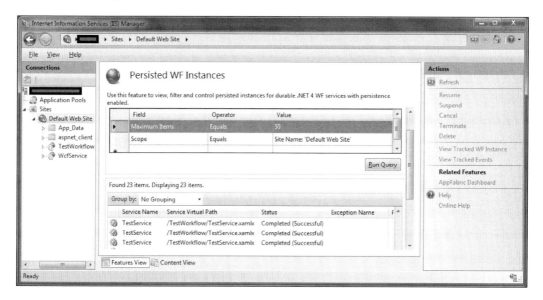

How it works...

There are three key parts of Windows Server AppFabric's persistence model:

▸ Instance Store Provider

▸ Instance Query Provider

▸ Instance Control Provider

Instance Store Provider, Instance Query Provider, and Instance Control Provider enable Windows Server AppFabric to persist, query, and control workflow instances. All these three providers are built as an abstraction running on top of .NET Framework's (v4.0) `SqlWorkflowInstanceStore`.

`SqlWorkflowInstanceStore` comes with .NET Framework 4 and provides persistence capabilities for workflows by storing state and relevant metadata in SQL Server 2005 or SQL Server 2008. For more details on `SqlWorkflowInstanceStore`, visit `http://msdn.microsoft.com/en-us/library/ee383994.aspx`.

The following code snippet shows how the `CreateInstanceStrore` is implemented by `SqlWorkflowInstanceStoreProvider`:

```
public override InstanceStore CreateInstanceStore()
{
    if (!string.IsNullOrEmpty(this.ConnectionString))
    {

        SqlWorkflowInstanceStore sqlWorkflowInstanceStore =
        new SqlWorkflowInstanceStore(this.ConnectionString);
        sqlWorkflowInstanceStore.HostLockRenewalPeriod =
        SqlWorkflowInstanceStoreProvider.LockRenewalPeriod;
        SqlWorkflowInstanceStore sqlWorkflowInstanceStore1 =
        sqlWorkflowInstanceStore;
        return sqlWorkflowInstanceStore1;
    }
    else
    {
        throw FxTrace.Exception.AsError(new
        InvalidOperationException(Resources.
        ProviderNotInitialized));
    }
}
```

We learned about configuring the persistence provider in *Chapter 1, Installing Windows Server AppFabric* with a recipe titled *Configuring Windows Server AppFabric (hosting and monitoring)*. Once the default persistence provider is configured, it gets registered in the root web. config file and is available to all the workflow services on the host machine, thus being available to all the workflow services on the host.

Use of provider model means clearer separation of concerns. It also allows abstracting implementation details of persistence from its client in Windows Server AppFabric hosting runtime. The following snippet shows the interface used to define `InstanceStoreProvider`:

```
public abstract class InstanceStoreProvider : ProviderBase
{
    protected InstanceStoreProvider();
    public abstract InstanceStore CreateInstanceStore();
    public abstract string UniqueProviderIdentifier();
}
```

There's more...

AppFabric Dashboard is not the only place that allows configuring persistence related parameters for Windows Server AppFabric. In fact, AppFabric Dashboard is a projection of values available in `web.config` file. This implies that all of the configuration can also be directly specified in `web.config` of the service host. Also, we can use Windows Server AppFabric cmdlets to configure workflow persistence as well. For more details on how to configure workflow persistence using Windows Server AppFabric cmdlets, visit `http://msdn.microsoft.com/en-us/library/ee677318.aspx`.

 Windows Server AppFabric allows configuring multiple persistence stores. For more details, visit `http://blogs.msdn.com/b/appfabriccat/archive/2010/09/23/windows-server-appfabric-how-to-adding-multiple-persistence-stores-to-an-appfabric-installation.aspx`.

Also, to learn more about using the Persisted WF Instance Page in IIS to view persisted WF instances visit MSDN at `http://msdn.microsoft.com/en-us/library/ee677370.aspx`.

Programmatically querying persisted workflow instances

In the previous recipe, we saw how the persisted instances can be queried via Windows Server AppFabric Dashboard. Although AppFabric Dashboard offers a simple and easy user experience, it is not the only way to query persisted workflow instances. In this recipe, we will learn about the Windows Server AppFabric's Instance Query Provider API, which can also be used to query persisted workflows.

 In fact, AppFabric Dashboard internally invokes Windows Server AppFabric cmdlets. And cmdlets internally instantiate and invoke the Windows Server AppFabric's API. Eventually, API is at the heart of the implementation and offers consistent feature set across AppFabric cmdlets and AppFabric Dashboard.

We will use the same Workflow Sample solution that we used in the previous recipe. The sample workflow that we are using is part of Windows Server AppFabric Samples and is available in the `yourSamplesDirectory\Hosting\InstanceQueryAndControl` folder. Windows Server AppFabric samples can be downloaded from `http://www.microsoft.com/download/en/confirmation.aspx?id=19603`.

Getting ready

We are using the same `TestWorkflow` sample that we used in the previous recipe. We will assume that persistence has been enabled for `TestWorkflow`. We will also assume that `TestWorkflow` has been invoked a few times from **WcfTestClient** (or any other client for that matter).

Launch Visual Studio with administrative privileges and open the `TestWorkflow` solution.

How to do it...

We will start with the Instance Query Provider and will follow it up with Instance Control Provider.

As the code is already available with the sample we will walk through the key steps as well as cover the changes that we are going to make for this sample to work in our scenario:

1. Initiate the instance of the `SqlConnectionStringBuilder` class and set the values for `DataSource`, `InitialCatalog`, and `IntegratedSecurity`. These values should point to your already available (and configured) persistence provider. The code, as available in the sample, should look like the following:

   ```
   SqlConnectionStringBuilder builder = new
   SqlConnectionStringBuilder();
               builder.DataSource = "sqlServerHost\\
   sqlServerInstanceName";
               builder.InitialCatalog = "PersistenceStoreV1";
               builder.IntegratedSecurity = true;
   ```

2. Note the hardcoded initialization in the preceding sample code.

    If SQL Persistence Store was not configured with Integrated Security Option then do set the `UserId` and `Password` properties of `SqlConnectionStringBuilder` with a profile that is part of the `AS_Administrators` group.

3. Create an instance of `InstanceQueryProvider` using `Activator.CreateInstance`:

   ```
   static string storeManagementDll = " C:\\Windows\\System32\\
   AppFabric\\Microsoft.ApplicationServer.StoreManagement.dll";

   Assembly storeManagementAssembly = Assembly.
   LoadFrom(storeManagementDll);
   ```

```
Type type = storeManagementAssembly.GetType("Microsoft.
ApplicationServer.StoreManagement.Sql.Query.
SqlInstanceQueryProvider");

InstanceQueryProvider factory = Activator.CreateInstance(type) as
InstanceQueryProvider;
```

 For 64-bit systems the file path for the `Microsoft.`
`ApplicationServer.StoreManagement.dll`
should be updated accordingly.

4. Now initialize the `factory` object by passing the store name and connection string as a `NameValueCollection`:

```
NameValueCollection collection = new NameValueCollection();
            collection.Add("ConnectionString",
            builder.ConnectionString);
            factory.Initialize("storeA", collection);
```

 `InstanceQueryProvider` will throw an `FxTrace.`
`Exception.ArgumentNull` exception if either of
the two parameters are passed as empty or null.

5. Using the factory object, create an instance of `SqlInstancQueryProvider`:

```
instanceQuery = factory.CreateInstanceQuery();
```

6. Create an instance of an `InstanceQueryArgs` and initialize it with the following values:

```
// Define query filter parameters.
            InstanceQueryArgs instanceQueryArgs = new
            InstanceQueryArgs();
            instanceQueryArgs.CreatedTimeFrom = null;
            instanceQueryArgs.CreatedTimeTo = null;
            instanceQueryArgs.ExceptionName = null;
            instanceQueryArgs.InstanceCondition = null;
            instanceQueryArgs.InstanceId = null;
            instanceQueryArgs.InstanceStatus = null;
            instanceQueryArgs.MachineName = null;
            instanceQueryArgs.ModifiedTimeFrom = null;
            instanceQueryArgs.ModifiedTimeTo = null;
            instanceQueryArgs.ServiceType = null;
            instanceQueryArgs.HostMetadata = new
            Dictionary<string, string>();
            instanceQueryArgs.HostMetadata.Add("SiteName", null);
// E.g., "Default Web Site".
```

```
instanceQueryArgs.HostMetadata.
Add("RelativeApplicationPath", null);
// E.g., /TestWorkflow".
instanceQueryArgs.HostMetadata.
Add("RelativeServicePath", null);
// E.g., /TestWorkflow/TestService.xamlx".
instanceQueryArgs.HostMetadata.Add
("VirtualPath", null);
// E.g., /TestWorkflow/TestService.xamlx".
```

7. Now, create an instance of `InstanceQueryExecuteArgs`, copy over the values from the `instanceQueryArgs` object by using a helper method called `CopyQueryArgs` (which literally copies value from one object to the other), and add values for two additional properties called `Count` and `OrderBy`:

```
InstanceQueryExecuteArgs instanceQueryExecuteArgs = new
InstanceQueryExecuteArgs();
CopyQueryArgs(instanceQueryExecuteArgs, instanceQueryArgs);
instanceQueryExecuteArgs.Count = 20;
instanceQueryExecuteArgs.OrderBy = Order.
LastUpdatedTimeDescending;
```

> `InstanceQueryExecuteArgs` is derived from `InstanceQueryArgs`, and it provides two additional properties of `Count` and `OrderBy`. `Count` is used to specify the maximum number of instances that can be returned and `OrderBy` specifies the sorting of results when the query is executed. We will talk about why we did not directly use `InstanceQueryExecuteArgs` later on in the *There's more...* section of this recipe. The following code shows the `InstanceQueryExecuteArgs` class:
>
> ```
> public class InstanceQueryExecuteArgs :
> InstanceQueryArgs {
>     public int? Count { get; set; }
>     public Order? OrderBy { get; set; }
> }
> ```

8. Use the `ExecuteQuery` helper method and pass the instance of `instanceQueryArguments`:

```
ExecuteQuery(instanceQueryExecuteArgs);
```

ExecuteQuery is a helper method available in the sample and simply registers a callback method called `ExecuteQueryCallback`. The following code shows how `ExecuteQuery` registers the callback with the `instanceQuery` object:

```
IAsyncResult asyncResult = instanceQuery.BeginE
xecuteQuery(instanceQueryExecuteArgs, TimeSpan.
FromSeconds(60), new AsyncCallback(ExecuteQueryCa
llback), null);
```

9. In `ExecuteQueryCallBack`, simply invoke `EndExecuteQuery` on the `instanceQuery` object and then iterate over the `IEnumerable<InstanceInfo>` to list down the values of available instances on the console. The following code shows how this is done:

```
public static void ExecuteQueryCallback(IAsyncResult result)
{
    foreach (InstanceInfo info in instanceQuery.
    EndExecuteQuery(result))
    {
        Console.WriteLine("Instance ID\t\t: " +
        info.InstanceId.ToString());
        Console.WriteLine("Status\t\t\t: " +
        info.InstanceStatus.ToString());
        Console.WriteLine("Condition\t\t: " +
        info.InstanceCondition.ToString());
        Console.WriteLine("ActiveBookmarks\t\t: " +
        info.ActiveBookmarks.ToString());
        Console.WriteLine("CreationTime\t\t: " +
        info.CreationTime.ToString());
        Console.WriteLine("LastUpdateTime\t\t: " +
        info.LastUpdateTime.ToString());
        Console.WriteLine("LastUpdatedBy\t\t: " +
        info.LastUpdatedBy.ToString());
        Console.WriteLine("StoreName\t\t: " +
        info.StoreName.ToString());
        if (info.ExceptionName != null)
        {
            Console.WriteLine("ExceptionName\t\t: " +
            info.ExceptionName.ToString());
            Console.WriteLine("ExceptionMessage\t: " +
            info.ExceptionMessage.ToString());
        }
    }
//..more code..
```

10. From Visual Studio 2010, build, execute, and start a new instance of our
    `InstanceQuery` project. You should get an output similar to the following
    screen capture:

How it works...

Windows Server AppFabric provides an implementation of `InstanceQueryProvider`
called `SqlInstanceQueryProvider`, which is responsible for instantiating objects of
`SqlInstanceQuery` class. The `SqlInstanceQuery` provides execution of queries on
an instance store and returns results to the calling client.

The `InstanceQueryProvider` implements `ProviderBase` (from the `System.`
`Configuration.Provider` namespace). The `SqlInstanceQueryProvider` in
turn inherits from `InstanceQueryProvider` as a sealed class to provide concrete
implementation of the query mechanism for persisted workflows.

The following code shows the skeleton of the `SqlInstanceQueryProvider` class:

```
public sealed class SqlInstanceQueryProvider : InstanceQueryProvider
{
    private string storeName;
    private NameValueCollection parameters;
    private string ConnectionString { get; set; }
    private string UniqueStoreIdentifier { get; set; }

    public override InstanceQuery CreateInstanceQuery()
    {
```

```
if (string.IsNullOrEmpty(this.ConnectionString))
throw FxTrace.Exception.AsError((Exception)
new SqlInstanceQueryException
(Resources.ProviderNotInitialized));
try
{
        return (InstanceQuery) new SqlInstanceQuery(this.
        storeName, new SqlConnectionStringBuilder(this.
        ConnectionString)
        {
            AsynchronousProcessing = true
        }.ConnectionString);
}
catch (Exception ex)
{
        if (!Fx.IsFatal(ex))
        throw new SqlInstanceQueryException(Resources.
        FailedToInstantiateQueryProvider, ex);
        throw;
}
}

public override string UniqueProviderIdentifier()
{
    //...more code here..
}

public override void Initialize(string name,
NameValueCollection config)
{
    //...more code here..
}
```

The `SqlInstanceQuery` is an implementation of `InstanceQuery`.

One of the key operations available on `SqlInstanceQuery` is `ExecuteQuery`.

Execute Query

Execute Query is responsible for returning a result set (comprising `IEnumerable<InstanceInfo>`) based on the selection criteria (implemented as `SqlInstanceQueryArgs`) to the calling client. `InstanceInfo` represents information associated with a persisted workflow instance. `InstanceInfo` has the following properties:

```
public abstract class InstanceInfo
{
    public virtual Guid InstanceId { get; protected set; }
    public virtual InstanceStatus InstanceStatus
    { get; protected set; }
```

```csharp
        public virtual InstanceCondition InstanceCondition { get;
        protected set; }

        public virtual string ActiveBookmarks { get; protected set; }

        public virtual DateTime CreationTime { get; protected set; }

        public virtual DateTime? LastUpdateTime { get; protected set; }

        public virtual string LastUpdatedBy { get; protected set; }

        public virtual string ExceptionName { get; protected set; }

        public virtual string ExceptionMessage { get; protected set; }

        public virtual string StoreName { get; protected set; }

        public virtual CommandInfo CommandInfo { get; protected set; }

        public virtual HostInfo HostInfo { get; protected set; }

        public virtual IEnumerable<PropertyInfo> PrimitiveProperties {
        get; protected set; }

        public virtual string UserData { get; protected set; }
    }
```

Finally, here is how the `SqlInstanceQuery` class is implemented:

```csharp
    internal sealed class SqlInstanceQuery : InstanceQuery
    {
        private string storeName;
        private readonly string connectionString;

        public SqlInstanceQuery(string storeName, string connectionString)
        {
          if (storeName == null)
            throw FxTrace.Exception.ArgumentNull("storeName");
          if (connectionString == null)
            throw FxTrace.Exception.ArgumentNull("connectionString");
          this.storeName = storeName;
          this.connectionString = connectionString;
        }

        public override IAsyncResult BeginExecuteQuery(InstanceQueryExecut
        eArgs args, TimeSpan timeout, AsyncCallback callback, object
        state)
    //more code…
```

```
        public override IEnumerable<InstanceInfo>
        EndExecuteQuery(IAsyncResult result)
//more code

        public override IAsyncResult BeginExecuteCount(InstanceQueryArgs
        args, TimeSpan timeout, AsyncCallback callback, object state)
//more code..

        public override int EndExecuteCount(IAsyncResult result)
//more code

        public override IAsyncResult BeginExecuteGroupCount
(InstanceQueryG roupArgs args, TimeSpan timeout,
AsyncCallback callback, object state)
//more code

        public override IEnumerable<GroupingResult> EndExecuteGroupCount
        (IAsyncResult result)
//more code

        public override void Cancel(IAsyncResult result)
//more code
}
```

There's more...

As you have seen in the preceding code, `SqlInstanceQuery` provides two additional methods on top of `ExecuteQuery`.

Execute Count

Execute Count returns an aggregate number such as the count of persisted workflow instances, based on the selection criteria. Selection criteria are specified via `InstanceQueryArgs`.

Execute Group Count

To execute Group Count we need to specify `GroupingMode` using `InstanceQueryGroupArgs`. `GroupingMode` is an enumeration and contains the following values:

```
public enum GroupingMode
{
    ExceptionName,
    Status,
    SiteName,
    MachineName,
    UniqueApplication,
    UniqueService,
```

```
    ServiceType,
    Condition,
}
```

The following code shows how the `GroupBy` clause can be specified:

```
List<GroupingMode> myGroupingMode = new List<GroupingMode>();
myGroupingMode.Add(GroupingMode.Status);
myGroupingMode.Add(GroupingMode.Condition);
instanceQueryGroupArgs.GroupBy = myGroupingMode;
```

Execute Group Count aggregates the count and returns an instance of `IEnumerable<GroupingResult>`.

Programmatically controlling persisted workflow instances

Along with Instance Query, Windows Server AppFabric also provides a default implementation of Instance Control Provider API for SQL Workflow Instance Store.

Instance Control commands are defined as a `CommandType` enumeration, as shown in the following code snippet:

```
public enum CommandType
{
    Suspend,
    Resume,
    Terminate,
    Cancel,
    Delete,
}
```

Instance Control Provider provides an asynchronous and durable command execution mechanism. All the issued commands are stored in a command queue in an Instance Store. Workflow Management Service (WMS) owns the execution of these commands by picking them up from the Instance Store and executing them against the specified workflow instance, following the First-In-First-Out (FIFO) algorithm.

WMS places a lock for 65 seconds on the instance for which it has picked up a command. If the command is executed successfully, it gets deleted from the queue and the lock is released immediately. In case of a failure WMS re-tries the failed command five times (based on a retry count that it maintains in the Instance Store) before removing it from the command queue.

 There can only be one command stored in the command queue for any given workflow instance. Newly issued commands will override existing commands as long as they are not locked or in pending state, in which case an error will be returned.

Workflow Management Service (WMS) plays an important role in Windows Server AppFabric's hosting capabilities. WMS is responsible for activation of persisted workflow service instances as well as execution of Instance Control commands.

In this recipe, we will learn about Instance Control Provider API and use it to issue commands against persisted workflow instances.

Getting ready

We are using the same `TestWorkflow` sample that we used in the preceding recipe. We will assume that persistence has been enabled for `TestWorkflow`. Copy one instance ID from the output of our last recipe (or copy one from IIS AppFabric Dashboard by querying persisted workflow instances) so that we can use it to issue commands against the corresponding workflow instance. Make sure that the workflow instance ID represents a workflow that is in the "running" state. This will help us invoke a "suspend" command against this selected workflow instance.

Launch Visual Studio with administrative privileges and open the `TestWorkflow` solution.

How to do it...

We will start by initializing the instance ID that represents a persisted workflow instance. Then we will issue a command against this instance and follow it up with validating the state of the persisted workflow instance.

1. Create a GUID using the value of a persisted workflow instance:

   ```
   Guid instanceId = new Guid("be65c1ce9ff14c9c99cf3252ae5d11e9");
   ```

2. Initialize a `SqlConnectionStringBuilder` using the `DataSource` and `InitialCatalog` properties. Use the `IntegratedSecurity` property or `UserId/Password` based on your own Persistence Store's configuration.

   ```
   SqlConnectionStringBuilder builder = new
   SqlConnectionStringBuilder();
   builder.DataSource = "localhost\\sqlexpress";
   builder.InitialCatalog = "ApplicationServerWorkflowInstanceStore";
   builder.IntegratedSecurity = true;
   ```

3. Create an object of type `InstanceControlProvider` (available in the `Microsoft.ApplicationServer.StoreManagement.Sql.Control. SqlInstanceControlProvider` namespace) using reflection. This is similar to the way we created `InstanceQueryProvider` in the previous recipe.

```
Assembly storeManagementAssembly = Assembly.
LoadFrom(storeManagementDll);
Type type = storeManagementAssembly.GetType("Microsoft.
ApplicationServer.StoreManagement.Sql.Control.
SqlInstanceControlProvider");
InstanceControlProvider factory = Activator.CreateInstance(type)
as InstanceControlProvider;
```

4. Now initialize the `factory` object by passing the store name and connection string as a `NameValueCollection`:

```
NameValueCollection collection = new NameValueCollection();
collection.Add("ConnectionString", builder.ConnectionString);
factory.Initialize("storeA", collection);
```

> `InstanceControlProvider` will throw an `FxTrace.Exception.ArgumentNull` exception if either of the two parameters are passed as empty or null.

5. Create an `InstanceCommand` object by passing `CommandType`, `InstanceId`, and `ServiceIdentifier` metadata:

```
InstanceCommand command = new InstanceCommand();
command.CommandType = CommandType.Suspend;
command.InstanceId = instanceId;

command.ServiceIdentifier = new Dictionary<string, string>();
command.ServiceIdentifier["SiteName"] = "Default Web Site";
command.ServiceIdentificr["RelativeApplicationPath"] =
    "/TestWorkflow";
command.ServiceIdentifier["VirtualPath"] = "/TestWorkflow/
TestService.xamlx";
```

> Note the use of hard-coded values in the previous sample code. In a production environment these values should come from a configuration file.
>
> `InstanceId` is the one that we initialized in step 1 and it represents a valid persisted workflow instance ID. `CommandType` is enumeration and we are issuing a `SuspendCommand`. `ServiceIdentifier`, which is metadata that helps Workflow Management Service (WMS) identify issues and execute commands against a particular workflow service.

6. Invoke a `BeginSend` using the `instanceControl` object's `CommandSend` property. The `BeginSend` method requires `command`, `timespan`, a callback method (`CommandSendCallback`) and `instanceControl`.

```
instanceControl.CommandSend.BeginSend(command, TimeSpan.
FromSeconds(60), CommandSendCallback, instanceControl);
```

> `CommandSendCallback` is a delegate that gets invoked when the command is executed. It is responsible for invoking `EndSend` to complete the execution of the issued command. The following code shows how `CommandSendCallback` is implemented in our example.

```
public static void CommandSendCallback(IAsyncResult result)
{
        InstanceControl instanceControl =
        (InstanceControl)result.AsyncState;
        try
        {
                instanceControl.CommandSend.EndSend(result);
                if (result.IsCompleted == true)
                {
                        Console.WriteLine("Command successfully
                        enqueued");
                }
        }
        catch (Exception ex)
        {
                Console.WriteLine(ex);
                return;
        }
}
```

7. Now, query against this instance ID to validate the state of the persisted workflow instance. It should be in `Suspended` state.

How it works...

Windows Server AppFabric provides a default implementation of
`InstanceControlProvider` called `SqlInstanceControlProvider`,
which is responsible for instantiating objects of `SqlInstanceControl`
class. `SqlInstanceControl` provides execution of commands on a
`SqlWorkflowInstanceStore`.

The `SqlInstanceControl` uses `SqlInstanceControlCommandSend` and
`SqlInstanceControlCommandRecieve` to issue and retrieve commands against
a configured SQL persistence store.

The following code shows the implementation of `SqlInstanceControl`:

```
public sealed class SqlInstanceControl : InstanceControl
{
    private readonly string connectionString;
    private SqlInstanceControlCommandSend commandSend;
    private SqlInstanceControlCommandReceive commandReceive;

    public override CommandSend CommandSend
    {
        get
        {
            if (this.commandSend == null)
                Interlocked.CompareExchange
                <SqlInstanceControlCommandSend>(ref this.
                commandSend, new SqlInstanceControlCommandSend
                (this.connectionString),
                (SqlInstanceControlCommandSend) null);
            return (CommandSend) this.commandSend;
        }
    }
}
```

```
public override CommandReceive CommandReceive
{
    get
    {
        if (this.commandReceive == null)
            Interlocked.CompareExchange
            <SqlInstanceControlCommandReceive>
            (ref this.commandReceive, new
            SqlInstanceControlCommandReceive
            (this.connectionString),
            (SqlInstanceControlCommandReceive) null);
        return (CommandReceive) this.commandReceive;
    }
}
public SqlInstanceControl(string connectionString)
{
    this.connectionString = connectionString;
}
}
```

The send and receive commands are issued asynchronously and are represented by the CommandSend and CommandRecieve classes respectively. CommandSend and CommandRecieve both implement BeginXXX and EndXXX methods to support asynchronous execution. connectionString gets passed from the InstanceControl provider to the CommandSend and CommandRecieve implementations. The database access however takes place in the SqlControlSendAsyncResult and SqlControlReceiveAsyncResult classes. The following code shows how SqlInstanceControlCommandSend is implemented:

```
internal sealed class SqlInstanceControlCommandSend : CommandSend
{
    private readonly string connectionString;
    public SqlInstanceControlCommandSend(string connectionString)
    {
        this.connectionString = connectionString;
    }
    public override IAsyncResult BeginSend(InstanceCommand command,
    TimeSpan timeout, AsyncCallback callback, object state)
    {
        SqlControlSendAsyncResult controlSendAsyncResult = new
        SqlControlSendAsyncResult(command,
        this.connectionString, callback, state);
        controlSendAsyncResult.BeginSendControl();
        return (IAsyncResult) controlSendAsyncResult;
    }
```

```
    public override void EndSend(IAsyncResult result)
    {
        SqlControlSendAsyncResult.End(result);
    }
}
```

The `SqlInstanceControlCommandReceive` also provides the following additional methods:

- ► `Begin/EndAbandon`
- ► `Begin/EndComplete`
- ► `DequeueAvailableControlCommand`

> It is also worth noting that `SqlInstanceControlCommandReceive` retrieves commands in batches of 10.
>
> This is defined via the `batchSize` property as shown:
>
> ```
> private readonly int batchSize = 10 * Environment.
> ProcessorCount;
> ```

The following block diagram shows the execution workflow for Instance Control Commands:

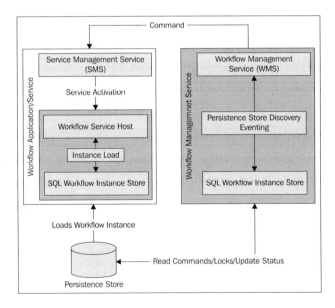

There's more...

To learn about controlling persisted workflow instances using AppFabric Cmdlets, visit `http://msdn.microsoft.com/en-us/library/ee677323.aspx`.

Windows Server AppFabric also allows viewing Tracked WF Instances through an IIS dashboard view. The view is aptly called **Tracked WF Instances Page**. To learn more about it go to `http://msdn.microsoft.com/en-us/library/ee677300.aspx`.

Developing an Instance Store provider

Windows Server AppFabric provides an API for implementing custom Instance Store, Query, and Control providers.

In the first recipe of this chapter, we have seen that Windows Server AppFabric provides a default `SqlWorkflowInstanceStoreProvider` which provides access to .NET Framework's `SqlWorkflowInstanceStore`. As Windows Sever AppFabric uses provider models we can implement a custom Instance Store provider.

In this recipe, we will focus on developing a custom Instance Store provider.

Getting ready

Start Visual Studio 2010 with administrative privileges and create a new class library project using C#.

How to do it...

We will add a new class named `CustomInstanceStoreProvider` which will implement an abstract base class called `InstanceStoreProvider`. We will then add the implementation details accordingly.

1. Rename the default class to `CustomInstanceControlProvider`.
2. Add the following assembly references to your project:
   - `System.Data.dll`
   - `System.Configuration.dll`
   - `System.Activities.DurableInstancing.dll`
   - `System.Runtime.DurableInstancing.dll`
   - `Microsoft.ApplicationServer.StoreProvider.dll`

3. Repeat steps 1 to 3 from the *Using optimistic concurrency* recipe in *Chapter 3, Windows Server AppFabric Caching – Advanced Use Cases*. This will initialize two instances of `DataCache`, definitions of key value pairs, as well as add an item to the cache based on the key-value pair definition.

4. Add the following using statements at the beginning of the file:

```
using Microsoft.ApplicationServer.StoreProvider;
using System.Runtime.DurableInstancing;
using System.Activities.DurableInstancing;
using System.Collections.Specialized;
using System.Data;
using System.Data.SqlClient;
```

5. Mark `CustomeInstanceControlProvider` as sealed and inherit it from the `InstanceStoreProvider` class. Your class declaration should like this:

```
public class CustomInstanceControlProvider : InstanceStoreProvider
```

6. Add a variable of type string called `connectionString` as well as the `Initialize` method to the class:

```
string ConnectionString { get; set; }
public override void Initialize(string name, NameValueCollection config)
{
    this.ConnectionString = config["connectionString"];
    base.Initialize(name, config);
}
```

7. Add a `CreateInstanceStore` method and create an instance of `SqlWorkflowInstanceStore` by passing `connectionString` to its constructor. Return this instance of `SqlWorkflowInstanceStore` to the calling client:

```
public override InstanceStore CreateInstanceStore()
{
    return (InstanceStore)new SqlWorkflowInstanceStore
    (this.ConnectionString);
}
```

8. Add an override method called `UniqueProviderIdentifier` that returns a string:

```
public override string UniqueProviderIdentifier()
{
    if (string.IsNullOrEmpty(UniqueStoreIdentifier))
    {
        UniqueStoreIdentifier =
        GetUniqueStoreIdentifier(this.ConnectionString);
    }
    return UniqueStoreIdentifier;
```

```
        }

        private string GetUniqueStoreIdentifier(string
        connectionString)
        {
            using (SqlConnection connection = new
            SqlConnection(connectionString))
            {
                using (SqlCommand command = new SqlCommand())
                {
                    command.CommandType =CommandType.Text;
                    command.CommandText = "SELECT TOP (1)
                    [StoreIdentifier] FROM
                    [Microsoft.ApplicationServer.
                    DurableInstancing].[StoreVersion]";
                    command.Connection = connection;

                    command.Connection.Open();

                    Guid identifier = (Guid)command.ExecuteScalar();
                    return identifier.ToString();
                }
            }
        }
```

 Note the use of the SQL query to retrieve the identity of the Instance Store. This SQL query is executed against the connection string which is passed as `NameValueCollection` in the `Initialize` method.

How it works...

Once you know the abstract base class (`InstanceStoreProvider`), implementation of a custom Instance Store provider is a straightforward task. In fact, our implementation of a custom Instance Store provider is fairly similar to the default `SqlWorkflowInstanceStoreProvider` from the Windows Server AppFabric API.

Once this implementation is complete, this Instance Store provider needs to be registered with Windows Server AppFabric. We will discuss this in detail later in this chapter under a recipe titled *Registering and configuring store, query, and control providers*.

There's more...

We have seen how a custom Instance Store provider can be built using Windows Server AppFabric API. In our implementation we still used the default SQL Server based store provider, which is available in .NET framework 4.0 as `SqlWorkflowInstanceStore`.

Use of SQL Server as a persistent store should work for most cases. However, in some instances it is imperative to be able to use a non SQL Server persistence store. As Windows Server AppFabric uses a provider model it is possible to build a custom instance store. To learn more about how to build an Oracle based persistence store for Windows Server AppFabric, visit MSDN at `http://blogs.msdn.com/b/appfabriccat/archive/2010/09/17/windows-server-appfabric-monitoring-works-with-oracle-10g-xe-database.aspx`.

Developing an Instance Query provider

We have already seen Windows Server AppFabric's API for a default `SqlInstanceQuery` in the first recipe of this chapter. In this recipe, we will learn about implementing a custom Instance Query provider.

Windows Server AppFabric provides an API based on a provider model that allows implementation of a custom Instance Query provider. The process is similar to how we created a custom Instance Store provider in the preceding recipe.

Getting ready

Start Visual Studio 2010 with administrative privileges and create a new class library project using C#.

How to do it...

We will add new class called `CustomInstanceStoreProvider`, which will implement an abstract base class called `InstanceStoreProvider`. We will then add the implementation details accordingly.

1. Rename the default class to `CustomInstanceControlProvider`.
2. Add the following assembly references to your project:
   - `System.Data.dll`
   - `System.Configuration.dll`
   - `Microsoft.ApplicationServer.StoreManagement.dll`

3. Inherit `CustomInstanceControlProvider` with `InstanceQueryProvider`:

```
public sealed class CustomInstanceQueryProvider :
InstanceQueryProvider
```

4. Add a new C# class and name it `CustomInstanceQuery`.

5. In the new `CustomInstanceQuery` class add the `using Microsoft.ApplicationServer.StoreManagement.Query` statement and inherit it from the `InstanceQuery` abstract base class:

```
public class CustomInstanceQuery : InstanceQuery
```

6. In the `CustomInstanceQuery` class add the following string variables and a constructor:

```
string storeName;
string ConnectionString { get; set; }
public CustomInstanceQuery(string storeName, string
connectionString)
{
    this.storeName = storeName;
    this.ConnectionString = connectionString;
}
```

7. In `CustomInstanceQuery` add the following default implementation of the `InstanceQuery` abstract base class:

```
public override IAsyncResult BeginExecuteCount(InstanceQueryArgs
args, TimeSpan timeout, AsyncCallback callback, object state)
{
    throw new NotImplementedException();
}


public override IAsyncResult BeginExecuteGroupCount
(InstanceQueryGroupArgs args, TimeSpan timeout,
AsyncCallback callback, object state)
{
    throw new NotImplementedException();
}


public override IAsyncResult BeginExecuteQuery
(InstanceQueryExecuteArgs args, TimeSpan timeout,
AsyncCallback callback, object state)
{
    throw new NotImplementedException();
}


public override void Cancel(IAsyncResult result)
{
```

```
        throw new NotImplementedException();
    }


    public override int EndExecuteCount(IAsyncResult result)
    {
        throw new NotImplementedException();
    }


    public override IEnumerable<GroupingResult>
    EndExecuteGroupCount(IAsyncResult result)
    {
        throw new NotImplementedException();
    }


    public override IEnumerable<InstanceInfo>
    EndExecuteQuery(IAsyncResult result)
    {
        throw new NotImplementedException();
    }
```

8. In the `CustomInstanceQueryProvider` class add two string variables, `storeName` and `connectionString`, and the following `Initialize` method:

```
string storeName;
string ConnectionString { get; set; }


public override void Initialize(string name, NameValueCollection config)
{

    storeName = name;
    ConnectionString = config["connectionString"];
    base.Initialize(name, config);

}
```

9. Add an `override` for the `CreateInstanceQuery` method that returns an instance of our own `CustomInstanceQuery` class, as shown in the following code snippet:

```
public override InstanceQuery CreateInstanceQuery()
{
    SqlConnectionStringBuilder connectionStringBuilder =
    new SqlConnectionStringBuilder(this.ConnectionString);
    return new CustomInstanceQuery(this.storeName,
    connectionStringBuilder.ConnectionString);
}
```

10. Add the following code to implement `UniqueStoreIdentifier`:

```
string UniqueStoreIdentifier { get; set; }

        public override string UniqueProviderIdentifier()
        {
    if (string.IsNullOrEmpty(this.UniqueStoreIdentifier))
    this.UniqueStoreIdentifier = GetUniqueStoreIdentifier
    (this.ConnectionString);

        return this.UniqueStoreIdentifier;
        }

    private string GetUniqueStoreIdentifier(string connectionString)
        {
        using (SqlConnection connection = new SqlConnection
        (connectionString))
        {
            using (SqlCommand command = new SqlCommand())
            {
                command.CommandType = CommandType.Text;
                command.CommandText = "SELECT TOP (1)
                [StoreIdentifier] FROM
                [Microsoft.ApplicationServer.
                DurableInstancing].[StoreVersion]";
                command.Connection = connection;

                command.Connection.Open();

                Guid identifier = (Guid)command.
                ExecuteScalar();
                return identifier.ToString();
            }
        }
    }
}
```

How it works...

Every time we issue a Windows Server AppFabric cmdlet such as `Get-AppServiceInstance`, it internally creates an instance of a registered Instance Query and executes queries against the registered Instance Store and returns results back to the cmdlet.

Once `InstanceQueryProvider` has been implemented it needs to be registered with Windows Server AppFabric. We will learn more about registering a custom provider later in this chapter in the recipe titled *Registering and configuring custom store, query, and control providers.*

There's more...

Our `CustomInstanceQuery` is just a skeleton code to show how we can add a custom `InstanceQuery` implementation for a custom Instance Query provider. Windows ServerAppFabric's implementation of `SqlInstanceQueryProvider` uses `SqlInstanceQuery` to execute queries against the SQL persistence store.

To use `SqlInstanceQuery` in our `CustomInstanceQueryProvider` we can use the following code:

```
public override InstanceQuery CreateInstanceQuery()
{
    return (InstanceQuery) new SqlInstanceQuery(this.storeName,
    new SqlConnectionStringBuilder(this.ConnectionString)
    {
        AsynchronousProcessing = true
    }.ConnectionString);
}
```

Developing an Instance Control provider

Windows Server AppFabric offers an Instance Control mechanism that allows issuing control commands to be executed against persisted instances. Instance Control also allows the ability to retrieve commands queued against a persisted workflow instance. This two-way communication enables a decoupled mechanism of handling, retrieving, and executing control commands against a persisted instance.

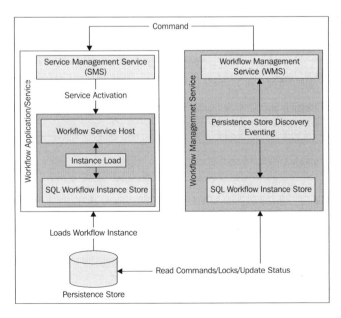

The Instance Control provider is responsible for providing access to an Instance Control object. Windows Server AppFabric provides a default implementation of the Instance Control provider called the `SqlInstanceControl` provider that runs on top of `SqlWorkflowInstanceStore`. We learned about `SqlInstanceControl` in our third recipe of this chapter, titled *Programmatically controlling persisted workflow instances*.

In this recipe, we will focus on building a custom Instance Control provider.

Getting ready

Start Visual Studio 2010 with administrative privileges and create a new class library project using C#; call it `CustomInstanceControlProvider`:

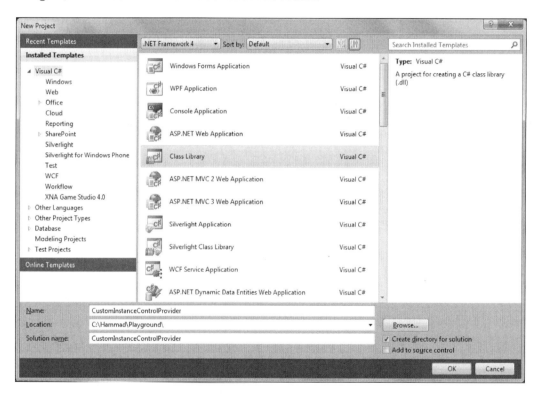

How to do it...

We will start by adding relevant assemblies and namespaces in our class library. Then we will implement the required Instance Control provider abstract base class provided by Windows Server AppFabric API and will add implementation details to our custom Instance Control provider. We will also implement underlying classes that allow control commands to work in Windows Server AppFabric to complete an end-to-end implementation.

1. Rename the `Class1` to `CustomInstanceControlProvider`.

2. Add reference to the `Microsoft.ApplicationServer.StoreManagement` and `System.Configuration` assemblies.

3. Add the following using statements:

```
using System;
using Microsoft.ApplicationServer.StoreManagement.Control;
using System.Collections.Specialized;
using System.Data.SqlClient;
```

4. Inherit `CustomInstanceControlProvider` from the `InstanceControlProvider` class and add the following skeleton code to implement the abstract base class:

```
public class CustomInstanceControlProvider :
InstanceControlProvider
{
    public override InstanceControl CreateInstanceControl()
    {
        throw new NotImplementedException();
    }

    public override string UniqueProviderIdentifier()
    {
        throw new NotImplementedException();
    }
}
```

5. Add a string property called `ConnectionString` along with the following `Initialize` method:

```
string ConnectionString { get; set; }

    public override void Initialize(string name,
    NameValueCollection config)
    {

    ConnectionString = config["connectionString"];

    base.Initialize(name, config);
    }
```

6. Add the following code to implement the `UniqueProviderIdentifier`:

```
public override string UniqueProviderIdentifier()
{
    this.UniqueStoreIdentifier =
    GetUniqueStoreIdentifier(this.ConnectionString);
    return this.UniqueStoreIdentifier;
}


private string GetUniqueStoreIdentifier
(string connectionString)
{
    using (SqlConnection connection = new
    SqlConnection(connectionString))
    {
        using (SqlCommand command = new SqlCommand())
        {
            command.CommandType =
            System.Data.CommandType.Text;
            command.CommandText = "SELECT TOP (1)
            [StoreIdentifier] FROM
            [Microsoft.ApplicationServer.
            DurableInstancing].[StoreVersion]";
            command.Connection = connection;

            command.Connection.Open();

            Guid identifier = (Guid)command.
            ExecuteScalar();
            return identifier.ToString();
        }
    }
}
```

7. To implement `CreateInstanceControl` add the following code. Note the use of a new class `CustomInstanceControl`, which we will implement shortly:

```
public override InstanceControl CreateInstanceControl()
{
    return (InstanceControl)new CustomInstanceControl
    (new SqlConnectionStringBuilder(this.ConnectionString)
    {
        AsynchronousProcessing = true
    }.ConnectionString);
}
```

8. Add a new class and name it `CustomInstanceControl` and inherit it from `InstanceControl` (from `Microsoft.ApplicationServer.StoreManagement.Control`):

```
public class CustomInstanceQuery : InstanceControl
```

9. In `CustomInstanceControl` class, add the `CommandRecieve` and `CommandSend` properties as shown in the following code:

```
public override CommandReceive CommandReceive
{
    get {
        if (this.commandReceive == null)
            this.commandReceive = new
            CustomInstanceControlCommandReceive
            (connectionString);

        return this.commandReceive;
    }
}


public override CommandSend CommandSend
{
    get
    {
        if (this.commandSend == null)
            this.commandSend = new
            CustomInstanceControlCommandSend
            (connectionString);

        return this.commandSend;
    }
}
```

 We will add implementation for `CustomInstanceControlCommandRecieve` and `CustomInstanceControlCommandSend` shortly.

10. Add a constructor for `CustomInstanceQuery` that takes in a `connectionString` parameter:

```
private readonly string connectionString;

public CustomInstanceControl(string connectionString)
{
    this.connectionString = connectionString;
}
```

11. Now let's add a new class and name it `CustomInstanceControlCommandRecieve`, and add the following implementation to it:

```
internal class CustomInstanceControlCommandReceive :
CommandReceive
{
        private string connectionString;

        public CustomInstanceControlCommandReceive
        (string connectionString)
        {
            this.connectionString = connectionString;
        }

        public override IAsyncResult
        BeginTryReceive(System.TimeSpan timeout,
        System.AsyncCallback callback, object state)
        {
            throw new NotImplementedException();
        }

        public override bool EndTryReceive
        (System.IAsyncResult result,
        out ReceivedInstanceCommand command)
        {
            throw new NotImplementedException();
        }
}
```

 Note that `BeginTryRecieve` and `EndTryRecieve` are throwing `NotImplementedException` so that the code can build successfully without any compilation errors.

12. Add another new class to the project, name it `CustomInstanceControlCommandSend` and add the following implementation to it.

```
internal sealed class CustomInstanceControlCommandSend :
CommandSend
{
        private readonly string connectionString;

        public CustomInstanceControlCommandSend(string
        connectionString)
        {
            this.connectionString = connectionString;
        }
```

```
mnb          public override IAsyncResult BeginSend
(InstanceCommand command, TimeSpan timeout,
AsyncCallback callback, object state)
{
    throw new NotImplementedException();
}

public override void EndSend(IAsyncResult result)
{
    throw new NotImplementedException();
}
}
```

Once again note that `BeginSend` and `EndSend` have not been implemented here. This is to keep this recipe focused on the custom Instance Control provider but also shows how the inner classes are implemented and can be further customized.

How it works...

Windows Sever AppFabric offers cmdlets that are used by IIS Manager / AppFabric Dashboard to control persisted workflow instances. Every time a cmdlet such as `Suspend-ASAppServiceInstance` is issued it internally creates an object of type `InstanceControlProvider` and executes the command against the specified persisted workflow instance.

Windows Server AppFabric uses an `InstanceCommand` type to abstract the command and instance related information. Once the command is issued against a persisted workflow instance, `InstanceControl` enqueues a command to the command queue. This command is then picked up by Workflow Management Service (WMS) and is executed against the specified workflows instance. The following code shows how `InstanceCommand` is implemented:

```
public class InstanceCommand
{
    public Guid InstanceId { get; set; }

    public CommandType CommandType { get; set; }

    [SuppressMessage("Microsoft.Usage",
    "CA2227:CollectionPropertiesShouldBeReadOnly",
    Justification = "Can be set by any user implementation of a
    Instance Control Command Queue")]
    public IDictionary<string, string> ServiceIdentifier { get; set; }
}
```

The `CommandType` is an enumeration and is defined as follows:

```
public enum CommandType
{
    Suspend,
    Resume,
    Terminate,
    Cancel,
    Delete,
}
```

Registering and configuring custom store, query, and control providers

After implementing custom providers, they need to be registered and configured with Windows Server AppFabric. Only the registered providers can be configured to be used by Windows Server AppFabric. Ideally, a custom provider's installation program should be responsible for registering and configuring the custom provider with Windows Server AppFabric.

In this recipe, we will learn about the following steps that are required to register and configure a custom provider with Windows Server AppFabric:

1. Add/Update registry values.
2. Create an Instance Store (physical database, and so on) and install binaries (containing custom provider implementations).
3. Add the Instance Provider details in the `Web.Config` file.
4. Add the Instance Store details in the `Web.Config` file.
5. Add the Instance Store Behavior in the relevant service configuration file.

Getting ready

Launch the **Registry Editor** and go to `HKEY_LOCAL_MACHINE\SOFTWARE\Microsoft\AppFabric\v1.0\Providers`. Assuming AppFabric is already installed, it should look as follows:

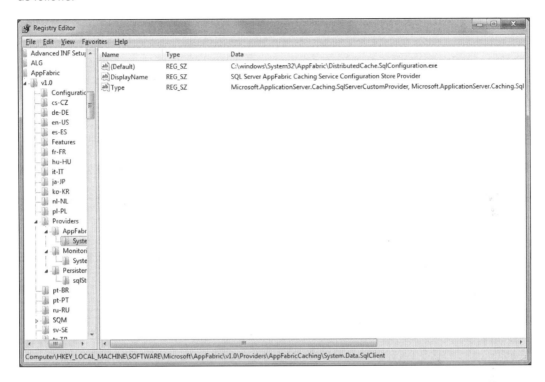

Under **Monitoring**, add a new subkey and name it **CustomMonitoring**. This is shown in the following screenshot:

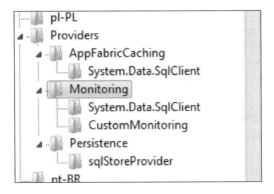

Select `CustomMonitoring` and for `(Default) Value` name, set **Value data** as `C:\windows\System32\AppFabric\Microsoft.ApplicationServer.SqlConfiguration.exe Monitoring`.

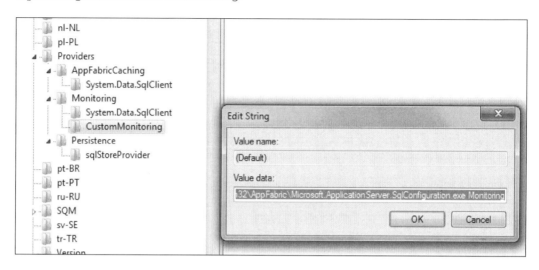

 We have used Windows Server AppFabric's default `Microsoft.ApplicationServer.SqlConfiguration` application but this can be replaced with a custom application specific to the provider that is being registered.

Likewise, we can add a custom key for the persistence provider and assign a **Value** data that maps to the persistence configuration application.

How to do it...

We will assume that the custom provider has already been registered with Windows Server AppFabric and the Instance Store as well as binaries have already been set up on the host machine. We will start with adding configuration settings for the Instance Store provider as well as the Instance Store. We will then proceed with the setup of the service behavior extension for the Instance Store to complete this recipe.

1. In the root `web.Config`, under `Microsoft.ApplicationServer/Persistence/instanceStoreProviders` add a new `storeProvider` by specifying fully qualified name of a .NET type that represents custom store, control, and query provider as shown in the following code:

```
<add name="CustomPersistenceStoreProvider"
storeProvider="fullyQualifiedTypeInformationForStoreProvider"
storeControlProvider="
fullyQualifiedTypeInformationForControlProvider "
```

```
storeQueryProvider=" fullyQualifiedTypeInformationForQueryProvider
" />
</instanceStoreProviders>
```

> Only `storeProvider` must have a fully qualified name of a .NET
> type that implements `StoreProvider` abstract base class from
> Windows Server Fabric API. The `storeControlProvider` and
> `storeQueryProvider` can either be an implementation of
> `ControlProvider` and `QueryProvider` respectively or they can
> be left empty for the cases where there is no implementation available.

2. Add an instance store under `Microsoft.ApplicationServer/Persistence/`
   `instanceStores` in the root `web.config` file such that it maps to the instance
   provider added in the previous step:

```
<instanceStores>
    <add
    name="AppFabricCustomDb"
    provider=" CustomPersistenceStoreProvider "
    connectionStringName="customConnectionString" />
</instanceStores>
```

> Additional descriptive attributes (for example, key-value pairs) can also be
> added to Instance Stores. `connectionString` must always be defined,
> otherwise Workflow Management Service (WMS) will not be able to connect
> to the persistence store. The following example shows how the additional
> key-value pairs can be added:

```
<instanceStores>
    <add
    name="AppFabricCustomDb"
    provider=" CustomPersistenceStoreProvider "
    connectionStringName="customConnectionString"
    value1="
    someValue1"
    value2="someValue2"
    value3="someValue2"/>
</instanceStores>
```

3. To define a custom Instance Store in `machine.config`, add a `behaviorExtension` under the `system.serviceModel/extensions/behaviorExtensions` element:

```
<add
name="customWorkflowInstanceStore"
type=" typeInfoHere"/>
```

> When Windows Server AppFabric is installed and its persistence store is configured, it adds the default `sqlWorkflowInstanceStore` entry in the `machine.config` file so that the services can readily use this behavior.
>
> ```
> <add name="sqlWorkflowInstanceStore"
> type="System.ServiceModel.Activities.
> Configuration.SqlWorkflowInstanceStoreElement,
> System.ServiceModel.Activities,
> Version=4.0.0.0, Culture=neutral, PublicKeyTok
> en=31bf3856ad364e35"/>
> ```

4. Add the following behavior in `web.config` to add persistence capabilities to an application or a service:

```
system.serviceModel>
    <behaviors>
      <serviceBehaviors>
        <behavior>
          < customWorkflowInstanceStore
          instanceCompletionAction="DeleteAll"
          instanceEncodingOption="None"
          instanceLockedExceptionAction="NoRetry"
          connectionStringName=" customConnectionString "
          hostLockRenewalPeriod="00:00:30"
          runnableInstancesDetectionPeriod="00:00:05" />
```

How it works...

Registration and configuration of instance, query, and control providers allow WCF and WF services and applications to leverage on Windows Server AppFabric's persistence capabilities using custom providers.

Once theses custom providers have been registered we can use the AppFabric configuration tool to use them to configure the Windows Server AppFabric installation. The following screen capture shows how a **customPersistence** provider is available as a **Persistence provider** in the Windows Sever AppFabric configuration wizard:

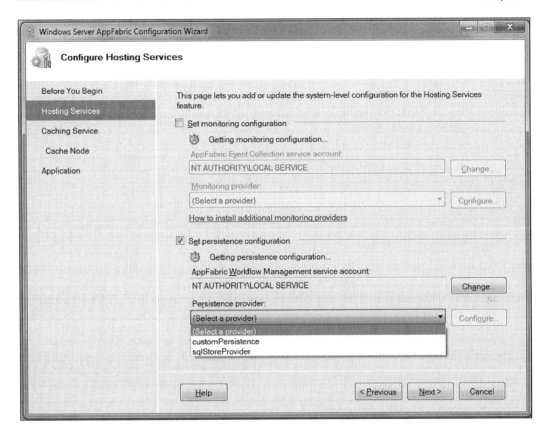

Once the custom provider is selected, the **Configure** option will launch the configuration tool that was specified in the registry during the setup phase.

There's more...

When using the default SQL Workflow Instance Store (rather than a custom Instance Store), Windows Server AppFabric configuration wizard can be used to:

> ▶ Add SQL Workflow Instance Store along with a connection string in the root web. config pointing to the selected persistence store

> ▶ Create a SQL server database instance for persistence

> ▶ Install Workflow Management Service (WMS) and add relevant configuration that points it to the configured persistence store

To learn more about using a non-SQL provider for Windows Server AppFabric, read this MSDN article at http://msdn.microsoft.com/en-us/library/ff383402.aspx.

7
Monitoring Windows Server AppFabric Deployment

In this chapter, we will cover:

- ▶ Collecting events from WCF and WF services
- ▶ Viewing and classifying events in the AppFabric Dashboard
- ▶ Enabling tracing and evaluating trace logs with WCF
- ▶ Creating a customized tracking profile for WF services
- ▶ Accessing the Monitoring DB
- ▶ Building a custom dashboard
- ▶ Using monitoring database cmdlets
- ▶ Monitoring cache cluster health

Introduction

One of the biggest benefits of Windows Server AppFabric is that it makes monitoring and troubleshooting WCF and WF4 services much easier by providing a core set of monitoring metrics that allow you to gain visibility into the status and health of your services, both at a glance and at a granular level of detail.

Enabling these monitoring capabilities is simply a matter of turning monitoring on and specifying the level of verbosity you are interested in by selecting a profile.

In addition, you can build your own tracking profiles for gaining a deep understanding of the events, messages, and information flowing in, through, and out of your services.

> Throughout this chapter, a sample WF service called "Reservation Service" is used to demonstrate various capabilities of Windows Server AppFabric.
>
> As the name of the application suggests, the Reservation Service simulates a real-world scenario that includes a restaurant reservation workflow service wherein a patron requests a reservation (perhaps from a web frontend or via an inbound automated call center agent), which is managed by the workflow service. The workflow service accepts the reservation and sends the "would be" patron an e-mail confirming the receipt of the reservation (but not the reservation itself). The service then awaits approval from the director of reservations (common in the hospitality space) or maître d to ensure that the requested accommodations can be met. If so, a second e-mail is sent to the patron welcoming them to the restaurant at the requested time, or notifying them that their request could not be accommodated.
>
> Please note this chapter assumes that you have already installed and configured Windows Server AppFabric. If you haven't, please refer to the recipe *Installing Windows Server AppFabric* in *Chapter 1, Installing Windows Server AppFabric*.

Collecting events from WCF and WF services

Windows Server AppFabric makes it very simple to configure monitoring for WCF and WF services. Gaining insight into the execution state of a WCF or WF service requires a considerable amount of configuration, which can be cumbersome to create initially and to manually maintain in the long run. Windows Server AppFabric signifantly simplifies things.

In this recipe, we will learn how to configure monitoring for WCF and WF services as well as develop an understanding of the different tracking profiles that are available.

Getting ready

We will use the Reservation Service sample WF application that is available for download as part of the resources available for this book.

How to do it...

As soon as you deploy your application to Windows Server AppFabric, you will immediately benefit from the enhanced monitoring and management capabilities of Windows Server AppFabric because by default, monitoring is automatically enabled for you.

1. Deploy your WF Service application to Windows Server AppFabric using your preferred deployment method and test the service by executing some operations on it to ensure that it is functional.

> In this example, I have deployed the Reservation Service that is available for download with this chapter; however, this recipe applies to any WF Service application deployed to Windows Server AppFabric.

2. Once the workflow service has been sufficiently exercised, open IIS and click on the application and select **Features View**.

3. Next, click on the **Services** icon under the AppFabric section to open the Services feature:

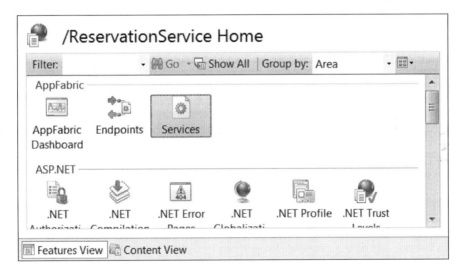

4. With the **Service** feature open, right-click on the **ReservationService** entry under the **Service Name** column and select **View Tracked Events**:

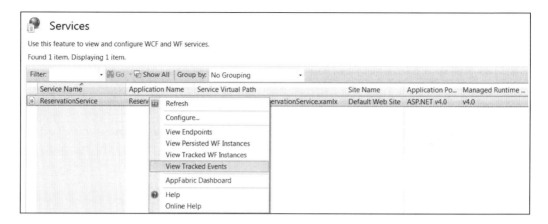

5. In the **Tracked Events** feature, notice that a number of events have been populated with various event types and useful information about the service is seamlessly available for each event record:

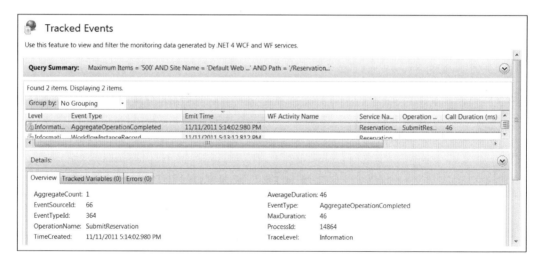

Without making any configuration changes whatsoever, monitoring is automatically enabled for any WCF or WF Service application that is deployed to Windows Server AppFabric.

There are a number of tracking profiles that are available, including the default level of "Health Monitoring" that monitors for errors and is typically appropriate for production scenarios. For more information on the tracking profiles that are available, see *How it works...* at the end of this recipe.

You can also create a custom tracking profile to only include the metrics and level of detail of interest. See the *Creating a customized tracking profile for WF services* recipe for details.

6. Now, right-click on the application and select **Manage WCF and WF Services** followed by **Configure**:

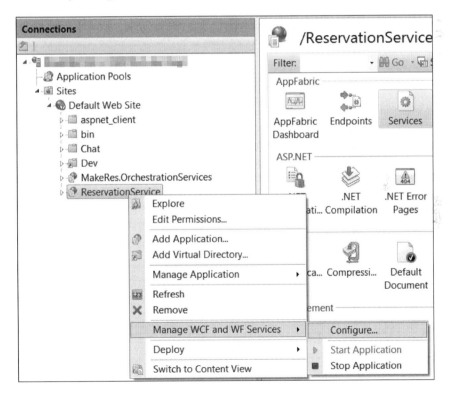

I'm using the Reservation Service sample application that is available for download with this chapter; however, this recipe applies to any WF Service application deployed to Windows Server AppFabric.

7. Next, click on the **Monitoring** tab and notice that monitoring has automatically been set to use the **Health Monitoring** tracking profile, and events are configured to be written to the Windows Server AppFabric monitoring database:

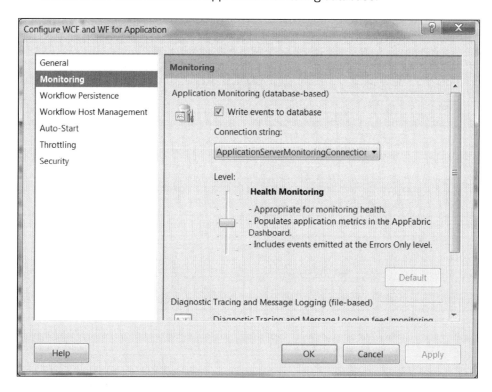

8. Experiment with the five available tracking profiles. Sliding the **Level** indicator all the way to the top enables the troubleshooting tracking profile, which is the most verbose, while sliding it all the way to the bottom results in turning monitoring completely off.

> Note that Windows Server AppFabric relies on the events that are tracked as defined in the Health Monitoring tracking profile in order to provide the monitoring capabilities provided in the AppFabric Dashboard. If you customize the profile or select one that is lower on this list, the dashboard may not show all of the events you would expect.

9. Enable the **Troubleshooting** tracking profile and click on **Apply**, accepting the warning that the application will be restarted.

10. Exercise the service again, and follow steps 3, 4, and 5. Notice that there are a significantly greater amount of events now being collected, including information on workflow instances and activity states.

 Studying tracked events in various tracking profile modes is an excellent way to gain a better understanding of the various events that take place in the life of a WCF or WF service call, and can be quite insightful.

How it works...

Windows Server AppFabric monitoring is useful both to WCF and WF Service application developers and those responsible for managing them once they have been deployed.

Although the monitoring metrics provided are much richer for WF Services, which has been the focus of this recipe, there is still value to enabling monitoring for WCF services. The AppFabric Dashboard (covered in the following recipe) provides WCF instance and error information and the tracked events feature includes useful information such as what operation was called, its process identifier, and other useful information for understanding what is happening within the workflow service.

The level of detail provided within the tracked events feature is determined by the tracking profile that is configured. Out of the box, there are five tracking profiles that are supported:

- **Off**, which disables the collection of any monitoring information
- **Errors Only**, which only includes unhandled exceptions, aborted instances, and faulted propagation events
- **Health Monitoring**, which includes the events tracked in the Errors Only tracking profile plus WF instance change events, including Started, Completed, Terminated, Canceled, Unsuspended, Persisted, Aborted, and UnhandledException as well as closed or faulted activity states and any CustomTrackingRecords emitted during execution
- **End to End**, which includes the events tracked in the Health Monitoring tracking profile, plus all WF instance event states, information on activity state, and any CustomTrackingRecords emitted during execution
- **Troubleshooting**, which includes all of the above and includes additional detail for certain events

Each of these tracking profiles leverages **Event Tracing for Windows** (ETW), which is a very robust, kernel level instrumentation feature that has a negligible impact on application performance.

It is important to note that while you can adjust these tracking profiles to suit your needs, the Health Monitoring tracking profile is required for the fundamental monitoring capabilities of Windows Server AppFabric within the AppFabric Dashboard to be available.

When you first deploy a WCF or WF Service application to Windows Server AppFabric, the Health Monitoring tracking profile is enabled by default and all events are written to the monitoring store that was configured during Windows Server AppFabric configuration.

When you modify the tracking profile, the corresponding entries are written to the `web.config`. For example, if I change the tracking profile to **Troubleshooting**, the following entries are written to the `web.config` file:

```
<microsoft.applicationServer>
    <monitoring>
        <default
            enabled="true"
            connectionStringName="ConnectionString"
            monitoringLevel="Troubleshooting" />
    </monitoring>
</microsoft.applicationServer>
<system.serviceModel>
    <diagnostics
        etwProviderId="f04b9909-6ada-4709-b683-48baf34f15c0">
        <endToEndTracing propagateActivity="true"
        messageFlowTracing="true" />
    </diagnostics>
    <behaviors>
        <serviceBehaviors>
            <behavior name="">
                <etwTracking
                    profileName="Troubleshooting Tracking Profile" />
            </behavior>
        </serviceBehaviors>
    </behaviors>
</system.serviceModel>
```

Thc monitoring element enables monitoring and determines the name of the monitoring store to which the events should be pushed once they have been picked up by ETW.

The diagnostics element sets up the ETW session by defining an `etwProviderId`, which identifies the source application as tracking participant, and lastly, a default service behavior is configured to enable the named tracking profile.

When events are emitted from WCF or WF Services that are configured for monitoring, the ETW Tracking Participant flows the events through an ETW trace listener to the ETW infrastructure, which in turn stores the events in an ETW session. A Windows NT service called the `AppFabricEventCollectionService` monitors the ETW session and forwards the events to the Windows Server AppFabric monitoring store, which feeds the AppFabric Dashboard and Tracked Events features:

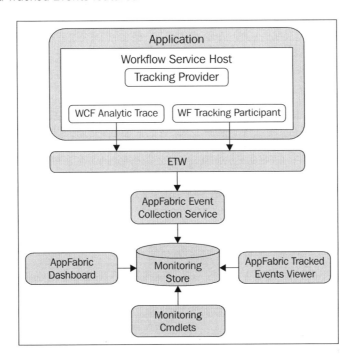

See also

Refer to the *Viewing and classifying events in the AppFabric Dashboard* recipe in this chapter to learn how to use the AppFabric Dashboard.

The code samples used in this recipe can be downloaded from the Packt website.

Viewing and classifying events in the AppFabric Dashboard

Windows Server AppFabric significantly enhances the management experience of WCF and WF services by providing fundamental monitoring capabilities out of the box, as well as providing tools for extending the monitoring metrics that are presented in the Windows Server AppFabric Dashboard.

In this recipe, we will walk through the Windows Server AppFabric Dashboard to provide an interactive orientation of the metrics captured for WCF and WF services.

 If you would like to learn how to enable monitoring for WCF and/or WF services, please refer to the recipes referenced at the end of this recipe in the section titled *See also*.

Getting ready

We will use the Reservation Service sample WF application that is available for download as part of the resources available for this book.

 As the name of the application suggests, the Reservation Service simulates a restaurant reservation workflow service wherein a patron requests a reservation (perhaps from a web frontend or via an inbound automated call center agent) that is managed by the workflow service and is used in several examples throughout this chapter.

Please note that the sample workflow service used in this recipe contains a custom activity that is implemented in the `SendEmail.cs` class, which simulates a confirmation email to a local directory (`C:\AppDev\Demos\Mail`).

Please make sure that you create a directory in `C:\AppDev\Demos\Mail`, or change the path in the SendEmail activity to a path of your choice: `smtpClient.PickupDirectoryLocation = @"C:\AppDev\Demos\Mail";`.

How to do it...

In this recipe, we will walk through the metrics that are captured in the Windows Server AppFabric Dashboard so that you can gain an understanding of the monitoring capabilities in Windows Server AppFabric.

 This recipe assumes that you have already configured monitoring on your application. If you haven't, please refer to the *See also* section at the end of this recipe for a reference to the recipe that covers this topic.

1. Once you have deployed the sample Reservation Service to Windows Server AppFabric, click on the **Content View** tab in Windows Server AppFabric and find the `.xamlx` file for the Reservation Service. Right-click on the file and click on **Browse** to launch the service page and verify that the service is hosted and ready.

2. Open a Visual Studio command prompt and type `wcftestclient`, hit **Space**, and paste the URL to the ReservationService:

This will launch the WCF Test Client, a lightweight test harness that ships with the framework SDK that is useful for exercising SOAP-based WCF and WF Services. Before following the next step, ensure that you have configured and enabled persistence for your service. See the *See Also* section for corresponding recipes in *Chapter 5, More Windows Server AppFabric Hosting Features*.

3. Expand the endpoint exposed over BasicHttpBinding and double-click on the **SubmitReservation** operation. Enter some test values for the reservation request and click on **Invoke**. Note the confirmation number that is returned (3155 in the following example):

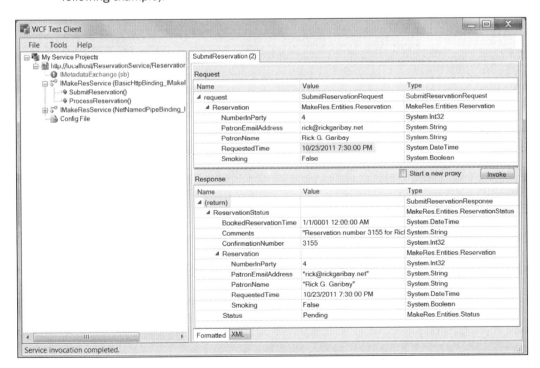

Minimize, but do not close the WCF Test Client window. We will come back to it shortly.

4. In IIS, double-click on the **AppFabric Dashboard** to view the collection of useful metrics for understanding what's going on with the Reservation Service:

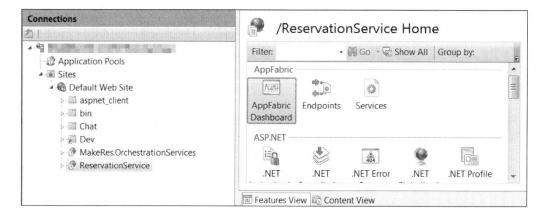

 Note that in order for the metrics to be visible, monitoring and persistence must be enabled for the ReservationService application. Please refer to the recipes for configuring WCF and WF monitoring and WF persistence in the section titled *See also* at the end of this recipe for more information.

5. The dashboard appears for the ReservationService application. Notice that:

- There is a single WF instance that is idle
- No workflow instances are currently active
- No workflow instances are suspended
- No workflow instances have been completed; however, there has been one activation
- One WCF call has completed

❑   There are currently no WCF or WF errors for the application

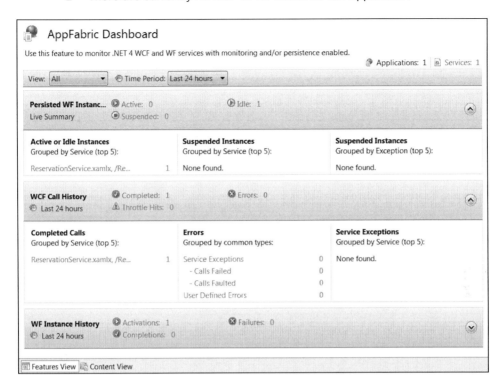

6. Click on the **Idle** link/icon to get more information on the workflow instance that is in an idle state. As you can see, that is our instance of the Reservation Service workflow, waiting for the approval message:

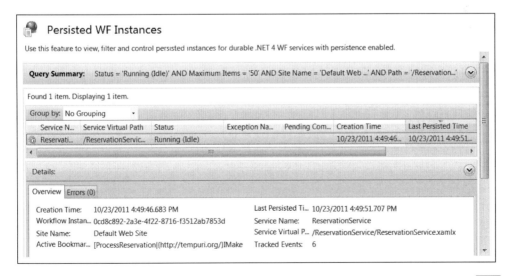

7. Next, open the `ReservationService.xamlx` file in Visual Studio and add a Throw activity just after the Receive activity inside the activity labeled "Process Reservation":

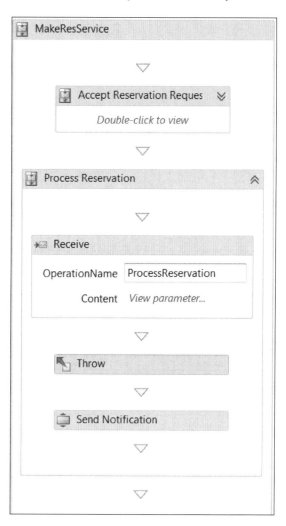

8. Set the Throw activity with an expression that instantiates a `System.Exception` to throw:

9. Re-deploy the ReservationService application to Windows Server AppFabric.

10. Now, go back to the WCF Test Client and double-click on the **ProcessReservation** operation. Paste in the confirmation number and set the status field to **Confirmed**. Click on **Invoke**. Click on **OK** on the one-way message delivery confirmation:

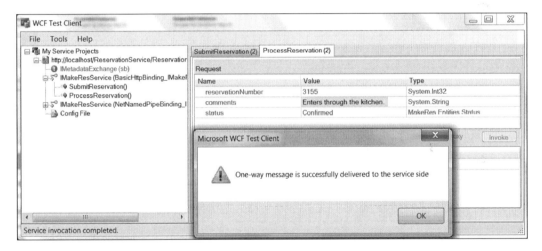

 The confirmation message is sent to the Reservation Service and no response is expected.

11. Now, go back to the AppFabric Dashboard and refresh it by pressing *F5*. Notice that the workflow instance is now suspended and that there is a failure recorded for the workflow:

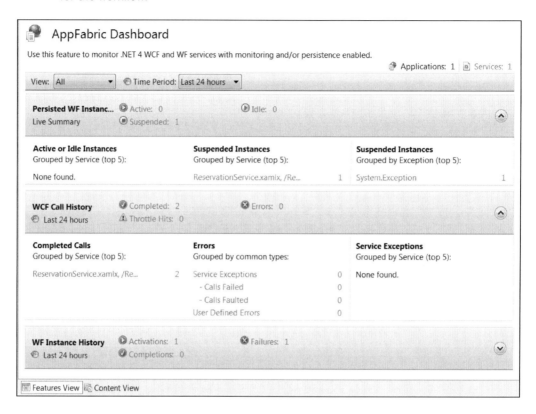

12. You will notice that in WCF Call History, the "Errors" metric is zero while the "Failures" metric in WF Instance History identifies a failure. Windows Server AppFabric distinguishes between a WCF error, that is an error that occurred in the messaging stack, and a failure that occurred while executing the workflow. Click on the **Suspended** link and click on the instance record that appears. The error tab reveals the problem:

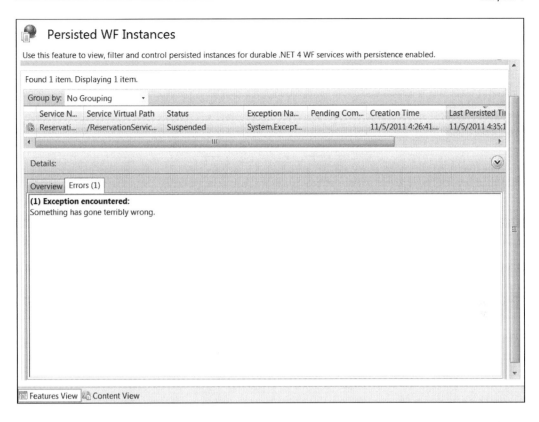

13. To fix the "bug", go back to the `ReservationService.xamlx` file, removing the Throw activity from the Process Reservation activity and re-deploying to Windows Server AppFabric.

14. Repeat steps 3 and 10, now that the issue has been fixed.

15. Now, go back to the AppFabric Dashboard and refresh it by pressing *F5*. Notice that there are no longer any idle workflow instances, but the **Completions** count under **WF Instance History** has been incremented, and the number of activations now matches completions with no additional persistence activity.

How it works...

Windows Server AppFabric provides monitoring and persistence capabilities in a very seamless manner compared to the traditional approach where the persistence database must be manually created and configured via XML. Furthermore, by default insight into application exceptions is very difficult to obtain.

Support for these capabilities requires that they have each been configured on the Windows Server AppFabric application. As the ReservationService workflow service requires support for long-running work, persistence must be enabled for the service to work as expected (see *Chapter 4*, *Windows Server AppFabric Hosting Fundamentals* and *Chapter 5*, *More Windows Server AppFabric Hosting Features* for recipes that cover WF Service hosting and persistence).

In addition, a valid monitoring profile ("Health Monitoring" at a minimum) is required for the non-persistence WCF and WF metrics to be available.

When the first message to request a reservation is received by the workflow service, the workflow instance is activated and begins executing the activities within the activity labeled "Accept Reservation Request". Once all activities are complete, the workflow goes into an idle state. By default, after 60 seconds, the workflow instance is unloaded from memory and persisted to the persistence store.

The Windows Server AppFabric Dashboard tracks the persisted state of workflow instances as well as activations, completions, or failures along with WCF metrics.

The persistence metrics are presented in the **Persisted WF Instances** section and provides visibility into the state of the instance, including **Active**, **Idle**, and **Suspended**. These metrics are read from the database that is configured for persistence.

WCF specific metrics are presented in the **WCF Call History** section, which provides information on **Completed Calls**, **Errors**, and **Throttle Hits**. These metrics, along with those in the **WF Instance History** section provide insights on **Activations**, **Failures**, and **Completions** of workflow instances for the application or website in scope and are read from the configured monitoring store.

The **Event Collection** service is responsible for gathering tracked events from the WCF or WF service and writing them to the configured monitoring store.

While most of the interaction in the AppFabric Dashboard is read-only, it is possible to perform some management tasks within the Persisted WF Instances section. For example, when the workflow instance was suspended in step 11 due to the exception that was thrown, the likely recourse would be to right-click the instance and either terminate, cancel, or delete it (see *Using common AppFabric hosting commandlets* in *Chapter 5*, *More Windows Server AppFabric Hosting Features* for a scripted alterative using the Windows Server AppFabric management commandlets).

It is important to note that if monitoring and persistence are not enabled for the WCF or WF service application or service, no data is gathered. However, if you choose to enable persistence but disable monitoring, data will still appear in the Persisted WF Instances section, and if you apply the inverse, data will be available in the remaining sections but not the former.

As all monitoring and persistence data is stored in SQL Server, multiple servers, applications and services can share the same persistence and monitoring stores and this is covered in greater detail in *Chapter 8, Scaling AppFabric Hosting, Monitoring, and Persistence*.

There's more...

Tracking Profiles are configured when you enable monitoring for an application. The profiles are canned configurations for the level (verbosity) of events you want to track. For example, you can configure Windows Server AppFabric to use the **Troubleshooting** tracking profile for the greatest level of verbosity or to not apply a tracking profile at all.

While the profiles that ship out of the box cover a broad range of needs, you can also write your own custom tracking profiles for Windows Server AppFabric. To learn more about custom tracking profiles, refer to the *See also* section at the conclusion of this recipe.

See also

For a step-by-step guide to installing Windows Server AppFabric, refer to the recipe *Installing Windows Server AppFabric* in *Chapter 1, Installing Windows Server AppFabric*.

Configuration of monitoring is covered in the first recipe of this chapter, *Collecting events from WCF and WF services*.

To learn about how to use AppFabric Dashboard, refer to the recipe in this chapter called *Viewing and classifying events in the AppFabric Dashboard*.

Deploying WF services is covered in detail in *Chapter 4, Windows Server AppFabric Hosting Fundamentals*, which provides the necessary steps to configure monitoring and persistence for a scenario with similar requirements that we covered in this recipe.

Chapter 6, Utilizing AppFabric Persistence provides a number of recipes that cover persistence related topics.

To learn about creating custom tracking profiles, please refer to the *Creating a customized tracking profile for WF services* recipe in this chapter.

The code samples used in this recipe can be downloaded from the Packt website.

Enabling tracing and evaluating trace logs with WCF

When something goes wrong with a WCF or WF service, it can be very difficult to determine what the problem is.

While the AppFabric Dashboard and Tracked Events viewer are a great first place to turn, sometimes, the only way to really understand what is going on is to probe more deeply into the messaging runtime.

For example, security and serialization exceptions often happen before a message even reaches your code, so relying on exception management inside your code does not always help. Infrastructure related issues such as security and transactions, or transport level issues related to reliable messaging are really out of the reach of what the AppFabric Dashboard is intended to provide.

In addition, sometimes you need to examine a message itself to really get an understanding of what is being sent on the wire.

Both WCF and WF services provide deep insights into what is really happening under the hood with support for diagnostic tracing via `System.Diagnostics`. Configuring tracing in WCF and WF service applications optionally requires some imperative code (in the event that you make use of the `Trace` class in your own service code), but at the very least requires a non-trivial amount of declarative mark up in the application or web configuration file.

In this recipe, we will learn how Windows Server AppFabric simplifies this significantly by providing the ability to enable tracing for WCF and WF services along with some of the most common configuration knobs.

Getting ready

You will want to ensure you have either a WCF or WF application deployed to Windows Server AppFabric before starting this recipe. The following examples use a WCF service called EchoService that is available for download as part of this book.

How to do it...

1. Windows Server AppFabric makes it simple to enable WCF tracing without the need for memorizing or looking up XML configuration schema or relying on the WCF Configuration Tool in Visual Studio.

2. In IIS, right-click on the WCF or WF application you want to enable tracing for and select **Manage WCF and WF Services** followed by **Configure**:

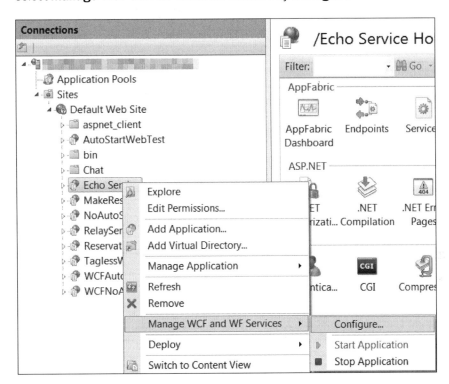

 The example is using the EchoService WCF service sample application that is available for download with this chapter; however, this recipe applies to any WCF service application deployed to Windows Server AppFabric.

3. Next, click on the **Monitoring** tab and scroll down until you see the **Diagnostic Tracing and Message Logging (file-based)** dialog. Click on **Configure...**:

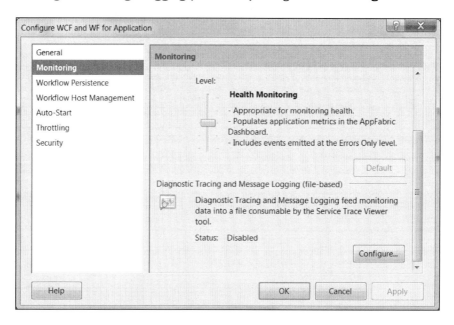

4. Notice that the **Configure Diagnostic Tracing and Message Logging** dialog is partitioned into two areas: **Tracing and Message Logging**. Set the WCF tracing level to the highest available by selecting the **Verbose** tracing level:

5. After choosing the tracing level, click on **Browse...** to pick a location on the disk for creating the log file and name the file (an extension of `svclog` will be automatically appended for you); click on **OK**:

6. Now, exercise the service by invoking an operation a few times and using Windows Explorer, navigate to the location of your `.svclog` file and open it with the `SvcTraceViewer.exe` tool, which is designed for reading the output.

 If the `SvcTraceViewer.exe` tool is not the default program for opening the `.svclog` file, you can find it in `C:\Program Files (x86)\Microsoft SDKs\Windows\v7.0A\Bin`.

7. Once the **Microsoft Service Trace Viewer** opens, you will notice one or more **Activity** sessions listed on the **Activity** tab, depending on the number of operations you exercised in step 6. The right pane includes information of each event within the activity session. Scroll up and down to note any information, warning or errors:

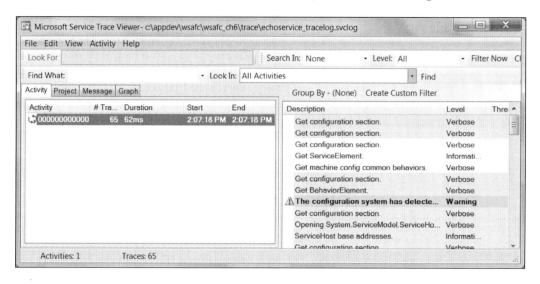

8. Next, double-click on one of the **Activity** sessions to load a **Graph** for the session (notice that the active tab is now **Graph**). Click on a few of the entries, which represent an event in the execution of the service operation and scroll down until you see an icon that depicts an incoming message; click the icon:

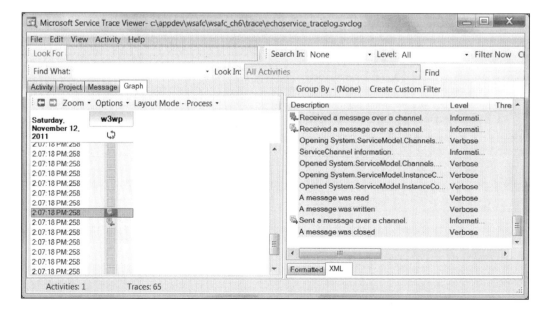

9. Notice that for each entry in the graph, a corresponding XML message is provided which contains information about the event and the level at which it is captured.

10. Now, go back to IIS and navigate to the **Monitoring** tab for the application again and click on **Configure...** to bring up the **Configure Diagnostic Tracing and Message Logging** screen. Enable message logging by checking the **Enable** checkbox under **Message Logging** and also check **Log entire message**. Provide a location and name for the message log file, ensuring that you distinguish it from the service trace file name, and click on **OK**:

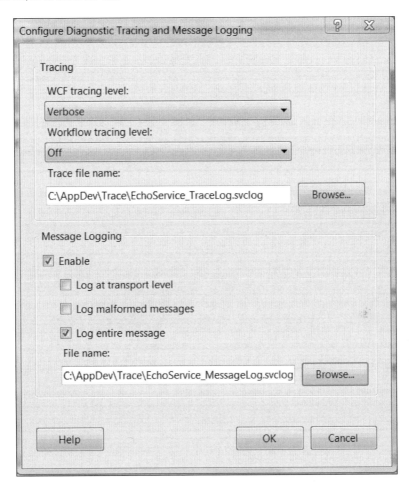

11. Once again, exercise the service by invoking an operation a few times and using Windows Explorer, navigate to the location of the `.svclog` file for your message logging, and open it with the `SvcTraceViewer.exe` tool.

12. As with the service trace session, the navigation is very similar, except that in this case, you are only seeing message information as opposed to channel stack events. If you click on one of the messages, you will see the original payload that the service received, along with any messages the service sent in response:

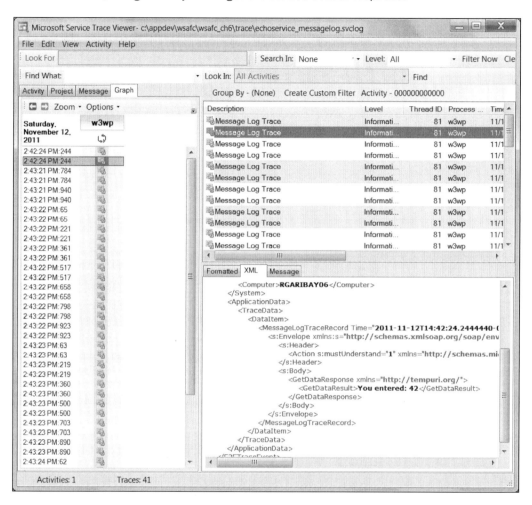

> If you are working with an encrypted message payload, as with the `WSHttpBinding` for example, you will notice that the trace log file is significantly more verbose with many more processing activities as the message makes its way through the channel stack.
>
>
>
> In addition, you will find a number of processing steps in which the **Message Log Trace** XML will contain a ciphered version of the message. To view the unencrypted payload, go the **Activities** tab and click on the first instance of action and response action being processed, and select **Message Log Trace** in XML view.

How it works...

When service tracing or message logging is enabled through Windows Server AppFabric, a number of entries are made to the `web.config` file for your application, including the `System.Diagnostics` configuration as well as the trace sources and the required elements for setting up and initializing the trace listeners for the service tracing and message logging.

While Windows Server AppFabric provides a number of common configuration options, there are a few options that are available to you, including the ability to configure the maximum number of messages to log and the limit on the size of messages to log. Both of these are useful because in addition to affecting performance, the log files can grow very quickly, creating a potential disk space problem if left unattended for too long.

By default, Windows Server AppFabric will only log up to 3,000 messages when enabling message logging. You can change this value by modifying the `maxMessagesToLog` attribute in the `messageLogging` element as shown in the following code:

```
<diagnostics>

    <messageLogging logEntireMessage="true"
                    logMalformedMessages="false"
                    logMessagesAtServiceLevel="true"
                    logMessagesAtTransportLevel="false"
                    maxMessagesToLog="3000" />

</diagnostics>
```

You can also specify the largest size of a message to log using the `maxSizeOfMessageToLog` attribute. This is useful when you are looking for a specific type of message and want to filter others out based on size, or when you are dealing with large binary messages or **MTOM (Message Transmission Optimization Mechanism)** encoded messages and want to preserve disk space by filtering those out.

See also

For a step-by-step guide for installing Windows Server AppFabric, refer to the recipe *Installing Windows Server AppFabric* in *Chapter 1, Installing Windows Server AppFabric*.

The code samples used in this recipe can be downloaded from the Packt website.

Creating a customized tracking profile for WF services

As covered in the *Collecting events from WCF and WF services* recipe of this chapter, Windows Server AppFabric provides a number of tracking profiles out of the box which allow you to monitor your WCF and WF service application with varying degrees of detail (to learn more about working with preconfigured tracking profiles, please see the references at the end of this recipe).

While the tracking profiles provided out of the box provide a wide range of coverage, sometimes it is helpful to gain a deeper insight, at the activity, variable, and argument level as to what is happening inside of the activities within a workflow.

Custom Tracking Profiles provide a way to extend Event Tracing for Windows (ETW) as a tracking participant, opting activities, variables, and arguments into a custom tracking profile defined by the `etwTracking` service behavior.

This means that the custom tracking profiles you build offer the same performance as the out of the box profiles, but offer a lower degree of granularity for gaining insight into your WF services.

As you will see in this recipe, you can define a custom tracking profile right within Windows Server AppFabric; once you have created it, you can interact with the events through Windows Server AppFabric just as you would for any other tracking profile.

Getting ready

We will use the Reservation Service sample WF application that is available for download as part of the resources available for this book.

As the name of the application suggests, the Reservation Service simulates a restaurant reservation workflow service wherein a patron requests a reservation (perhaps from a web frontend or via an inbound automated call center agent) that is managed by the workflow service and is used in several examples throughout this chapter.

Please note that the sample workflow service used in this recipe contains a custom activity that is implemented in the `SendEmail.cs` class, which simulates a confirmation email to a local directory (`C:\AppDev\Demos\Mail`). Please make sure that you create a directory in `C:\AppDev\Demos\Mail`, or change the path in the SendEmail activity to a path of your choice: `smtpClient.PickupDirectoryLocation = @"C:\AppDev\Demos\Mail";`

How to do it...

First, we will create a tracking profile file using Visual Studio and then load the tracking profile into Windows Server AppFabric:

1. Deploy your WF Service application to Windows Server AppFabric using your preferred deployment method and test the service to ensure that it is functional.

> In this example, I've deployed the Reservation Service that is available for download with this chapter; however, this recipe applies to any WF service application deployed to Windows Server AppFabric.

2. Once you have verified that everything is functioning properly, in Visual Studio, create an XML file by right-clicking on the project, selecting **Add, New Item**, and then **XML File** and add the following elements:

```
<trackingProfile name="CustomTrackingProfile">
    <workflow activityDefinitionId="*">
    </workflow>
</trackingProfile>
```

> The workflow element includes an `activityDefinitionId` which scopes the name of the activity that you want to track. The asterisk indicates that all activities will be included in the tracking.

3. Next, add an `activityStateQueries` and `activityStateQuery` element right under the `workflow` element, along with the `states` and `variables` elements:

```
<activityStateQueries>
    <activityStateQuery activityName="*">
        <states>
            <state name="Closed"/>
        </states>
        <variables>
            <variable name="reservationRequest"/>
        </variables>
    </activityStateQuery>
</activityStateQueries>
```

> The `activityStateQuery` element defines a query that will filter based on the state of the activity. In this case, we want to only look at activities that have completed executing.
>
> In addition, the `variables` element defines one or more variables to be tracked based on the `name` attribute. In this case, we are only interested in tracking the `reservationRequest` variable.

4. The full configuration should resemble the following screenshot, which includes the necessary queries for tracking the named variable that is assigned when the workflow is executed:

```xml
<?xml version="1.0" encoding="utf-8" ?>
    <trackingProfile name="CustomTrackingProfile">
        <workflow activityDefinitionId="*">
            <activityStateQueries>
                <activityStateQuery activityName="*">
                    <states>
                        <state name="Closed"/>
                    </states>
                    <variables>
                        <variable name="reservationRequest"/>
                    </variables>
                </activityStateQuery>
            </activityStateQueries>
        </workflow>
    </trackingProfile>
```

5. Change the file extension from XML to TP.

6. Now, in Windows Server AppFabric, with the **ReservationService** sample WF Service application in scope, double-click on the **Services** icon:

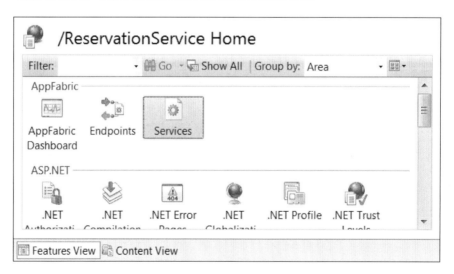

7. Right-click on the service entry, click on **Configure...** and click on the **Monitoring** tab. On the **Monitoring** screen, click on **Configure...** to open the **Workflow Tracking Profile** screen:

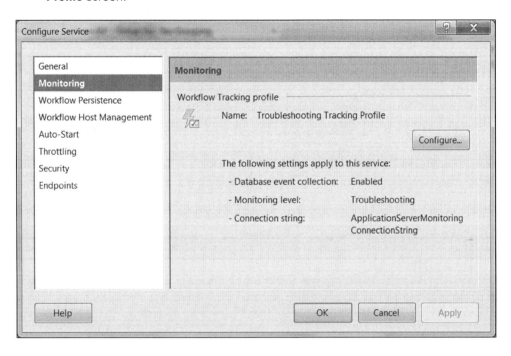

8. On the **Workflow Tracking Profile** screen, click on **Add new**, and then click **Browse** to load to the `.tp` file that contains your custom tracking profile. Give your tracking profile a name and check the boxes to set as the current profile and overwrite it if the profile already exists. Click on **OK**, then on **OK** again, and finally **OK** once more:

9. With the custom tracking profile you created configured, exercise the service to create tracking data, select the service, right-click it, and select **View Tracked Events**:

10. Click on any of the activity state records, and review the information on the **Overview** tab. Notice that the **Tracking Profile** field is set to the **CustomTrackingProfile** you created at the bottom of the **Overview** tab:

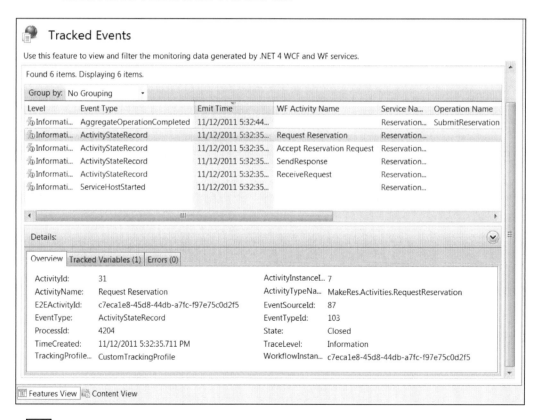

11. Now, take a look at the configured custom variable you enabled for tracking. Click on a couple of activity state records until you find one that has at least one tracked variable showing on the **Tracked Variables** tab. Notice the name of the variable and hover your pointer to the right of the field and you will see a complete XML serialized representation of the payload:

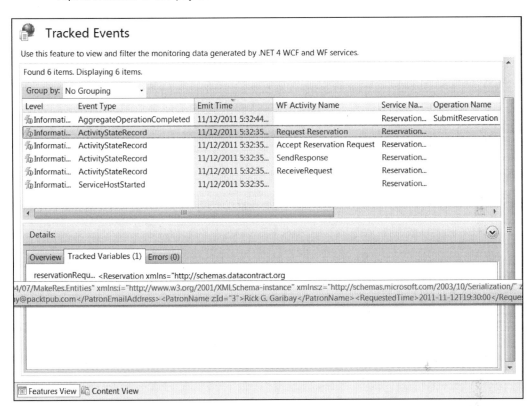

How it works...

In step 4, we defined the elements required to author a custom tracking profile. First, we give the custom tracking profile a name by setting the `name` attribute in the `trackingProfile` element. Next we scope the tracking we want to do to include the workflow, activities, and variables we want to track. The configuration in step 4 declares that we are interested in tracking all activities in all workflow instances, and are specifically interested in the `reservationRequest` variable, regardless of what activity it appears in.

Once we load the custom tracking profile, Windows Server AppFabric creates the necessary configuration in the application's `web.config` file, including the `etwTracking` service behavior which configures an ETW tracking participant that will receive the events defined in the custom tracking profile.

These events are captured in tracking records, which represent a tracked event that occurs within a workflow, activity, or custom query. For example, workflow tracking records may fire when a workflow starts or completes, whereas activity tracking records track the state of variables and/or arguments at various stages of activity execution such as executing, closed, or faulted.

As discussed in the *Collecting events from WCF and WF services* recipe of this chapter, the ETW tracking participant consumes the workflow events and emits them to an ETW session, which is then fed to the Windows Server AppFabric monitoring store.

Once the tracked events are in the store, they are treated the same way as events from any of the out of the box tracking profiles and made available for review in a consistent manner within the Tracked Events viewer.

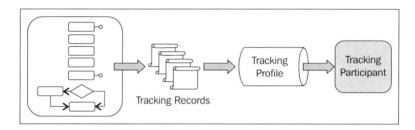

There's more...

Sometimes it is useful to add custom events inside activities that you create yourself. For example, you may want to increment how many times a custom activity has been executed, or test for a certain region of code within the custom activity being hit. You can use a **Custom Tracking Queries** to do just that. See `http://msdn.microsoft.com/en-us/library/ee513989(v=VS.110).aspx` for more information.

See also

For a step-by-step guide for installing Windows Server AppFabric, refer to the recipe *Installing Windows Server AppFabric* in *Chapter 1, Installing Windows Server AppFabric*.

To learn how to configure WCF and WF services to use the built-in tracking profiles, refer to the *Collecting events from WCF and WF services* recipe of this chapter.

The code samples used in this recipe can be downloaded from the Packt website.

Accessing the Monitoring DB

When you install and configure Windows Server AppFabric to support monitoring, (as discussed in *Chapter 1, Installing Windows Server AppFabric*) Windows Server AppFabric automatically provisions a database for storing all of the monitoring events that are captured based on the tracking profile you have selected.

This database is based on a schema that is defined specifically for Windows Server AppFabric, and while it is important that you don't tamper with the schema itself, as it is created on a SQL Server database, information can be gleaned from it by connecting to it using any number of SQL Server tools.

In this recipe, we will look at connecting to the Windows Server AppFabric monitoring database using Visual Studio to familiarize you with some of the most useful data definition objects that are created and used by the Windows Server AppFabric monitoring infrastructure, including the AppFabric Dashboard, Tracked Events viewer, and PowerShell cmdlets (each of which is covered within this chapter).

Getting ready

A basic understanding of Windows Server AppFabric monitoring capabilities will help you appreciate this recipe more fully. Take a look at the *Collecting events from WCF and WF services* and *Viewing and classifying events in the AppFabric Dashboard* recipes in this chapter if you aren't already familiar with the monitoring capabilities that Windows Server AppFabric provides.

How to do it...

The first thing we need to do is determine the location of the monitoring store. From there, we will connect to it via Visual Studio and explore some of the most useful objects:

1. To determine the name and location of the monitoring store for your application, open IIS and double-click on the **Connection Strings** icon, which should list all of the connection strings that have been configured at the website level:

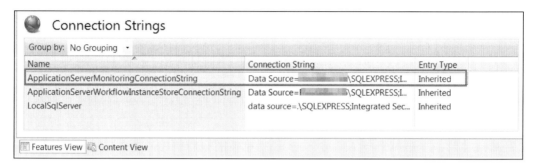

2. If you are not sure which connection string you configured for the monitoring store, start the Windows Server AppFabric configuration tool, which is located at `C:\Windows\system32\AppFabric\Microsoft.ApplicationServer. Configuration.exe` to verify. You can follow the first recipe in *Chapter 1, Installing Windows Server AppFabric* for more details on working with the Windows Server AppFabric configuration tool.

3. Open Visual Studio and press *Ctrl+W* and *Ctrl+L* to launch Server Explorer.

4. Right-click on the **Data Connections** root and select **Add Connection**:

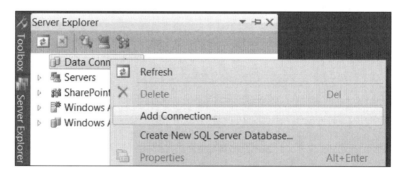

5. Enter the connection information from the connection string you resolved in step 1 and click on **Test Connection** to verify that you can connect to the database. Click on **OK** to dismiss the confirmation dialog and then click on **OK** again to close the connection dialog:

6. Notice that there are several dozen objects, including tables, views, stored procedures, and functions. Expand the **Views** node to enumerate the views:

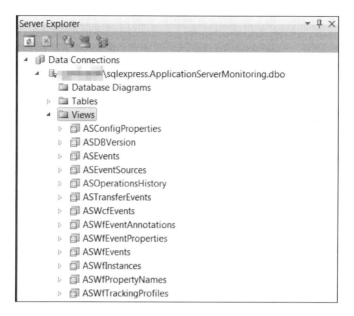

7. Right-click on the `ASWcfEvents` view and select **Show Results** to view the contents of the table.

8. Let's write some custom T-SQL against these views by starting a new query connection. In Visual Studio, click on **Data | Transact-SQL Editor | New Query Connection**. If prompted for database information, provide the server name and your credentials and click **Connect**.

9. Type the following T-SQL code to associate the WCF events from the `ASWcfWEvents` view with the event source from the `ASEventSources` view:

```
SELECT e.EventTypeId, s.Name, e.EventType, s.VirtualPath,
e.Duration FROM  ApplicationServerMonitoring.dbo.ASWcfEvents e
LEFT JOIN ApplicationServerMonitoring.dbo.ASEventSources s
ON e.EventSourceId = s.Id
ORDER by e.Duration DESC;
```

The query results include the name of the application, the type of event, the path to the application in IIS, and the duration, in milliseconds of each event ordering by events with the longest duration.

10. Take some time to explore some of the other views, including the following views that apply to WF Services: `ASWfEvents`, `ASWfInstances`, `ASWfEventProperties`, and `ASWfTrackingProfiles`.

How it works...

As all of the monitoring information that is gathered by the Windows Server AppFabric tracking profiles is stored in SQL Server, accessing it is directly is pretty useful should you wish to do so.

The AppFabric Dashboard, Tracked Events viewer, and Poweshell cmdlets such as the `Get-ASAppMonitoring` cmdlet all use the monitoring store as the source of information once the events have made it from the ETW session to the store.

See also

For a step-by-step guide to installing Windows Server AppFabric, refer to the recipe *Installing Windows Server AppFabric* in *Chapter 1, Installing Windows Server AppFabric*.

To learn more about how to configure monitoring from within Windows Server AppFabric, take a look at the *Collecting events from WCF and WF services* and *Viewing and classifying events in the AppFabric Dashboard* recipes of this chapter.

The code samples used in this recipe can be downloaded from the Packt website.

Building a custom dashboard

As covered in the previous recipe, by default, all monitoring data collected by Windows Server AppFabric is stored in SQL Server. This provides a number of possibilities for querying, exposing, and analyzing the monitoring data in a variety of interesting ways.

In this recipe, I am going to show you how to expose this data across a variety of user interfaces by exposing select views from the monitoring store via WCF Data Services. As OData is a cross platform standard for sharing resources, it is a perfect choice for expanding the reach of this data as far and wide as possible.

From there, we will build a simple dashboard using ASP.NET MVC 3, which consumes our service and provides some common ways for interacting with tracked events collected for a WF Service that has been hosted in Windows Server AppFabric.

While not comprehensive, this recipe will show you all the things you need to get started. In fact, all of the code in this sample is available in the download contents for you to learn from and extend as you wish.

Getting ready

Before getting started with this recipe, you will want to ensure that you have exercised the service and introduced some tracking events into the monitoring store to ensure that you have some events to monitor. See the *Collecting events from WCF and WF services* along with *Creating a customized tracking profile for WF services* recipes if you are not sure how to do so.

This recipe assumes that you are familiar with Visual Studio and the ASP.NET MVC 3 project template, and have a general understanding of Entity Framework and WCF Data Services. If this is not the case, please refer to the resources referenced at the end of this recipe in the *See also* section.

MVC 3 shipped after Visual Studio 2010 was released. If you don't already have MVC 3 installed, please visit the download page to install the "ASP.NET MVC 3 Tools Update": `http://www.microsoft.com/download/en/details.aspx?displaylang=en&id=1491`. Lastly, this recipe makes use of the Microsoft NuGet Package Manager, which provides a simple way to include additional libraries offered by Microsoft, third-party vendors and the community at large. If you have not installed NuGet, you can do so by using the Microsoft Platform Installer or downloading the tool directly from: `http://visualstudiogallery.msdn.microsoft.com/27077b70-9dad-4c64-adcf-c7cf6bc9970c`.

To run the samples in this recipe, you will need to download a free 60-day trial of the Telerik Extensions for ASP.NET MVC. This trial license will allow you to run local copies of demos that use the Telerik Grid for ASP.NET MVC. To obtain your free trial license, visit `http://www.telerik.com/aspnet-mvc`. Once the trial is installed, it will add all of the necessary assembly references and install the needed JavaScript and CSS files to support.

 For information on using NuGet, please refer to the NuGet overview documentation for getting started: `http://docs.nuget.org/docs/start-here/overview`.

How to do it...

We will follow a number of code-intensive steps to build out our custom dashboard. First, we will build an entity model using Entity Framework 4 and then expose it as OData by wrapping the entity model in a WCF Data Service.

From there, we will create an ASP.NET MVC 3 web application to serve as a simple dashboard for consuming the resources from the WCF Data Service and presenting them in a meaningful way.

1. To get started, create an **ASP.NET MVC 3 Web Application** project called **CustomDashboard** (when prompted for the type of application, choose **Intranet**, as we will be running this dashboard locally):

2. Next, add an **Entity Data Model** by right-clicking on the **Custom Dashboard** project and adding an **ADO.NET Entity Data Model** item type. Name the item template `AppFabricMonitoringStore` and click on **Add**:

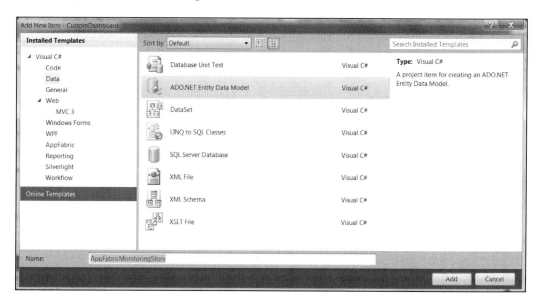

3. When prompted to choose the data **Model Contents**, select the **Generate from database** option and click on **Next**:

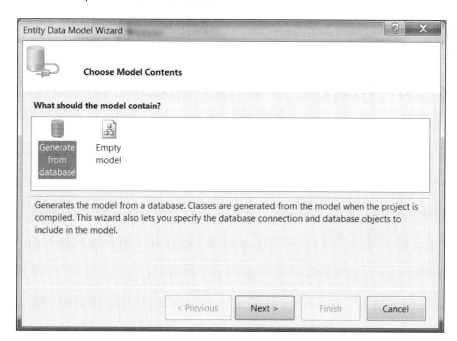

4. On the **Choose Your Data Connection** screen, select the connection string for the monitoring store as configured on your machine. Ensure the checkbox next to **Save entity connection settings in Web.config** is checked and name the connection string **ApplicationServerMonitoringEntities**. Click on **Next**:

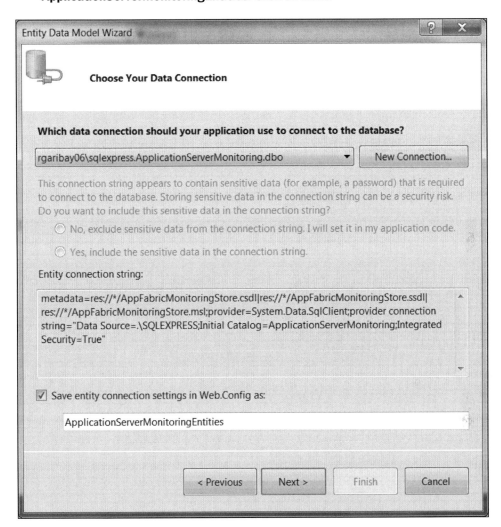

5. Next, on the **Choose Your Database Objects** screen, check the box next to **Views** and ensure that both checkboxes at the bottom are checked. Name the **Model Namespace** as **ApplicationServerMonitoringModel** and click on **Finish**.

The `AppFabricMonitoringStore.edmx` file is created within the CustomDashboard project, which contains a class that has been generated for each view and an entity context for interacting with the views.

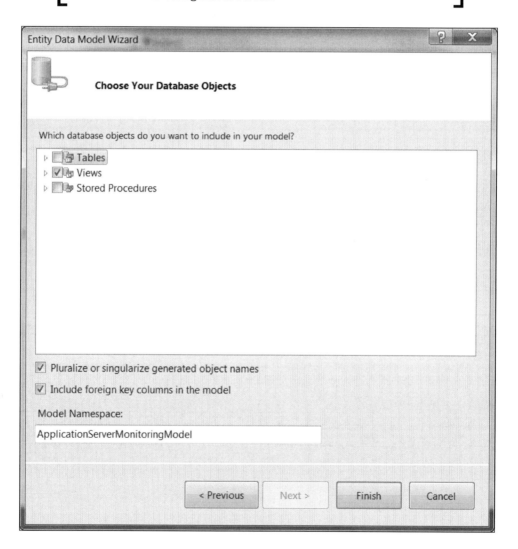

6. Now, create the WCF Data Service, which will wrap the entity model we just created by adding a WCF Data Service item to the CustomDashboard project, and name it **MonitoringStoreService.svc**:

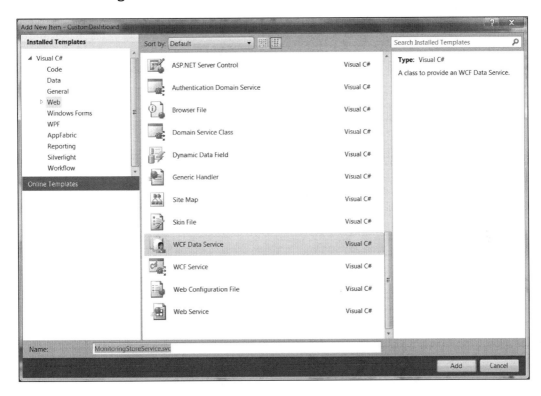

7. Double-click the newly created `MonitoringStoreService.svc` file and overwrite line 11 with the following code:

```
public class MonitoringStoreService : DataService<ApplicationServe
rMonitoringEntities>
```

8. Do the same for line 18, replacing the default code with the following:

```
config.SetEntitySetAccessRule("*", EntitySetRights.AllRead);
```

9. Deploy the CustomDashboard project to Windows Server AppFabric using the deployment method of your choice (see *Chapter 4, Windows Server AppFabric Hosting Fundamentals* if you aren't sure how to do this).

10. Now, test the `MonitoringStoreService` by browsing to the URL in your browser. Doing so should resemble the following, which shows the default response that lists each of the entities that have been exposed:

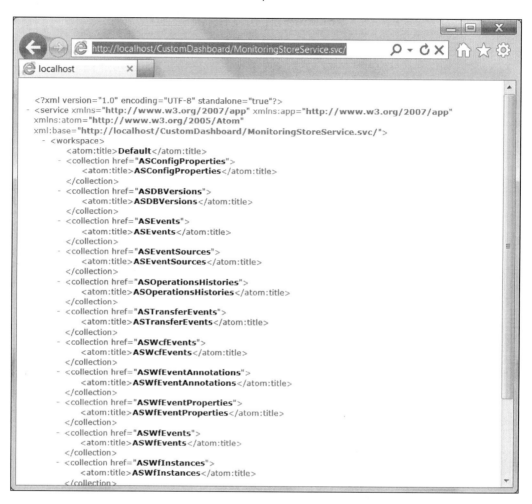

11. To request the records for a particular resource, append the name of the view to the URL. For example, to see the records provided by the **ASWfEvents** resource, append it to the URL as follows: `http://localhost/CustomDashboard/MonitoringStoreService.svc/ASWfEvents`.

12. With our WCF Data Service complete, it's now time to build out a view on our dashboard. To do so, we are going to use a grid control provided by Telerik. The easiest way to get a hold of the control is to install the Telerik Extensions for ASP.NET MVC via NuGet. To do so, right-click on the CustomDashboard project and select **Manage NuGet Packages...**. Search for `telerik` and install the `TelerikMvcExtensions` package:

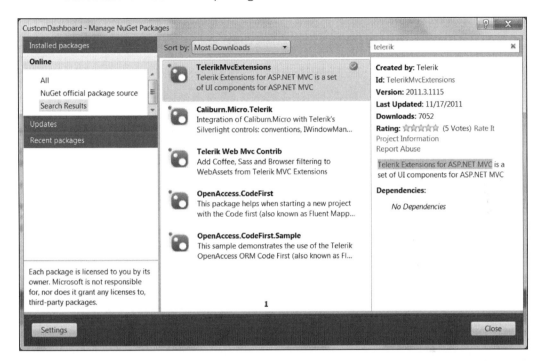

To run some demos in this chapter, you will need to download a free 60-day trial of the Telerik Extensions for `ASP.NET` MVC. This trial license will allow you to run local copies of demos that use the Telerik Grid for `ASP.NET` MVC. To obtain your free trial license, visit `http://www.telerik.com/aspnet-mvc`.

Once the trial is installed, it will add all of the necessary assembly references and install the needed JavaScript and CSS files to support.

13. In the CustomDashboard project, find the `Site.Master` file by expanding the `Views` folder and expanding the `Shared` folder. Double-click on the `Site.Master` file to open it.

14. Copy the following code into the head element, which registers the stylesheets that are specific to the Telerik controls:

```
<%= Html.Telerik().StyleSheetRegistrar()
    .DefaultGroup(group => group.Add("telerik.common.css")
                                .Add("telerik.vista.css"))
%>
```

15. Next, scroll to the bottom of the Site.Master file and add the following snippet just before the closing body element, which ensures that all JavaScript helper files are registered:

```
<%= Html.Telerik().ScriptRegistrar() %>
```

 A fully functional sample is available with the download contents of this chapter. Feel free to reference it as you go.

16. Now, let's work on the view for our dashboard. Open the Index.asp page and paste the following code in the asp:Content element:

```
<% Html.Telerik().Grid<CustomDashboard.Models.Event>(Model)
    .Name("Events")
    .Columns(columns =>
    {
            columns.Bound(e => e.Id);
            columns.Bound(e => e.EventSource);
            columns.Bound(e => e.EventType);
            columns.Bound(e => e.ActivityName);
            columns.Bound(e => e.TimeCreated);
    })
    .DetailView(detailView => detailView.Template(e => // Set
    the server template
    {
            // Display the details for the Employee
    %>
    <table>
    <tr>
    <td>
        <ul>
        <li>Activity Id: <%= e.ActivityId%> </li>
        <li>Activity Name: <%= e.ActivityName%> </li>
        <li>Virtual Path: <%= e.VirtualPath%> </li>
        <li>Event Type: <%= e.EventType%> </li>
        <li>Process Id: <%= e.ProcessId%> </li>
        <li>Time Created: <%= e.TimeCreated%> </li>
        <li>Trace Level: <%= e.TraceLevel%> </li>
        </ul>
    </td>
```

```
            <td>
            <ul>
                 <li>Variable: <%= e.Variable%> </li>
                 <li>Value <%= e.ValueBlob%> </li>

                 </ul>
            </td>
            </tr>
            </table>

            <%
    }))
    .RowAction(row =>
    {
            // Expand initially the detail view of the
            // first row
            if (row.Index == 0)
            {
                    row.DetailRow.Expanded = true;
            }
    })
    .Pageable()
    .Filterable()
    .Sortable()
    .Render();
    %>
```

There is quite a bit going on here and I'll explain it in detail in the *How it works...* section; however, to summarize, we are declaring the Telerik Grid control, which will bind the results from our calls to the `MonitoringStoreService` in the Controller.

When we declare the Grid, we are referencing a class that is part of our Model called Event, which will be hydrated by our OData service and served by the controller.

Everything else is really formatting and enabling features that the Grid control supports such as paging, sorting, and filtering.

We will see all of this in action in just a few more steps...

17. Next, we need to define some classes that will model the information we want to represent. Create three C# class files in the `Model` folder: `Event.cs`, `EventProperties.cs`, and `Source.cs`.

18. Paste the following code into the `Event.cs` file just after the opening bracket on line 9 to define the properties that describe an `Event` type:

```
public long Id { get; set; }
public string ActivityId { get; set; }
public string EventSource { get; set; }
public string VirtualPath { get; set; }
public string EventType { get; set; }
public string ActivityName { get; set; }
public long ProcessId { get; set; }
public string TraceLevel { get; set; }
public string Variable { get; set; }
public string ValueBlob { get; set; }
public DateTime TimeCreated { get; set; }
```

19. Do the same for the `EventProperties.cs` file just after the opening bracket on line 9 to define the properties that describe the `EventProprties` type:

```
public long EventId { get; set; }
public string WfDataSource { get; set; }
public string ValueBlob { get; set; }
```

20. Again, paste the following code in the `Source.cs` file just after the opening bracket on line 9 to define the properties that describe the `Source` type:

```
public long Id { get; set; }
public string Name { get; set; }
public string Computer { get; set; }
public string Site { get; set; }
public string VirtualPath { get; set; }
public string ApplicationVirtualPath { get; set; }
public string ServiceVirtualPath { get; set; }
```

21. In order to work with OData as easily as possible, I've included a library called OData Helper that greatly simplifies working with OData services from a client perspective. To install the OData Helper, install the OData Helper NuGet package just as you did for the Telerik controls in step 12.

22. With our view and model complete, all that's left now is to wire it up within the `HomeController.cs` file that has already been created for us by the ASP.NET MVC 3 Web Application project template. Open the `HomeController.cs` file and replace the contents of the `Index` method with the following code:

```
ViewData["Message"] = "Custom Dashboard Example.";

List<Event> eventList = new List<Event>();
var events = OData.Get("http://localhost/
CustomDashboard/
MonitoringStoreService.svc/ASWfEvents");
```

```
var sources = OData.Get("http://localhost/
CustomDashboard/
MonitoringStoreService.svc/ASEventSources");
var props = OData.Get("http://localhost/
CustomDashboard/
MonitoringStoreService.svc/ASWfEventProperties");


foreach (dynamic eventRecord in events)
{
    Event e = new Event();
    e.Id = eventRecord.Id;
    foreach (dynamic sourceRecord in sources)
    {
        if (sourceRecord.Id == eventRecord.
        EventSourceId)
        {
            e.EventSource = sourceRecord.Name;
            e.VirtualPath = sourceRecord.VirtualPath;
        }

    }

    foreach (dynamic propsRecord in props)
    {
        if (propsRecord.EventId == eventRecord.Id)
        {
            e.Variable = propsRecord.WfDataSource;
            e.ValueBlob = propsRecord.ValueBlob;
            e.ValueBlob.ToString();
        }

    }

    e.ActivityId = eventRecord.ActivityId;
    e.ActivityName = eventRecord.ActivityName;
    e.EventType = eventRecord.EventType;
    e.ProcessId = eventRecord.ProcessId;
    e.TraceLevel = eventRecord.TraceLevel;
    e.TimeCreated = eventRecord.TimeCreated;

    eventList.Add(e);
}

return View(eventList);
```

The previous code block makes use of the OData Helper library, invoking our `MonitoringStoreService` OData service that we deployed to IIS in step 9 and hydrating each of the entities in our model before returning the Event collection to the view.

Notice that the controller knows nothing about the view or the Telerik control, which demonstrates the agility of the Model-View-Controller design pattern.

Also, notice that as the data from the Windows Server AppFabric monitoring store is returned as OData, it can be consumed by literally any client capable of issuing an HTTP GET request.

23. Now, let's run the application by hitting *F5* to see the dashboard in action:

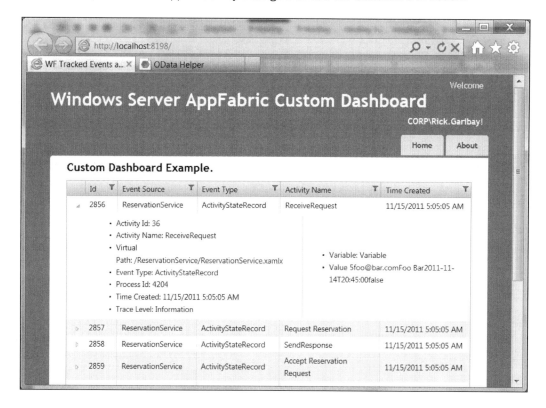

A composite record resulting from the `ASWfEvents`, `ASEventSources`, and `ASWfEventProperties` OData resources is returned for each event in the ASWfEvents view.

Support for paging, sorting, and filtering is provided by the Telerik Grid control.

How it works...

To say the least, we accomplished a ton in this recipe!

We started by creating a default ASP.NET MVC 3 Web Application which provides everything we needed to design a view on our custom dashboard. When the project was created, it provided default project artifacts including the views and a default controller to serve the "Home" and "About" views.

With all of that out of the way, we created an entity set using Entity Framework 4 which generated entities for each of the views we specified in step 5, including a special class called `ApplicationServerMonitoringEntities` that provides a context for querying (and even updating records, which of course we would not want to do in this scenario). All of these classes were created in the `AppFabricMonitoringStore.edmx` file. If you click on this file, you will see a nice designer that shows you all of the entity sets that were generated in a graphical way. If you want to look at the code itself, you can expand the file and click on the `AppFabricMonitoringStore.Designer.cs` file to view the code that was automatically generated.

With our entity model created, we added a WCF Data Service called `MonitoringStoreService`, which exposes our entity model over OData for cross-platform reach. In step 7, we told the WCF Data Services runtime what context class to use to query and work with the entity model we created. From there, in step 8, we gave WCF Data Services permission to expose all of the entities in our entity container.

Since our `MonitoringStoreService` is a WCF service, it is a great candidate for hosting in Windows Server AppFabric. As such, before we built out the user interface, we deployed the CustomDashboard project, which just happens to host the service to IIS. In reality, it is very likely that you would encapsulate the service in a different application dedicated to serving requests, but for the purpose of simplicity I kept everything in one project.

With our `MonitoringStoreService` returning the records from the monitoring store views over OData, we added the necessary assemblies, script files, and stylesheets for working with the Telerik Grid control to our project using NuGet, which greatly simplifies the process of installing third-party components without a heavy installation process. When the `TelerikMvcExtensions` package was installed, it added all of the necessary assemblies and copied the necessary JavaScript files into the `Scripts` directory along with CSS files used by the Telerik controls into the `Content` folder.

Next, following some basic configuration to ensure that these files are available to our view, we went to work on our view which showed the same kind of information you would expect to see graphically in the Windows Server AppFabric Tracked Events feature in IIS or by using the Windows Powershell Application Server cmdlets.

Let's look at the code we added to the `Index.aspx` view in closer detail.

The first thing the code does is declare the Grid control using the generic Grid type, which takes the name of the class we created when we added the three files to our `Model` folder. Combined with the `Model` argument, this initialization tells the Grid control to ask for the collection of `Event` objects from the default method in the `HomeController`. In addition, we name the instance of the Telerik Grid control and provide a fluid definition of the columns we want to show in the initial record view, as shown in the following code:

```
<% Html.Telerik().Grid<CustomDashboard.Models.Event>(Model)
        .Name("Events")
        .Columns(columns =>
        {
                columns.Bound(e => e.Id);
                columns.Bound(e => e.EventSource);
                columns.Bound(e => e.EventType);
                columns.Bound(e => e.ActivityName);
                columns.Bound(e => e.TimeCreated);
        })
```

Next, we set the `DetailView` property on the Grid control, which includes simple HTML markup for nesting the details in a detail view for each event record. A simple Lambda expression is used to inject the markup into the `DetailView` property:

```
.DetailView(detailView => detailView.Template(e => // Set the
server template
{
        // Display the details for the Employee
        %>
        <table>
        <tr>
        <td>
                <ul>
                <li>Activity Id: <%= e.ActivityId%> </li>
                <li>Activity Name: <%= e.ActivityName%> </li>
                <li>Virtual Path: <%= e.VirtualPath%> </li>
                <li>Event Type: <%= e.EventType%> </li>
                <li>Process Id: <%= e.ProcessId%> </li>
                <li>Time Created: <%- e.TimeCreated%> </li>
                <li>Trace Level: <%= e.TraceLevel%> </li>
                </ul>
        </td>
        <td>
        <ul>
                <li>Variable: <%= e.Variable%> </li>
                <li>Value <%= e.ValueBlob%> </li>
```

```
                    </ul>
                </td>
                </tr>
                </table>

            <%
    }))
```

The next piece of code sets the `RowAction` property, which provides the effect of selecting the first row in the Grid and enabling the detail view:

```
        .RowAction(row =>
        {
                // Expand initially the detail view of the first row
                if (row.Index == 0)
                {
                    row.DetailRow.Expanded = true;
                }
        })
```

At the end of the Grid declaration, we enable paging, sorting, and filtering as follows:

```
        .Pageable()
        .Filterable()
        .Sortable()
        .Render();
```

Within the `HomeController.cs` file, we do all of our communication, querying, and wiring up of the resources returned from our `MonitoringStoreService`.

To simplify consuming our service, we installed the OData Helper, available at CodePlex (see URL at the end of this recipe), which wraps the entire client communication stack into a class called ODataHelper.

After declaring a variable to hold our collection of Event objects, we issued three distinct calls to the `MonitoringStoreService`:

```
List<Event> eventList = new List<Event>();
var events = OData.Get("http://localhost/CustomDashboard/
MonitoringStoreService.svc/ASWfEvents");
var sources = OData.Get("http://localhost/CustomDashboard/
MonitoringStoreService.svc/ASEventSources");
var props = OData.Get("http://localhost/CustomDashboard/
MonitoringStoreService.svc/ASWfEventProperties");
```

The `Get` method returns an `IList` of dynamic types, so since we need to bind these types to the `Event` class we defined in our Model, we iterate through each OData entry and hydrate an instance of the Event class for each record returned.

In addition, we look up key fields from the `ASEventSources` and `ASWfEventProperties` so that we can compose the results from our three composite service calls into a single Event instance and add that instance to the `eventList` we defined earlier:

```
foreach (dynamic propsRecord in props)
{
    if (propsRecord.EventId == eventRecord.Id)
    {
        e.Variable = propsRecord.WfDataSource;
        e.ValueBlob = propsRecord.ValueBlob;
        e.ValueBlob.ToString();
    }

}

e.ActivityId = eventRecord.ActivityId;
e.ActivityName = eventRecord.ActivityName;
e.EventType = eventRecord.EventType;
e.ProcessId = eventRecord.ProcessId;
e.TraceLevel = eventRecord.TraceLevel;
e.TimeCreated = eventRecord.TimeCreated;

eventList.Add(e);
}
```

Finally, the `eventList` is returned to the view:

```
return View(eventList);
```

Of course, this is just one example of how you can surface the monitoring information provided by Windows Server AppFabric. Additional interesting scenarios might include empowering information workers to access monitoring data via Excel, or making this important information available on the go to mobile consumers.

There's more...

Entire books have been dedicated to ASP.NET MVC, Entity Framework, and WCF Data Services. I've provided some links to popular resources on the Web in the *See also* section.

Another way to consume the events that we've exposed via OData is to use the PowerPivot plug in for Microsoft Excel (see the *See also* section for more information).

Consuming monitoring data from Microsoft Excel

To consume monitoring data right within Microsoft Excel, follow these steps:

1. Start Microsoft Excel and click on the **PowerPivot** ribbon. On the left-hand of the ribbon, find the icon called **PowerPivot Window** and click on it:

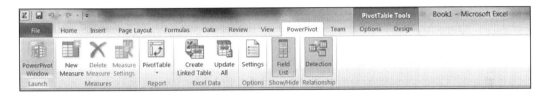

2. Now, look for the **Get External Data** group on the **Home** ribbon and click on the **From Other Sources** icon that looks like a grey database:

3. In the **Table Import Wizard**, select the **Other Feeds** option and click on **Next**:

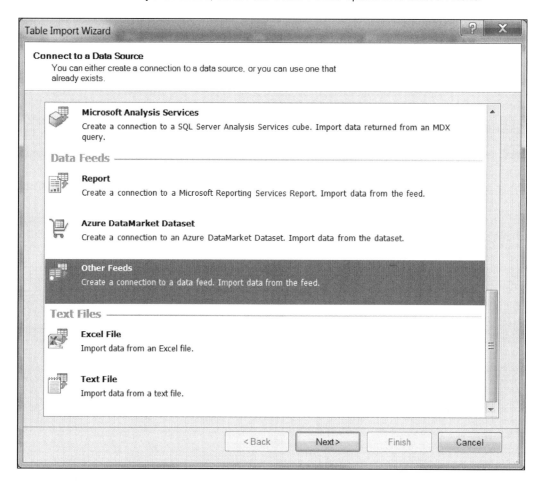

4. Now, type the URL to our `MonitoringStoreService.svc` and click on **Test Connection** to ensure that all is well. Then click on **Next**:

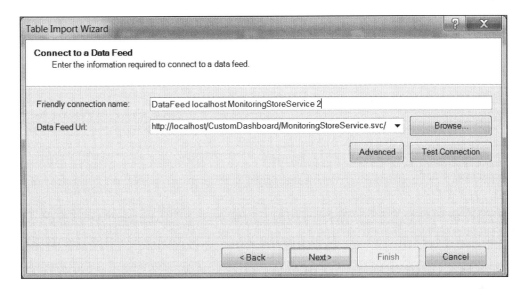

5. Now, select the views (entity set resources) you want to interact with and click on **Finish**:

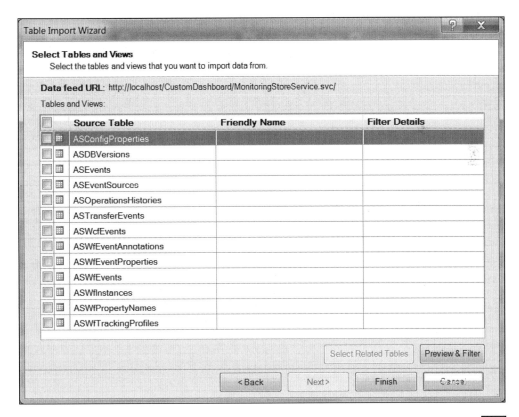

6. You will notice a tab for each resource you selected that allows you to interact with the data in a linear manner.

7. Now, if you go back to Excel, you can start to build your pivot charts by clicking on fields within the resources to add dimensions and slice and dice the information in a variety of interesting ways:

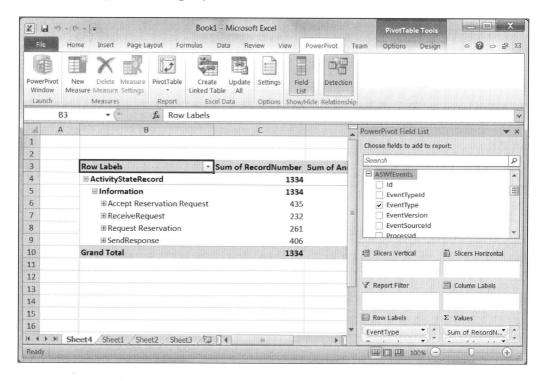

See also

For a step-by-step guide for installing Windows Server AppFabric, refer to the recipe *Installing Windows Server AppFabric* in *Chapter 1, Installing Windows Server AppFabric*.

To learn how to enable monitoring so that monitoring events are produced for analysis, refer to the *Collecting events from WCF and WF services* recipe in this chapter.

ASP.NET MVC is an alternative to traditional ASP.NET code-behind. To learn more about ASP. NET MVC, visit `http://www.asp.net/mvc`.

To learn more about Entity Framework, Microsoft's ORM technology now in its second major release, see `http://msdn.microsoft.com/ef`.

If you are interested in learning more about how to build OData producers by exposing your Entity Framework models using WCF Data Services, you will find many resources, tutorials, and videos for getting started at `http://msdn.microsoft.com/en-us/data/bb931106`.

While the OData Helper library is available via NuGet, you may want to download the source and supporting documentation via CodePlex to aid you in any future projects where you might want to make use of this helpful tool: `http://odatahelper.codeplex.com/`.

OData is supported natively in Excel via the PowerPivot plugin. To learn more, visit `http://www.microsoft.com/bi/en-us/solutions/pages/powerpivot.aspx`.

The Telerik Extensions for ASP.NET MVC controls, including the Grid control in this recipe, are made available to owners of this book under a GPL licensing model. Please review the details of the license if you have any question on appropriate usage of the controls: `http://www.telerik.com/aspnet-mvc`.

The code samples used in this recipe can be downloaded from the Packt website.

Using monitoring database cmdlets

There are a number of ways to configure monitoring and consume monitoring information with Windows Server AppFabric. As covered by the recipes in this chapter, you can configure monitoring with the Windows Server AppFabric configuration tool in IIS and use IIS-based Windows Server AppFabric features, including the AppFabric Dashboard and Tracked Events viewer to consume monitoring events and information.

These capabilities are great for managing monitoring configuration aspects interactively, but Windows Server AppFabric also supports the ability to automate monitoring configuration while providing a user experience that system administrators or IT Pros are most comfortable with.

In this recipe, we will cover the most common Windows Powershell cmdlets for configuring monitoring for Windows Server AppFabric applications.

How to do it...

The first thing we need to do is import the ApplicationServer module so that it is accessible from the Windows PowerShell console. From there, we will walk through some of the most helpful commands for managing monitoring in your Windows Server AppFabric applications.

1. Start Windows PowerShell in Administrator mode, and at the prompt enter `Import-Module ApplicationServer` to import the `ApplicationServer` module so that we can begin working with it.

2. Issue the following command to get acquainted with the different commands that are available in the ApplicationServer module: `Get-Command –module ApplicationServer`.

The **Get**, **Set**, **Add**, **Clear, Enable**, **Disable**, and such other prefixes for each command are referred to as verbs and the noun is the physical or logical entity that the command will operate on. Not all names are intuitive, and most have several parameters, so feel free to use the following command to get more information on the purpose and intended use of each command of interest: `cmdlet: Get-Help [ModuleName]:`

3. To check the monitoring configuration for an application, issue the following command:

```
Get-ASAppMonitoring -SiteName "Default Web Site" -VirtualPath /
ReservationService
```

A result similar to the following is returned:

The `-SiteName` and `-VirtualPath` properties scope the command to an application called Reservation Service, which is part of the default website.

Replace the `-VirtualPath` property with the application you want to get the monitoring information for.

If you want to target the website scope, omit the `-VirtualPath` property completely.

4. Notice that the **MonitoringLevel** is currently set to the **Health Monitoring** tracking profile. Let's change it to the most detailed tracking profile by issuing the following command:

```
Set-ASAppMonitoring -SiteName "Default Web Site" -VirtualPath /
ReservationService -MonitoringLevel Troubleshooting
```

A result similar to the response shown in the preceding screenshot is returned. Notice that the `-MonitoringLevel` property has now been set to `Troubleshooting Tracking Profile`.

The `-MonitoringLevel` property sets the tracking profile to one of the following available tracking profiles: `EndToEndMonitoring`, `ErrorsOnly`, `HealthMonitoring`, `Off`, `Troubleshooting`, or `Custom`.

5. To start monitoring, issue the following command, which enables the propagation of monitoring events to the monitoring store:

```
Start-ASAppMonitoring -SiteName "Default Web Site" -VirtualPath /
ReservationService
```

6. After running these three commands, the monitoring level is configured to use the Troubleshooting tracking profile with publishing to the monitoring store enabled, just as you would do through the GUI-based configuration tool. You can verify these settings by right-clicking on the application you configured previously, by selecting **Manage WCF and WF Services**, clicking on **Configure**, and then by clicking on the **Monitoring** tab:

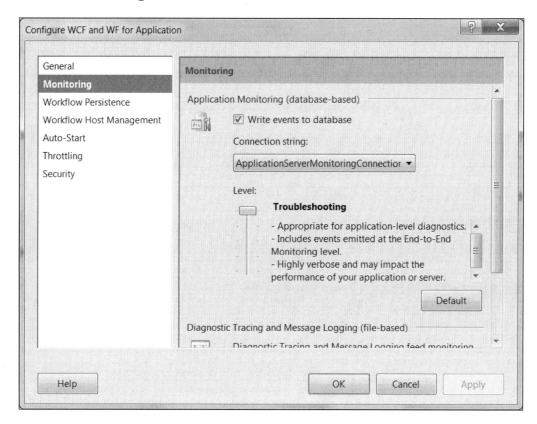

How it works...

Windows Server AppFabric packages the management cmdlets into a Windows PowerShell module called ApplicationServer, which is installed in the following path when Windows Server AppFabric is installed: `C:\Windows\System32\WindowsPowerShell\v1.0\Modules\ApplicationServer`.

Each cmdlet serves a distinct function, given a verb and noun. For example, cmdlets with a Get verb are known as query cmdlets and may traverse configuration files and configured database stores to return information about the application or a service.

Interestingly, much of the GUI-based configuration features supported through the IIS extensions actually use the Powershell cmdlets we've just explored, making for a very consistent experience regardless of what management/configuration tool you use.

Cmdlets such as the `Get-ASAppMonitoring`, `Set-ASAppMonitoring`, and `Start-ASAppMonitoring` act on configuration stores such as `web.config`, `machine.config`, or `applicationhost.config`, depending on the level (application/service) or feature you are managing.

There's more...

The *Creating a customized tracking profile for WF services* recipe of this chapter covers how to create and load a custom tracking profile into Windows Server AppFabric at the service scope. Alternatively, you can use the `Import-ASAppServiceTrackingProfile` cmdlet to accomplish the same result and it can be used to configure a tracking profile at the service scope.

See also

For a step-by-step guide to installing Windows Server AppFabric, refer to the recipe *Installing Windows Server AppFabric* in *Chapter 1, Installing Windows Server AppFabric*.

The code samples used in this recipe can be downloaded from the Packt website.

Monitoring cache cluster health

As covered in *Chapter 2, Getting Started with AppFabric Caching* and *Chapter 3, Windows Server AppFabric Caching – Advanced Use Cases*, Windows Server AppFabric provides a robust, highly available distributed caching feature which allows you to store objects that change somewhat infrequently in a fast, logically centralized but physically distributed in-memory cache, known as a cache cluster.

Each cache cluster has one or more cache hosts which store the objects you want to store in memory. When your application requests an object, the cache cluster checks to see if the object is available and if so, returns it to the application.

Optionally, you may choose to implement a local cache as part of your application. This has the advantage of keeping the cached objects as close to your application as possible and only asking the cache cluster for the object when it is not available in the local cache.

As you can imagine, it is very important that the memory allocated to these cache hosts is adequate for the needs of your application(s) and while careful planning should be done in advance of deploying your Windows Server AppFabric cache-enabled application, it is important to be proactive about understanding the health of your cache hosts and the cache cluster itself.

In this recipe, we will look at some of the most useful Windows Powershell Cmdlets for gaining visibility to the health of your cache hosts along with some key commands you will need to make adjustments should that become necessary.

How to do it...

The first thing we need to do is import the `ApplicationServer` module so that it is accessible from the Windows PowerShell console. From there, we will start with common commands for managing at the cache host level and move our way down to the lowest level of granularity for managing cache health.

Start Windows PowerShell in Administrator mode, and at the prompt enter `Import-Module ApplicationServer` to import the `ApplicationServer` module so that we can begin working with it:

1. A quick way to get visibility to the health of your cache cluster is to quickly inspect the state of each of the cache hosts. You can do this by issuing the `Get-CacheHost` command, which will enumerate each cache host in the cache cluster and whether the AppFabric Caching Service is up or down:

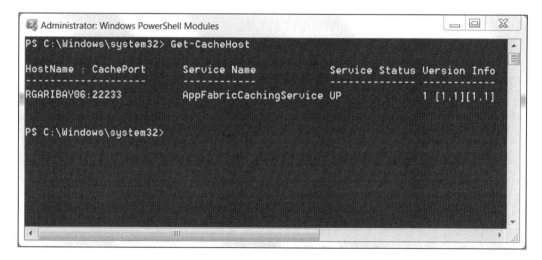

```
PS C:\Windows\system32> Get-CacheHost

HostName : CachePort       Service Name            Service Status Version Info
-------------------        ------------            -------------- ------------
RGARIBAY06:22233           AppFabricCachingService UP                1 [1,1][1,1]


PS C:\Windows\system32>
```

2. Once you have a reference to all the cache hosts in your cache cluster, you can inspect the details for each cache host by entering the following command, which will return some useful configuration information:

```
Get-CacheHostConfig -HostName LOCALHOST -CachePort 22233
```

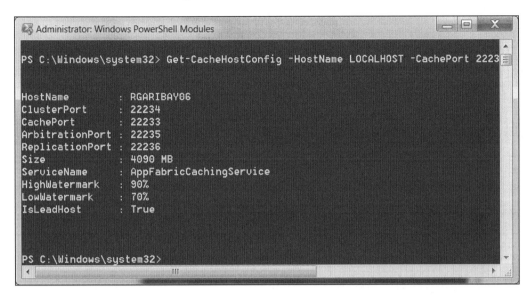

3. To inspect the health of the named caches in your cache cluster issue the `Get-CacheClusterHealth` command, which will report on the health of each named cache in the cache cluster:

4. Another useful command is the `Get-CacheStatistics` cmdlet, which provides information at the named cache level of detail. For example, issuing the `Get-CacheStatistics –CacheName default` returns information on the total amount of bytes being taken up by the objects in the cache, the number of objects currently cached, the regions created by the system (or custom regions), and the number of requests and misses (if any):

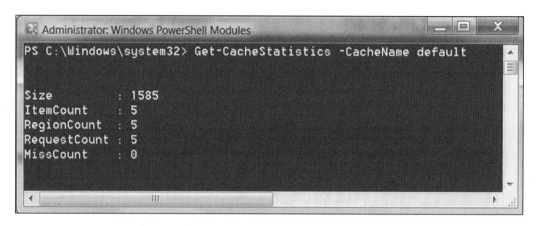

How it works...

In step 1, we verified that the AppFabric Caching Service, which is responsible for serving cache requests and cache management, is up and running for all cache hosts. In my development environment, I only have one cache host, but in a production environment you would likely have at least two.

When Windows Server AppFabric caching is configured, there are a number of TCP ports that are created for managing inter/intra cache cluster communication. In addition, an initial default memory allocation of 4 GB is made for the server acting as a cache host. Running the `Get-CacheHostConfig` command in step 2 returns these values along with the name of the caching service. In addition, an indication of whether the cache host is the lead host is provided along with the lower and upper thresholds that influence how eviction policies are applied by Windows Server AppFabric. Every cache cluster has one or more lead hosts which is a management role that is assigned to one of the cache hosts for managing the cache cluster and coordinates the hosts in the cluster. On my development machine, as my machine is the only host in the cluster, it is by default the lead host. In addition, as the Low Watermark memory threshold is set to 70%, when 70% of the 4 GB allocation is consumed, Windows Server AppFabric will begin evicting objects in the cache that have expired. Similarly, when the High Watermark of 90% is reached, objects are evicted regardless of their expiration until the normal allocation is reached.

Evicted objects can result in cache misses in your application, so careful planning is recommended to make sure that there is enough memory available for each cache host. For this reason, Microsoft recommends that cache hosts be dedicated. While there is nothing to stop you from setting up a cache cluster using multi-purpose machines, this scenario is not supported by Microsoft.

> Be sure to review the Windows Server AppFabric capacity planning guidance provided by Microsoft in planning your cache deployment strategy: `http://msdn.microsoft.com/en-us/library/gg186017.aspx`.

To manage these settings, you can use the `Set-CacheHostConfig` command. See *Chapter 3, Windows Server AppFabric Caching – Advanced Use Cases* for more information.

Issuing the `Get-CacheClusterHealth` command to assess the health of each named cache in the cache cluster results in five metrics that are assigned a percentage, where that percentage represents the amount of total cache cluster partitions. In the example provided in step 3, there is a single named cache called `default`, of which 100% of its cache partitions are healthy. You can think of a cache partition as memory allocation across cache hosts dedicated to caching.

In a nutshell, you want to see all of the percentages in the Healthy indicator. If you see percentages in the other indicators, it could be a benign temporary condition or something more serious. Refer to the following MSDN documentation for more information: `http://msdn.microsoft.com/en-us/library/ff921010.aspx`.

As there is only one named cache in this cluster, it is representative of all of the partitions in the cache cluster, which are healthy. As you add more named caches, the available partitions will distribute equally. For example, if you add another named cache, you would expect to see it now occupy 50% of the cache partitions, add a third, 33%, and so on. A fun exercise is to add a couple of named caches using the `Add-Cache` command and then call the `Get-CacheClusterHealth` cmdlet repeatedly after deleting them with the `Remove-Cache` command. You will see the percentages being redistributed as the partition space allocated to the named caches start to be reclaimed and distributed.

When we ran the `Get-CacheStatistics` cmdlet, it returned information on the total amount of bytes being taken up by the objects in the cache as well as the number of objects currently being cached. It also includes the regions that were either created by the system or custom regions created by a user. A region is a container inside of a named cache which provides some additional benefits, such as tagging which is covered in *Chapter 3, Windows Server AppFabric Caching – Advanced Use Cases*. In addition, the cmdlet returns the number of requests and misses. In this case, there have been five requests to the cache and zero cache misses.

There's more...

While the dashboard and cmdlets offered with Windows Server AppFabric provide a number of options for monitoring both single and multiple Windows Server AppFabric IIS deployments, it is also important to consider proactive monitoring measures for automating the process of identifying and alerting operations staff when an issue is encountered.

Microsoft offers a product called System Center Operations Manager (SCOM), which is designed to monitor key metrics across one or many Windows Server instances. In addition to metrics for monitoring key components such as CPU, memory, and disk space, SCOM offers packages that are specific to products and extensions such as Windows Server AppFabric, called "management packs".

The Windows Server AppFabric Management Pack enables proactive monitoring of key services such as the Event Collection Service, Workflow Management, and Caching Service along with Windows Server AppFabric specific SQL databases such as the persistence and monitoring store. It is also capable of monitoring WCF and WF services hosted in IIS with the Windows Server AppFabric extension installed.

While SCOM is beyond the scope of this book, you can learn more about the "Windows Server AppFabric Management Pack" here: `http://technet.microsoft.com/en-us/library/ff755962.aspx`.

See also

For a step-by-step guide to installing Windows Server AppFabric, refer to the recipe *Installing Windows Server AppFabric* in *Chapter 1, Installing Windows Server AppFabric*.

To learn more about Windows Server AppFabric caching, refer to *Chapter 3, Windows Server AppFabric Caching – Advanced Use Cases*.

The code samples used in this recipe can be downloaded from the Packt website.

8
Scaling AppFabric Hosting, Monitoring, and Persistence

In this chapter, we will cover:

- ▶ Creating an initial base configuration
- ▶ Adding and removing servers from the farm
- ▶ Application deployment on the farm
- ▶ Configuration and management on the farm
- ▶ Automating deployment with scripts

Introduction

Windows Server AppFabric was designed to support a variety of customer scenarios, ranging from small shops with a handful of developers to larger, more sophisticated environments that require support for scalable and highly available hosting and management of mission critical composite applications and services.

While designing for high availability could fill several chapters of this book, a good starting point is to demonstrate an approach for scaling Windows Server AppFabric with Microsoft Network Load Balancing (NLB). NLB is a capability that is battle proven since its release with Windows NT 4.0 and provides a relatively simple way to scale Windows Server AppFabric.

 NLB is a clustering technology which is available in Windows Server and is designed to provide high availability, reliability, and scalability of TCP/IP based hosts, such as IIS.

NLB is particularly well suited for scaling traffic across multiple hosts in a cluster (known as cluster hosts) and supporting automatic failover by detecting healthy hosts in a cluster and redistributing traffic accordingly.

As NLB is a software-based solution, it is relatively simple to install, configure, and maintain and is well suited for managing IIS/Windows Server AppFabric servers at scale.

While software-based load balancing certainly has its benefits (and liabilities), NLB is fairly approachable for most IT professionals and provides an inexpensive way to get started with scaling Windows Server AppFabric.

 There are a number of software and hardware-based load balancing products on the market, so be sure to do some research when planning your scale out strategy.

The recipes in this chapter serve as a foundation for building a classic "2+1" Windows Server AppFabric farm/cluster. The "2+1" design provides scale at the application tier with two instances of Windows Server AppFabric serving as a single logical application server and one instance of SQL Server serving as the persistence and monitoring store. The SQL Server instance can also be clustered, but that level of detail is beyond the scope of this chapter.

For the recipes in this chapter, I've provisioned two application servers and a single database server (all running Windows Server 2008 R2, with the database server also running SQL Server 2008 R2) as depicted in the following diagram which shows the 2+1 design. In addition, I'm working with a Windows Server 2008 R2 domain called AppFabricam.

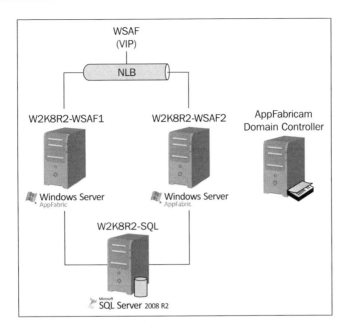

The 2+1 design includes two application server instances (W2K8R2-WSAF1 and W2K8R2-WSAF2) fronted by Windows NLB, that are part of a domain called AppFabricam. The application server instances rely on a dedicated database server running SQL Server 2008 R2 for monitoring and persistence support. Client applications interact with a virtual IP and/or host name provided by NLB which allows you to scale the farm out as needed while introducing reliability and high availability.

In this chapter, I'll first show you how to create a baseline configuration including the first application server instance along with a separate SQL Server instance for providing monitoring and persistence storage capabilities.

From there, you'll learn how to load balance both application server instances using Microsoft NLB, introducing scalability, reliability, and resilience to your Windows Server AppFabric application services.

We'll also cover how to remove an application server from the farm as well as management and configuration considerations on the farm, followed by a walkthrough of deploying applications to the farm.

Lastly, we'll wrap up with a recipe that will show how to automate deployment to both servers using the Microsoft Web Deployment Tool and how you can use Windows Powershell to automate some common Windows Server AppFabric configuration chores accross the farm in a consistent and reliable manner.

Creating an initial base configuration

The first thing you want to do when preparing a Windows Server AppFabric environment for scale-out is to prepare a fully functional base installation.

The base installation is simple, but will vary slightly from the standalone design covered in *Chapter 1, Installing Windows Server AppFabric* because we'll need to separate the application server—which will handle hosting- and the database server which will provide persistence and monitoring support. In addition to provisioning each of these servers with the requisite Windows Server AppFabric components, we will also want to ensure that the application layer can talk to the monitoring and persistence stores that will reside on separate servers.

In addition, the security model will also vary from what you might be accustomed to because we'll want to shift from a purely local security model to a domain model since among other things, more than one application server will be communicating with the SQL Server databases.

In addition, this fully functional base configuration can be used to establish the baseline or template for the rest of the servers that will be added to the farm throughout the progressive recipes in this chapter.

Getting ready

One of the first things we'll do in this recipe is design a domain-based security model so that each host in the farm can function as expected.

 In order to complete this recipe, you will need to have access to Active Directory on a Domain Controller or ask someone with domain administrator privileges to assist you.

In addition, you will need to have a Windows Server 2008/2008 R2 machine with SQL Server Database Engine Services ready to go. This machine will be used to provide monitoring and persistence store services to the application server(s).

Lastly, you will need a Windows Server 2008/2008 R2 machine, which will serve as the base Windows Server AppFabric server. Once you get the base configuration working correctly, each subsequent server can be added with ease.

Please note that both application and database server instances will need to be a part of the domain and I'll assume that's already done as we jump right in.

> I recommend Windows Server 2008 R2 for the application server and database server instance along with SQL Server 2008 R2 for the database server. As such, these are the versions I use in this chapter, but check the system requirements for Windows Server AppFabric 1.1, which covers other supported OS options: `http://www.microsoft.com/download/en/details.aspx?id=27115`.

How to do it...

Scaling IIS and Windows Server AppFabric requires moving to a domain-based security model. Follow these steps to prepare the initial host which will become part of the NLB cluster.

1. First, create the necessary domain security groups in Active Directory to model the Windows Server AppFabric security model. This includes creating accounts and groups for the Administrators, Observers, and Users roles:

> Create the following Global groups in Active Directory:
> - APPFABRIC_ADMINS
> - APPFABRIC_OBSERVERS
> - APPFABRIC_USERS
>
> Then, create the following accounts, adding them to the respective groups you just created:
> - APPFABRIC_ECS domain account, member of the APPFABRIC_ADMINS group, which will be used to run the AppFabric Event Collection Service.
> - APPFABRIC_WMS domain account, member of the APPFABRIC_ADMINS group, which will be used to run the AppFabric Workflow Management Service.
> - APPFABRIC_WRITER domain account, member of the APPFABRIC_ADMINS group, which will be used for read and write operations against the monitoring and persistence stores as required.
> - APPFABRIC_READER domain account, member of the APPFABRIC_OBSERVERS group, which will be used for read operations against the monitoring and persistence stores as required.
> - APPFABRIC_IIS_USER domain account, member of the APPFABRIC_USERS group, which will be used to run the application pools for similar applications/services deployed across the farm.

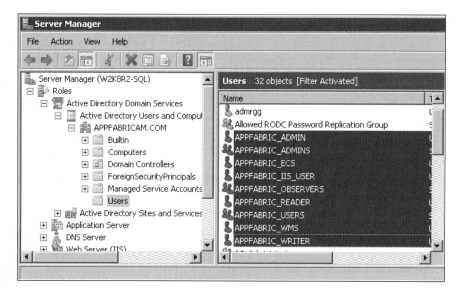

2. Next, grant each account the **Log on as a Service right** at the domain level by typing `secpol` in the start menu textbox and navigating to the **Log on as a service** policy under **Local Policies**, **User Rights Assignment** and adding the **APPFABRIC_ADMINS** group.

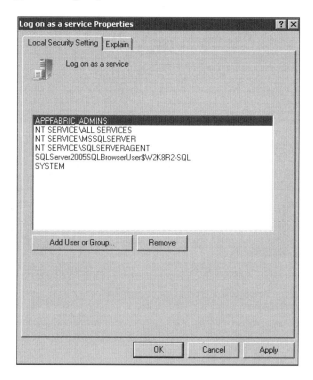

3. Next, Install Windows Server AppFabric on the SQL machine identified as the Windows Server AppFabric SQL Server store. Follow the *Installing Windows Server AppFabric* recipe in *Chapter 1, Installing Windows Server AppFabric* as a guide.

4. Next, configure the SQL Server machine by running the AppFabric Configuration wizard, which is covered in the *Configuring Windows Server AppFabric (hosting and monitoring)* recipe in *Chapter 1, Installing Windows Server AppFabric*, to provision the persistence and monitoring stores. For the monitoring and persistence configuration steps, use the domain accounts you created in step 1 as follows:

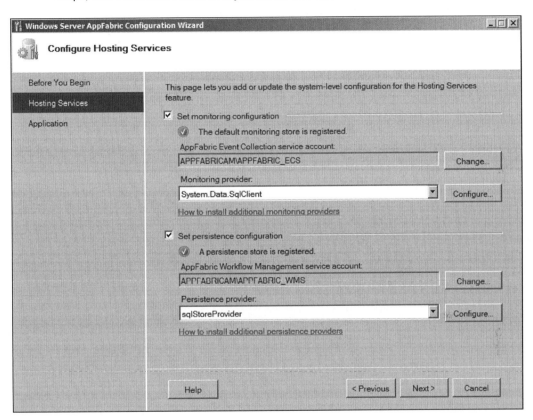

5. On the SQL Server machine, add the APPFABRIC_ADMINS, APPFABRIC_ECS, and APPFABRIC_WMS groups to the AS_Administrators local group as their domain member accounts will be used:

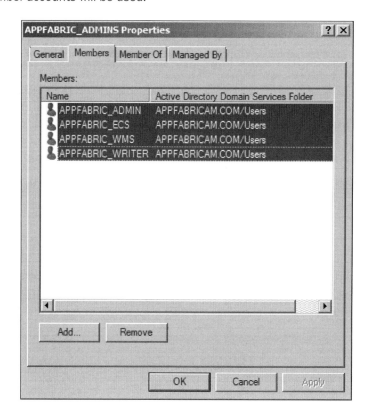

6. Add the APPFABRIC_OBSERVERS Global group to the local AS_OBSERVERS group as well.

The Windows Server AppFabric installation and configuration steps will create the local groups and add the accounts you specified in step 4 earlier. However, you must add the domain groups you created in step 1 to the respective groups as outlined in step 5 before the proceeding group, as their domain member accounts will be used.

7. Next, provision the monitoring provider, ensuring that you select both checkboxes to make entries into the root `web.config` as well as actually creating the monitoring database. Choose the local server as the server name and provide a name for the database along with the local group mappings, as shown in the following screenshot:

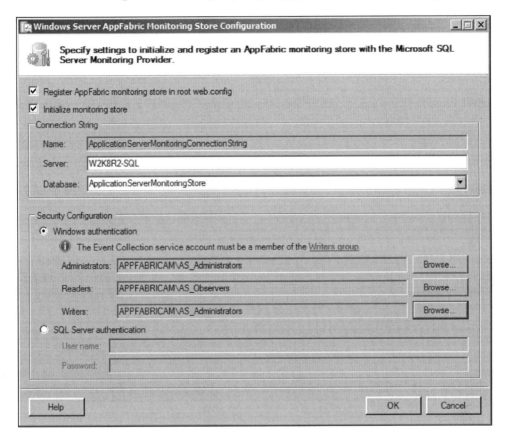

8. Repeat the same steps for provisioning the persistence provider, mapping the groups accordingly.

9. Now, install Windows Server AppFabric on the Windows Server 2008/2008 R2 machine identified as the application server, using the *Installing Windows Server AppFabric* recipe in *Chapter 1, Installing Windows Server AppFabric* as a guide.

10. Once you have installed Windows Server AppFabric on the application server, configure it just as with steps 7 and 8 earlier, but do not select the **Initialize...** checkbox as the databases have already been provisioned.

 In this step, be sure to point the server to the SQL machine you configured in steps 7 and 8.

11. Now, deploy a WCF or WF service application to the application server and test to ensure that hosting and monitoring is working correctly. You can verify this by exercising the service a few times and reviewing the AppFabric Dashboard as outlined in *Chapter 4, Windows Server AppFabric Hosting Fundamentals*. I will also show you how to manage a Windows Server AppFabric farm using the AppFabric Dashboard, Tracked Events, and so on in the *Configuration and management on the farm* recipe of this chapter.

How it works...

Scaling out Windows Server AppFabric requires moving to a domain model so that the infrastructure services on multiple hosts can share the same credentials when accessing shared resources such as the persistence and monitoring stores. This is necessary from a distributed computing perspective and also aids in manageability because the accounts and groups can be managed from a central location.

Windows Server AppFabric implements a straightforward role-based security policy based on the trusted subsystem model. In steps 1 and 2, you applied the security model at the domain level.

The Event Collection service and Workflow Management service use a named service account for communicating with the lower level infrastructure (you can learn more about persistence and monitoring in *Chapter 6, Utilizing AppFabric Persistence* and *Chapter 7, Monitoring Windows Server AppFabric Deployment* respectively) and the other groups and accounts are established to model the single server configuration.

We installed and configured a standalone SQL Server machine for managing the persistence and monitoring chores. Breaking out this machine in a scale-out scenario is a best practice because it allows you to dedicate the necessary resources to the database server without having to share resources with other roles or applications. In addition, though not covered in these recipes, SQL Server can be clustered to use a highly performant and resilient storage fabric, which aids in performance and high availability.

As part of the SQL Server provisioning process, we supplied the same local accounts for creating the necessary monitoring and persistence databases, which also resulted in the configuration wizard mapping the necessary groups to the SQL Server roles.

Next, we configured the application server role with Windows Server AppFabric, in much the same way we would if we were configuring a standalone server. The main difference is that we substituted the typical local machine accounts for domain accounts. For example, when we configured the service accounts for the Event Collection service and Workflow Management service, we explicitly set these services to run as each respective domain account. Again, this is key because in a scale out scenario, SQL Server will be on a separate machine, making a local security strategy inadequate.

See also

For step-by-step guidance for installing and configuring Windows Server AppFabric refer to the recipes in *Chapter 1, Installing Windows Server AppFabric*.

For guidance on streamlining Windows Server AppFabric application deployment, refer to the first two recipes of *Chapter 4, Windows Server AppFabric Hosting Fundamentals*.

While scaling SQL Server is beyond the scope of this chapter, please refer to the architectural guidance for enterprise scaling of SQL Server, provided here: `http://msdn.microsoft.com/en-us/library/gg132881.aspx`.

Adding and removing servers from the farm

This recipe will walk you through the process of setting up Windows Network Load Balancing (NLB) and adding one or more Windows Server AppFabric application server hosts to a cluster.

The first thing we'll do is install the NLB feature on the first server that we will be configuring for the NLB cluster, then create the cluster, and add the first server to the cluster. This is the server we configured in the preceding recipe (*Creating an initial base configuration*), and in this recipe and those that follow, I refer to the first server in the cluster as W2K8R2-WSAF1. From there, we will verify that that we can reach the server via its own host name and IP address as well as the new NLB virtual host name and IP address that we'll configure in this recipe.

From there, we will add a second host to the cluster (W2K8R2-WSAF2), and test it both individually and via the NLB cluster.

At that point, the logical view of our application layer will resemble the following, with independent, yet identical instances of IIS/WAS and the AppFabric Workflow Management and AppFabric Event Collection services:

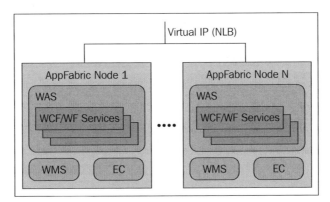

Following the successful configuration of both Windows Server AppFabric application server hosts, I will also demonstrate how to remove the server from the cluster and ensure that both the cluster and the server itself continue to function.

Getting ready

In order to complete this recipe, you will need to have completed the *Creating an initial base configuration* recipe of this chapter or have an environment ready that is comparable to the design depicted in the introduction of this chapter. This environment should include two application server instances running Windows Server AppFabric, configured with a separate, standalone server running SQL Server 2008 for providing persistence and monitoring capabilities.

If you don't already have two application server instances along with a separate, dedicated SQL Server instance, I recommend that you follow the preceding recipe before continuing, repeating the process for provisioning an application server twice as you'll need two instances of each for this recipe and those that follow.

As a reminder, all three machines will need to be a part of the domain and the security model will need to resemble the guidance provided in the aforementioned recipe of this chapter.

 Windows Server 2008 R2 is recommended for all server instances along with SQL Server 2008 R2 for the database server; however, check the system requirements for Microsoft AppFabric 1.1 for Windows Server for the latest information on supported operating systems `http://www.microsoft.com/download/en/details.aspx?id=27115`.

How to do it...

As summarized in the beginning of the chapter, an NLB cluster comprises two or more cluster hosts. With the initial base configuration of our first host in place, we are ready to proceed. Let's begin by installing and configuring NLB and adding our two Windows Server AppFabric application servers to the cluster:

1. The first step to configuring Windows Server AppFabric for scale out is to install NLB on the base application server host (W2K8R2 WSAF2), if it is not already installed. In Windows Server 2008 R2, open **Server Manager**, right-click on **Features**, and click on **Add Features**. About half way down the list, check **Network Load Balancing** and click on **Next** to complete the wizard.

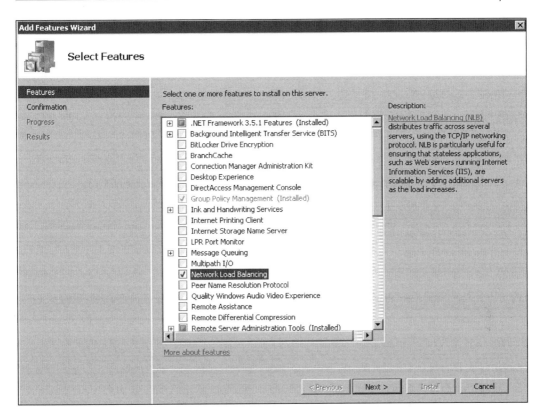

 Network Load Balancing is a big topic, to which an entire book could be dedicated. Rather than covering NLB in any detail beyond the basics for getting the farm up and running, I've included some references at the end of this recipe in the *See also* section.

2. With NLB installed on the base application server, open the **Network Load Balancing Manager** tool under **Administrator Tools** and click on **Cluster, New Cluster**. Enter the name of the base application server in the **Host** field and click on **Connect**. Once the IP address is bound, click on **Next**:

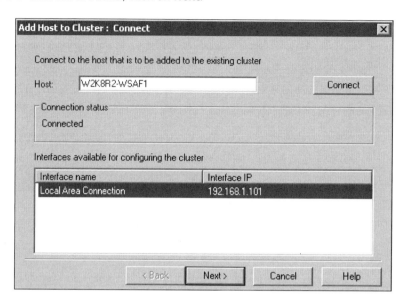

3. Accept the defaults on the next screen and click on **Next** again.

4. Next, enter the IP address that you want to virtualize for the cluster and enter it in the **IPv4 address** field along with its subnet mask in the **Subnet mask** field and click on **OK**, followed by **Next**:

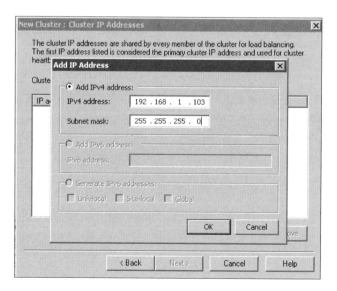

In this case, I have chosen an IP address of 192.168.1.103. I have also configured the IP address for the W2K8R2-WSAF1 application service instance to 192.168.1.101 and W2K8R2-WSAF2 to 192.168.1.102 to help me remember which IP is assigned to which host.

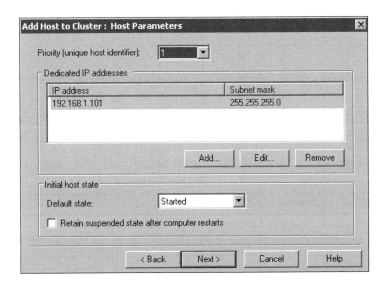

5. Now, provide the DNS name you want to use to logically refer to the cluster (in this case I have chosen WSAF) and set that in the **Full Internet name** field; choose the **Multicast** option below and click on **Next**:

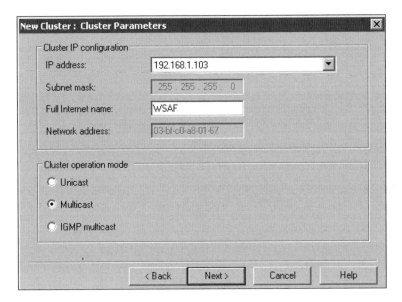

The choices between operation modes will vary depending on your environment, router/firewall rules, and so on. As I am working off my own network and domain, Multicast offers great flexibility and performance, but you will want to read up on the NLB documentation to choose the mode that is right for your environment.

6. On the next screen, edit the first entry which represents a port rule, and change **Protocols** to **TCP**, **Affinity** to **None**, and then click on **OK**:

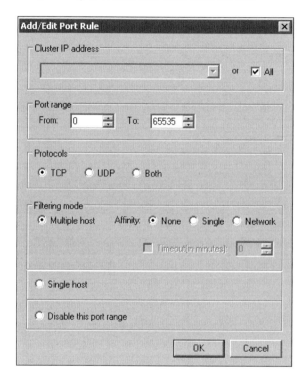

7. Wait a few seconds and monitor the status of the host. The host is created successfully when it turns green, with a **Status** of **Converged**:

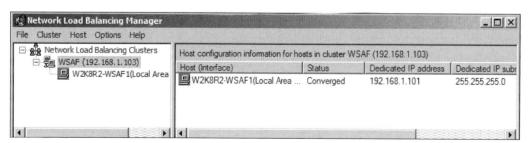

8. Now, point your browser to the URI for the WCF or WF service that is deployed to the first host (of W2K8R2-WSAF1) to ensure that we can still reach the server directly:

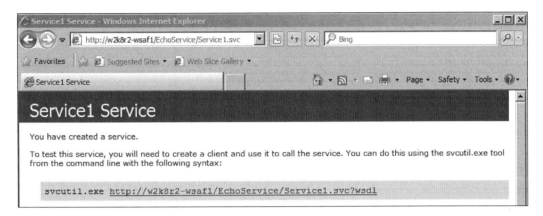

9. Now let's test the same service on the first host, only this time, we will use the cluster host address of WSAF instead of the server name of W2K8R2-WSAF1:

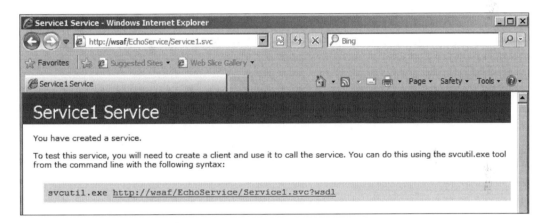

In this example, I have loaded the help page for the same WCF 4 service I deployed to the base host in the last step of the *Creating an initial base configuration* recipe, only this time I am using the cluster host name of WSAF instead of the machine's name of W2K8R2-WSAF1, which indicates that the cluster is functioning correctly.

10. Now it is time to add the second application host. You will want to configure it just as you did with the base configuration host (of W2K8R2-WSAF1), ensuring that it is pointing to the SQL Server instance (in my case W2K8R2-SQL). Once you have verified that it has been configured correctly as discussed in the preceding recipe, proceed to the next step.

11. Log in to the first host in the NLB cluster, open the **Network Load Balancing Manager** tool under **Administrator Tools,** and right-click on the cluster you created in step 2; select **Add Host To Cluster:**

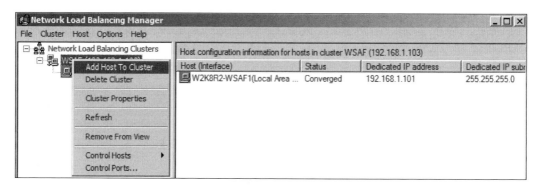

12. Next, enter the name of the second Windows Server AppFabric application server (W2K8R2-WSAF2 in my case). Click on **Connect** followed by **Next:**

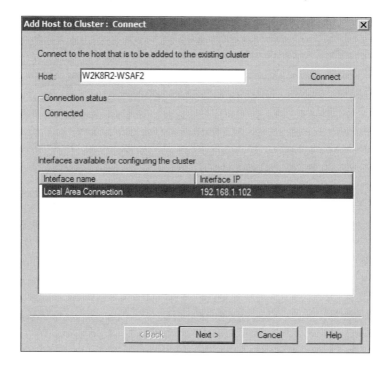

The **Interface name** and **Interface IP** should appear with the correct adapter and IP, indicating that the host can be reached and identified. If you have more than one network interface, ensure that the correct one is selected.

13. Click on **Next** on the following screen, noting that the priority has defaulted to 2, as this is the second host in the cluster. Accept the defaults and click on **Finish** on the **Port Rules** screen.

14. While the host is being converged as part of the cluster, you will see an hour glass. After about 30 seconds, the second host should be added to the cluster, which will be indicated by the second host turning green with a **Status** of **Converged**:

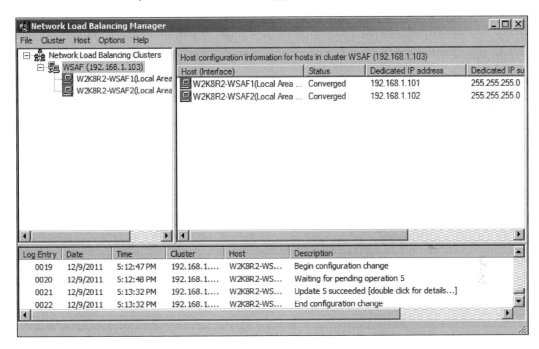

 The second host has been successfully added when it turns green and the **Status** shows as **Converged**.

15. Now that we have both hosts configured on the cluster, repeat the test you conducted in steps 8 and 9, ensuring that you can reach the second server by its own name and IP and that using the host name (WSAF) results in a response from the WCF or WF service, as shown in the following example:

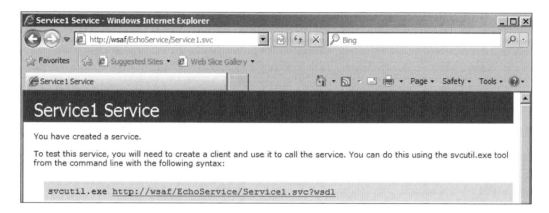

16. To remove a host, simply right-click on the host name in the cluster and select **Delete**. You will be prompted to confirm, and clicking on **Yes** will remove the host you have chosen from the cluster:

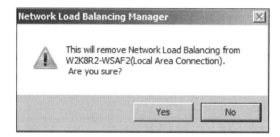

How it works...

When configuring a server with NLB, an intermediate layer is added to the TCP stack on each cluster host that intercepts all packets directed to the cluster host and filters the packets based on the NLB algorithm.

After we created our NLB cluster by adding the first application server host (of W2K8R2-WSAF1) and testing it using the virtual host name and IP address, we assigned a priority and configured a **Port Rule**. Each host has a priority, which is numerical. The first host we added had a priority of 1 and the second host we added had a priority of 2. The first host (in my case the W2K8R2-WSAF1 host) is known as the **Default Host**. The **Default Host** handles all of the cluster traffic that is not otherwise constrained by a **Port Rule**. This basically means that given an equal distribution of traffic, and no further granularity specified by a **Port Rule**, load will attempt to be distributed equally to both hosts.

If the first host were to go down or no longer be available, then the host with the next highest (really lowest) priority would become the **Default Host** and all traffic would be handled by it.

For example, in step 6 of this recipe, we configured **Port Rules** for the cluster, specifying no affinity, meaning that the algorithm will attempt to distribute all traffic equally across the cluster hosts. This is the most effective way to distribute traffic across hosts but has some liabilities that you must consider. As requests from one client may very well be distributed across each host in the cluster, careful considerations must be made around session state and cookies. If your services use session state or cookies, then you may want to either consider using out of process session state instead (an excellent approach is to leverage Windows Server AppFabric Caching, which is covered extensively in *Chapter 2, Getting Started with AppFabric Caching* and *Chapter 3, Windows Server AppFabric Caching – Advanced Use Cases*), or changing the affinity to network or single, which will attempt but not necessarily guarantee that all requests from a client always go to a specific host. For more information on NLB, see the link provided in the *See also* section.

In addition, while your application will still benefit from high availability and reliability, the choice you make on affinity may impact the degree to which you benefit from scalability because if all requests from one client go to one host, the load on the logical application is not necessarily optimally distributed.

NLB monitors the health of the cluster by looking for heartbeats emitted from each host. If more than 5 seconds has elapsed since a heartbeat, the cluster begins a process known as convergence, which recalibrates the cluster to no longer direct traffic to the failed host. In the event that one of the hosts in the cluster goes down, all traffic will be redistributed automatically. The same process is used when adding new hosts as well, and, just as we did in this recipe, when adding a new host, you want to configure the **Port Rules** to either distribute load equally across the hosts (as with the no affinity choice) or select the **Single** or **Network** option.

There's more...

In step 16, I showed you how to explicitly remove a host from the cluster. While you may want to do this from time to time to perform maintenance on a host without impacting application availability, the same effect can result when a host is no longer available due to it being inadvertently shut down (it happens), or due to a catastrophic OS or hardware failure which renders the host unreachable.

These things can and do happen, which is one of the main reasons to configure Windows Server AppFabric for high availability and scale out.

To get a sense of what a failure scenario might look like, ensure both Windows Server AppFabric hosts are accessible and start a ping from the command prompt of a client machine that can reach the cluster using the `ping WSAF -t` command. The `-t` parameter ensures that the ping request is repeated. After a few seconds, you should see a consistent response indicating that the cluster host is reachable.

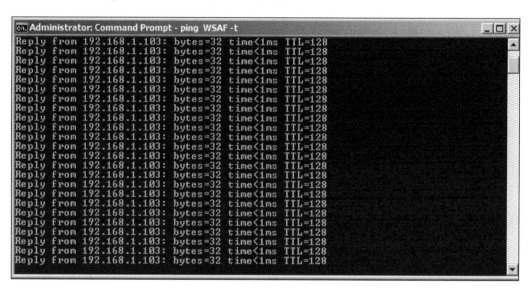

Now, with the ping command to the cluster host still running, shut down the second host (W2K8R2-WSAF2 in my environment) gracefully by simply following the Windows shut down procedure:

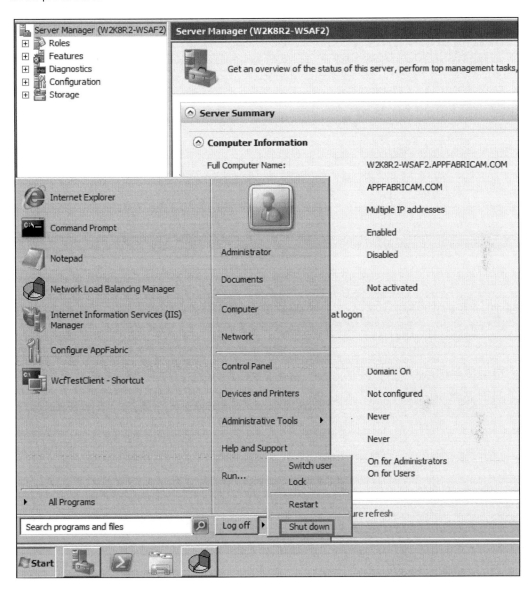

After a few seconds, you should see the **Status** of the second host change from **Converged** to **Unreachable**:

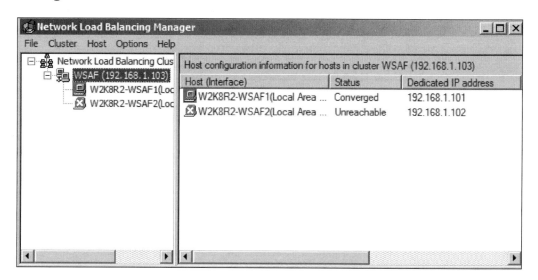

Now, bring up the command window you started before you simulated a host failure and you should see that the client is still successfully getting ping responses from the cluster host. While degraded, the cluster is still operational and your applications deployed to Windows Server AppFabric continue to be available despite a failure of the second host.

At this point, even though the second cluster host is offline, the application continues to be responsive even though it is in a degraded state. While as in the preceding example, this is transparent to the client, it is important to become aware when such a failure happens as soon as possible so that performance, scalability, reliability, and availability of the solution are not compromised.

When you bring up the second host again, it will be converged to the cluster and NLB will automatically redistribute all traffic across the cluster.

See also

For step-by-step guidance for installing and configuring Windows Server AppFabric, refer to the recipes in *Chapter 1, Installing Windows Server AppFabric*.

For guidance on streamlining Windows Server AppFabric application deployment, refer to the first two recipes of *Chapter 4, Windows Server AppFabric Hosting Fundamentals*.

To learn how to use caching for session state and as an alternative to cookies, check out *Chapter 2, Getting Started with AppFabric Caching* and *Chapter 3, Windows Server AppFabric Caching – Advanced Use Cases.*

Network Load Balancing has been around since NT4, and if you don't want to spend big bucks on hardware load balancing solutions, it's worth exploring. You can find a good introduction to NLB here: `http://technet.microsoft.com/en-us/library/bb742455.aspx`.

Application deployment on the farm

The preceding recipes have covered how to prepare and configure servers running Windows Server AppFabric for high availability and scale using a 2+1 design topology with Microsoft NLB.

By adding two application servers, high availability, scalability, and redundancy are introduced as your WCF and WF services are now virtualized via a logical endpoint exposed by the NLB cluster.

In addition to properly configuring your application servers and database server as covered in this chapter, care must be taken to ensure that all applications are synchronized on each host in the cluster, along with any changes to configuration.

Fortunately, the Microsoft Web Deployment tool (also known as Web Deploy) covered in *Chapter 4, Windows Server AppFabric Hosting Fundamentals*, and the ability to import the packages it generates to IIS/Windows Server AppFabric in a standard and consistent manner, makes the process of keeping the applications deployed to each application server much easier than using alternatives such as XCOPY or time consuming MSIs.

In this recipe, I'll highlight some considerations you should think about when deploying your applications to a Windows Server AppFabric farm. As the Microsoft Web Deployment tool is covered in detail in *Chapter 4, Windows Server AppFabric Hosting Fundamentals*, I'll refer you to the first two recipes of that chapter throughout this recipe.

Getting ready

Take a few minutes to read the *Installing the Web Deployment tool (Web Deploy)* and *Packaging services for deployment with Web Deploy* recipes in *Chapter 4, Windows Server AppFabric Hosting Fundamentals*, and make sure you have installed the tool on both application servers (W2K8R2-WSAF1 and W2K8R2-WSAF2 in the examples of this chapter) before continuing.

How to do it...

The most important thing to remember about working with a Windows Server AppFabric farm is that every application you deploy must be deployed to all servers in the farm. Let's see how the Microsoft Web Deployment tool makes this process a lot easier:

1. Follow the *Packaging services for deployment with Web Deploy* recipe in *Chapter 4, Windows Server AppFabric Hosting Fundamentals* to package your application into a Microsoft Web Deployment tool's ZIP file package and place it on a share or a location that is accessible by all servers on the farm.

2. Log in to each server on the farm and deploy the application by using the **Import Application** feature in IIS:

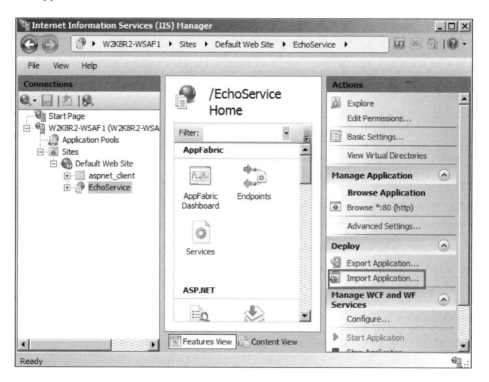

3. As covered in the *Packaging services for deployment with Web Deploy* recipe in *Chapter 4, Windows Server AppFabric Hosting Fundamentals*, browse to the location of the application package and follow the wizard to completion.

4. Smoke-test the application by running it, or by executing a simple operation that can give you feedback on the health of the deployment. This should be done on the machine it is deployed to, as well as remotely from a client using both the machine host and cluster host name.

5. Repeat steps 2 through 4 for each sever in the farm.

How it works...

Farms introduce a number of benefits but carry additional management consideration as everything you do to one server in the farm, you must do to every server.

Deployment is a key consideration which can be streamlined significantly by using Web Deploy with the **Import Application** feature in IIS/Windows Server AppFabric.

It is essential that the process of deploying the application package is repeated for each application server in the farm and that you test the application both directly using the host's IP address and host name, as well as through the NLB cluster host name and IP.

See also

Information and guidance on the using the Microsoft Web Deploy tool is covered in the _Installing the Web Deployment tool (Web Deploy)_ and _Packaging services for deployment with Web Deploy_ recipes in _Chapter 4, Windows Server AppFabric Hosting Fundamentals._

Configuration and management on the farm

The preceding recipes have covered how to prepare and configure servers running Windows Server AppFabric for high availability and scale using a 2+1 design topology as well as guidance for deploying applications to a Windows Server AppFabric farm.

When managing a Windows Server AppFabric farm environment, it is important that each server in the farm uses the standalone SQL Server database server for monitoring and persistence, which ensures that the application servers are allocated to do what they do best, leaving the persistence and monitoring chores to the dedicated SQL instance. This ensures that all WF instances are managed in one logical location and that you can get full visibility to all metrics and tracked events for all servers in the farm from any server in the farm.

In this recipe, we'll look at how to ensure that each server's persistence and monitoring store is configured correctly and walk through the AppFabric Dashboard and Tracked Events Viewer to look at events generated from multiple servers in the farm.

Getting ready

This recipe assumes that you have either completed the _Creating an initial base configuration_, _Adding and removing servers from the farm_, and _Application deployment on the farm_ recipes in this chapter or have an environment ready that is comparable to the design depicted in the introduction of this chapter.

How to do it...

1. Let's start by confirming that each application server is configured to use the separate SQL Server database server for persistence and monitoring. From there, we will place some load on an application and inspect the results in the AppFabric Dashboard and Tracked Events Viewer.

2. On each application server, open IIS and select the **Web Site** or **Application level** on the left and double-click on the **Connection Strings** icon under ASP.NET to bring up the connection strings that have been configured in either the root or the specific application's `web.config` file:

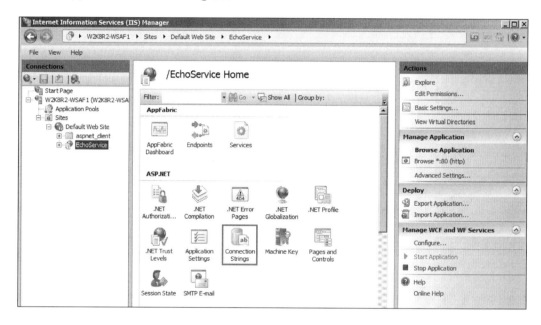

3. Ensure that the connection strings for the monitoring and persistence stores are configured to use the SQL Server database server that is dedicated to the farm:

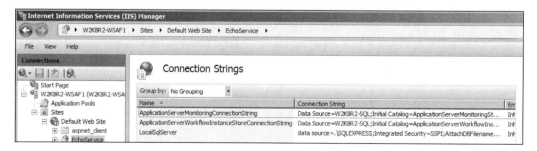

4. Next, verify that the application pool identity that is configured for the application(s) in your farm uses an account (preferably a domain account) that has permission to read and write from/to the persistence store.

5. Verify that the domain accounts for the AppFabric Event Collection service and AppFabric Workflow Management service have been configured for each service in accordance with the *Creating an initial base configuration* recipe of this chapter:

6. Now, apply some load on the application you have deployed to each host in the farm (the `wcftestclient.exe` tool is a simple way to do so) and open the AppFabric Dashboard to inspect the latest metrics:

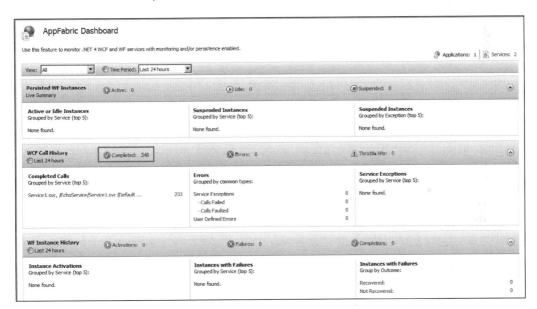

7. Click on the **Completed** calls under **WCF Call History** to load the **Tracked Events Viewer** and notice that entries have been collected from both hosts in the farm:

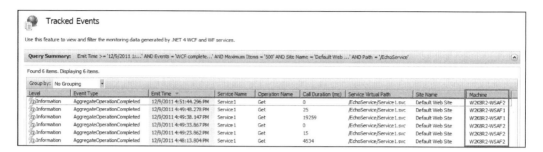

 For the recipes in this chapter, I have deployed the EchoService WCF application, which is available with the code for this book.

How it works...

When managing a Windows Server AppFabric farm, it is important to ensure that the monitoring and persistence stores are configured correctly so that monitoring events and workflow instances are written to the shared SQL Server database server instead of the local database if one happens to be present on the application server.

The standalone security model for Windows Server AppFabric uses local groups and accounts which are configured within the application and management scope for securing Windows Server AppFabric. In a farm scenario, the application servers and database server are still managed by the AppFabric Event Collection service and AppFabric Workflow Management service; however, you must shift the security design from a local model to a domain model, using domain accounts that have the necessary permissions for accessing the monitoring and persistence infrastructure.

The AppFabric Event Collection service is responsible for streaming monitoring events to the monitoring store based on the tracking profile that has been selected for the application, so the service account must have the ability to write events as they occur. Similarly, the AppFabric Workflow Management service is responsible for managing persistence and communicating with the persistence store, so its identity must have the appropriate access. In addition, the application pool that is configured for each Windows Server AppFabric application must have the ability to publish events as well as read and write from/to the persistence store.

The management scope organizes security based on those who are administering Windows Server AppFabric and Windows Server AppFabric applications. This includes the ability to use the interactive AppFabric Dashboard and Tracked Events Viewer for gaining insight into the health and activity of the applications. As prescribed in the *Creating an initial base configuration* recipe in this chapter, domain groups are created for supporting read-only "observers" who might use the AppFabric Dashboard and Tracked Events Viewer, and an administrative role which in addition supports the ability to manage workflow instances via the Tracked Workflow Instances feature.

When we applied load on the logical Windows Server AppFabric application, the requests were distributed to each host on the farm as indicated by the Tracked Events viewer.

It is also important to remember any changes you make to one application's configuration (such as changing the autostart behavior of a service, increasing or decreasing a monitoring tracking profile, or configuring WCF throttling) must be repeated for each server in the farm.

See also

Be sure to read the *Creating an initial base configuration* recipe of this chapter to understand the recommended security groups and accounts that must be created to effectively manage Windows Server AppFabric security.

More details on the Windows Server AppFabric security model can be found here: `http://msdn.microsoft.com/en-us/library/ee677290.aspx`.

For guidance on streamlining Windows Server AppFabric application deployment, refer to the first two recipes in *Chapter 4, Windows Server AppFabric Hosting Fundamentals*.

It is also important to consider disaster recovery for the SQL Server database instance. See `http://msdn.microsoft.com/en-us/library/ms178094.aspx` for guidance and considerations for SQL Server disaster recovery as well as `http://msdn.microsoft.com/en-us/library/ms189134.aspx`, which covers SQL Server clustering.

The last recipe in this chapter, *Automating deployment with scripts* shows you how to leverage the Microsoft Web Deploy tool to automate deployment across servers on the farm.

Automating deployment with scripts

While developers who program WCF and WF services for Windows Server AppFabric spend most of their time writing and testing the code that will become an application within Visual Studio, the application must eventually be deployed and managed.

While manually deploying and managing an application on a single server is not without challenges, doing so on a distributed farm is simply untenable. In addition to ensuring that mistakes are not made in copying the necessary files and assemblies, configuration changes such as enabling metadata and setting throttling thresholds at the application or service level and setting tracking profiles based on the needs for different levels of information manually can be cumbersome and error prone.

In the *Application deployment on the farm* recipe of this chapter, I cover how to use the Microsoft Web Deployment tool (Web Deploy) to streamline the application packaging and deployment process, simplifying the deployment experience and reducing friction between developers who build applications for Windows Server AppFabric and the IT professionals who must maintain them. Additionally, in *Chapter 6, Utilizing AppFabric Persistence*, I cover a number of powerful Windows Powershell cmdlets that are useful to administrators for quickly and easily gaining insight into the health of Windows Server AppFabric applications while simplifying routine administrative tasks.

The combination of Web Deploy and Windows Server AppFabric Powershell cmdlets arm the administrator with a powerful set of tools for automating these deployment and monitoring chores.

In this recipe, I will cover some of the most common tasks, including using Web Deploy to remotely deploy an application to one or more servers in the farm, along with some Powershell cmdlets provided out-of-the-box and in the Windows Server AppFabric 1.1 samples for simplifying some common management tasks in a farm environment.

Getting ready

This recipe assumes that you have either completed the *Creating an initial base configuration*, *Adding and removing servers from the farm*, and *Application deployment on the farm* recipes in this chapter or have an environment ready that is comparable to the design depicted in the introduction of this chapter.

In addition, the Microsoft Web Deployment Tool (Web Deploy) must be installed on each machine, including the **Remote Agent service**, which allows administrators to use the `msdeploy.exe` command to deploy application packages to the server remotely. To enable the Remote Agent, you must either select it when installing the tool or add it via **Add and Remove Programs** in the control panel of each machine. For more information on packaging application for deployment with Web Deploy, please refer to the *See also* section at the end of this recipe.

Lastly, you must be logged into a machine with an account that has administrative permissions to each machine on the farm (this could be a local administrator account or a domain account with administrative privileges). See the *Creating an initial base configuration* recipe of this chapter for guidance on establishing a domain based security model in a farm environment.

How to do it...

Let's start by using Web Deploy to deploy an `MSBuild` package to each server in the farm. From there, we'll explore some Powershell cmdlets that can be used in batch mode to enable metadata, change the tracking profile for monitoring, and configure throttling on each server in the farm.

1. After packing your WCF or WF application for deployment, place it in a location that is accessible from the machine from which you will be conducting your remote deployment and start a command window.

   > Note that adding the path to the executable located in `C:\Program Files\IIS\Microsoft Web Deploy V2\msdeploy.exe` to the `Path` environment variable on the machine from which you will conducting the remote deployment will make the following steps much simpler as you won't need to deal with multiple locations on the file system.

2. Issue the following command, substituting `EchoService.zip` with the path to your application package and `W2K8R2-WSAF1` with the server that you want to deploy to:

   ```
   msdeploy.exe -verb:sync -source:package=EchoService.zip
   -dest:auto,computername=W2K8R2-WSAF1
   ```

3. Repeat this command for each server in the farm that you want to deploy the application to. For example, in the farm depicted in this chapter, I would repeat the same command, replacing `W2K8R2-WSAF1` with `W2K8R2-WSAF2`.

   > When working with scripts on the command line, it can often be helpful to pipe the results to a log file. For example, to have the command in step 2 output its results to a file named `DeployResult.log` instead of the console, add `>` `DeployResult.log` to the end of the command as follows:
   >
   > ```
   > msdeploy.exe -verb:sync
   > -source:package=EchoService.zip
   > -dest:auto,computername=W2K8R2-WSAF1 >
   > DeployResult.log
   > ```

4. Ensure that Windows Remote Management has been configured on each machine by running the `Winrm quickconfig` command on each machine in the farm and selecting yes when promoted, as shown in the following screenshot:

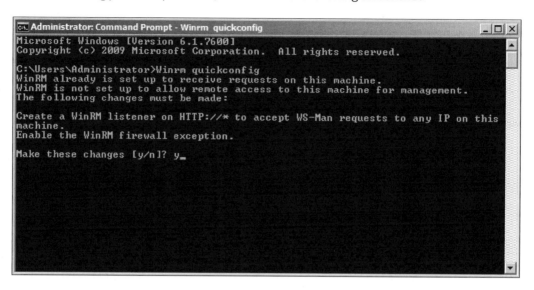

5. Ensure you are logged in with a domain administrator account and issue the following command in a Powershell console to enable metadata exchange for the given app on each host in the farm, substituting the `-ComputerName` parameter with your server names and the `-VirtualPath` parameter with the application you want to configure:

```
Invoke-Command -ComputerName W2K8R2-WSAF1,W2K8R2-WSAF2
-ScriptBlock {Import-Module ApplicationServer; Set-
ASAppServiceMetadata -SiteName "Default Web Site" -VirtualPath /
EchoService -httpGetEnabled 1}
```

6. To increase the verbosity of the monitoring feature, you can set the tracking profile to the **Troubleshooting Tracking Profile** by issuing the following command:

```
Invoke-Command -ComputerName W2K8R2-WSAF1,W2K8R2-WSAF2
-ScriptBlock {Import-Module ApplicationServer; Set-ASAppMonitoring
-Sitename "Default Web Site" -VirtualPath "/EchoService"
-MonitoringLevel Troubleshooting}
```

7. Lastly, to change the throttling configuration for all applications on each host in the farm, issue the following command, which will limit the maximum number of concurrent calls allowed to 200 (as an example):

```
Invoke-Command -ComputerName W2K8R2-WSAF1,W2K8R2-WSAF2
-ScriptBlock {Import-Module ApplicationServer; Set-
ASAppServiceThrottling -root -MaxConcurrentCalls 200}
```

How it works...

MSBuild and Web Deploy make a powerful duo for streamlining the packing and deployment process to servers running IIS or Windows Server AppFabric and we put this to use by taking an existing package and automating the deployment from the command line. While this can be done manually in single machine scenarios, the power of the command line is realized by scripting this process out, which is particularly useful when targeting more than one machine because the command can be easily repeated, substituting only the names of the target servers with each invocation.

In step 2, we used the command line options for working with Web Deploy, including the `sync` verb which ensures that a reference (or source) and target destination are both identical by identifying any differences between source and target and reconciling them. This ensures that the target is synchronized with the contents of the source application package. We also specified the type of source and target by using the `-source` and `-dest` parameters.

The commands we used can be organized into scripts for supporting loops and the ability to iterate through reference files to further automate deployment. Microsoft has an excellent example of this in the Windows Server AppFabric samples that are referenced at the end of this chapter.

In step 4, we verified that Windows Remote Management (WinRM) is configured. WinRM is a SOAP-based implementation of the WS-Management specification which standardizes a set of interfaces that support the ability to manage various hardware and software configurations of a host remotely. When working with Windows Powershell cmdlets in a remote capacity, WinRM is required.

In the remaining steps, we used the Windows Powershell cmdlets that are provided with Windows Server AppFabric to enable metadata exchange on an application by using the `Set-ASAppServiceMetadata` cmdlet in conjunction with the `Invoke-Command` cmdlet; this accepts a `ComputerName` and `ScriptBlock` parameter that allow us to specify each application host in the Windows Server AppFabric farm, along with the Windows Server AppFabric specific Powershell cmdlet to invoke.

This is a very powerful combination that dramatically simplifies the process of managing configuration settings on remote Windows Server AppFabric hosts. The best thing about it is that any configuration that is accessible by the Powershell cmdlets can be used in this manner.

We saw this by also using the `Set-ASAppMonitoring` and `Set-ASAppService Throttling` cmdlets to change the active tracking profile to Troubleshooting as well as limiting the maximum number of concurrent calls that will be accepted to 200 (as mentioned in step 7, you can set this to whatever number is realistic based on your scenario and available resources).

Again, any Windows Server AppFabric cmdlet can be used in this manner, which significantly simplifies management across each host in the farm.

See also

To learn more about packaging applications for deployment with Microsoft Web Deploy, refer to the *Installing the Web Deployment tool (Web Deploy)* and *Packaging services for deployment with Web Deploy* recipes in *Chapter 4, Windows Server AppFabric Hosting Fundamentals*.

Microsoft provides an excellent reference for automating deployment via scripts in the Windows Server AppFabric Management samples available here `http://www.microsoft.com/download/en/details.aspx?displaylang=en&id=19603`.

A complete list of Windows Server AppFabric Powershell cmdlets is documented extensively at `http://msdn.microsoft.com/en-us/library/ee767662(v=WS.10).aspx`.

9

Configuring Windows Server AppFabric Security

In this chapter, we will cover:

- ▶ Running caching services using Domain accounts
- ▶ Setting up security for persistence stores
- ▶ Securing Windows Server AppFabric's monitoring store
- ▶ Securing the Event Collection service

Introduction

Applications and services running on Windows Server AppFabric need to be secured at two levels. First and foremost, the application and services must be developed using best practices outlined by Microsoft Security Development Lifecycle (SDL). Considering the breadth and depth of SDL, discussing what it entails for developing WCF and WF applications is beyond the scope of this book.

 For more details on Microsoft's Security Development Lifecycle, visit http://www.microsoft.com/security/sdl/default.aspx.

Secondly, it is also very important to secure the hosting and monitoring infrastructure of Windows Server AppFabric itself. In this chapter, we will solely focus on securing Windows Server AppFabric.

Windows Server AppFabric is built on top of Windows OS and Internet Information Services (IIS) to provide a scalable, durable, and secure hosting and monitoring infrastructure for Windows Communication Foundation (WCF) and Workflow Foundation (WF) applications and services. Windows Server AppFabric supports development of applications and services using the all too familiar and powerful Microsoft.NET Framework and Visual Studio. Use of SQL Server database for persistence and configuration storage (while supporting a provider model that allows usage of other databases and XML configurations) allows a streamlined mechanism for data access. This integration allows Windows Server AppFabric to rely on existing security paradigms of the Microsoft platform, making it simple for developers to reuse their existing knowledge for securing Windows Server AppFabric WCF and WF applications.

Windows Server AppFabric security building blocks

Windows Server AppFabric Security has the following four building blocks:

- **Windows security**: Windows Server AppFabric relies on Windows Server's security groups and filesystem security for common authentication and authorization for resources (for example, file access for configuration files and SQL Server database access). Windows Server AppFabric also uses Windows Server based accounts for running its caching and hosting services.

- **.NET Framework security**: WCF and WF applications support a robust and highly configurable security model that supports message and transport level security scenarios. In addition Windows authentication and X509 certificate-based autentication is supported for securing both clients and services. Windows Server AppFabric relies on WCF and WF security for application level security.

- **IIS security**: Windows Server AppFabric uses a subset of IIS (and Windows Activation Service – WAS) security features to offer a secure hosting environment for WCF and WF applications and services. IIS uses Windows based Access Control Lists (ACLs) to provide tight control over file and directory access to secure service deployments, configuration and corresponding assets, and so on. Windows Server AppFabric also uses the IIS based application pool identity to access underlying SQL Server databases for hosting and monitoring scenarios.

- **SQL server security**: Windows Server AppFabric uses SQL Server accounts and roles to control access to the database assets such as monitoring and persistence schemas as well as stored proceduresand other DDL and DML objects.

Simplicity is the key when it comes to securing Windows Server AppFabric. Since it's built on tried and tested security paradigms highlighted in the preceding section, it allows developers to focus on what matters most: implementing the logic that drives business value.

In this chapter, we will learn about security on Windows Server AppFabric.

Running caching services using Domain accounts

A caching service account is used for the Caching Service Configuration Provider. The caching service account must be a member of Administrators Groups and must have administrative access over caching configuration database. Windows Server AppFabric v1.0 used NT AUTHORITY\NETWORK SERVICE as a default and did not allow changing this account for Domain environments.

 For a Workgroup environment, Windows Server AppFabric v1.0 allowed changing the account as long as the all participating machines in the cluster had the same user/password combination (with administrative privileges) defined.

In Windows Server AppFabric v1.0 we could not change the NT AUTHORITY\NETWORK SERVICE. This led to scenarios where domain level security principles could not be applied, and created security issues for IT Administrators.

The good news is that with AppFabric 1.1 for Windows Server, we can now use the Domain accounts to run caching services.

In this recipe, we will assume that a Windows Server AppFabric caching service is already installed and we want it to use a Domain account instead of the default NETWORK SERVICE account.

Getting ready

To begin, launch **Caching Administration Windows PowerShell** with administrative privileges.

The simple process required for updating the Windows Server AppFabric caching service to use a Domain account involves the following four step approach:

1. Stop existing cache service(s).
2. Unregister and remove the cache host(s) from the cache cluster.
3. Change the service credentials.
4. Register and add the cache host to the cache cluster.

To execute the steps previously highlighted we can either use the Windows Server AppFabric Configuration Wizard (called **Configure AppFabric**) or the **Caching Administration Windows PowerShell** commandlets..

How to do it...

Follow these steps to run a caching service using a Domain account.

In this recipe we will use the **Caching Administration Windows PowerShell**.

1. Stop the cache host using the following PowerShell commandlet:

   ```
   Stop-CacheHost hostName1 22233
   ```

    Stop-. CacheHost requires HostName and the CachePort.

2. Once the cache service is stopped, we will Unregister it from the Windows Server AppFabric Cache Cluster using the following AppFabric PowerShell commandlet:

   ```
   Unregister-CacheHost -Provider System.Data.SqlClient
   -ConnectionString "Data Source=YourSQLServer;Initial Catalog=Cachi
   ngServiceDb;Integrated Security=True" -HostName hostName1
   ```

3. Now remove the cache host from the Cluster by executing the following AppFabric PowerShell commandlet:

   ```
   Remove-CacheHost
   ```

    Remove-CacheHost must be executed from the cache host that needs to be removed from the cluster (and hence, no need to specify the HostName and CachePort).

4. Change the Windows Server AppFabric Caching Service's credentials using the following Service Control (SC.exe tool).

   ```
   sc.exe config AppFabricCachingService obj= YOURDOMAIN\YourUser
   password= yourPassword
   ```

    SC is a command line program used for communicating with the Service Control Manager and services.

5. Now, add the cache host and use the Domain account specified in the previous step:

   ```
   Add-CacheHost -Provider System.Data.SqlClient -ConnectionString
   "Data Source=YourSQLServer;Initial Catalog=CachingServiceDb;Integr
   ated Security=True" -Account "YourDOMAIN\YourUser"
   ```

6. Register the cache host using the following Windows Server AppFabric PowerShell commandlet:

```
Register-CacheHost -Provider System.Data.SqlClient
-ConnectionString "Data Source=YourSQLSERVER;Initial Catalog=Ca
chingServiceDB;Integrated Security=True"  -Account "yourDOMAIN\
yourUser" -CachePort 22233 -ClusterPort 22234  -ArbitrationPort
22235 -ReplicationPort 22236 -HostName YourCacheHost
```

7. Start the cache host (from the cache server itself):

```
Start-CacheHost
```

How it works...

AppFabric 1.1 for Windows Server allows using Domain accounts to run caching services. This recipe highlights how easy it is to move existing caching services from the default NT AUTHORITY\NETWORK SERVICE to a relevant Domain account.

AppFabric PowerShell commandlets, being extremely flexible and useful, enable a simple strategy of stopping the services, removing them from the cache cluster, and then changing the service credentials using sc.exe tool. Once the credentials are changed it is just a matter of adding the cache host and registering it back with Windows Server AppFabric Cache Cluster.

 To manage sites, applications, and/or services deployed on a remote server you can use PowerShell Remoting. You can also use PowerShell Remoting to run Windows PowerShell cmdlets remotely.

To learn more about PowerShell Remoting please visit http:// msdn.microsoft.com/en-us/library/ee677232.aspx.

There's more...

The approach highlighted previously can also be executed for the whole cluster at once. This will imply that the caching services will be unavailable while the changes are being made. If the downtime is not acceptable (which will be the case for most of the production environments), then each and every cache host must be acted upon one by one.

For more information on configuration commands, see http://msdn.microsoft.com/ en-us/library/hh351341.aspx.

Setting up security for persistence stores

A persistence store, also known as the Instance Store, is a SQL Server database repository that Windows Server AppFabric uses to preserve workflow instances, enabling durable/long running Workflow scenarios in .NET 4.0. In order to secure Windows Server AppFabric deployment, it is paramount to secure its persistence store as it contains business critical workflow information.

> Although Windows Server AppFabric allows the use of custom persistence providers (see *Chapter 5, More Windows Server AppFabric Hosting Features* for more details) this recipe will solely focus on the default SQL Server implementation of a persistence provider.

Windows Server AppFabric relies on Microsoft SQL Server's security model to secure the persistence database. Implementation-wise access to the persistence store is secured via the following five SQL Server roles:

- `InstanceStoreUsers`
- `InstanceStoreObservers`
- `WorkflowAdministrators`
- `WorkflowActivationUsers`
- `WorkflowManagementServiceUsers`

> The granularity of access control based on SQL Server roles is such that a user who has access to a persistence store will be able to access all instances (of all services) persisted in that particular store. This leads to a practice of segregating instance stores on the basis of services, that is, configuring one persistence store per service.

In this recipe, we will execute the following steps to secure the Windows Server AppFabric persistence store:

- Configure separate persistence stores (one for each service)
- Configure an identity for multiple Workflow Management Services (WMS)
- Configure security configuration for:
  - Instance Control Endpoint (ICE)
  - Workflow Management Service (WMS)
  - Service Management Endpoint (SME)

Getting ready

We will need to have access to SQL Server ready. We will also need to open service configuration files so that we can edit the relevant configuration sections.

Have two SQL Server databases configured for Windows Server AppFabric persistence. For the sake of simplicity, we will call them `StoreA` (representing a persistence store for `ServiceA`) and `StoreB` (representing a persistence store for `ServiceB`). Also create Windows users `UserA` and `UserB`, as well as Windows user groups `UserGroupA` and `UserGroupB`. We will use these users, groups, and databases in the following steps to set up security for the Windows Server AppFabric persistence store.

Have multiple instances of WMS ready, that is, one for each persistence store such that their Security Identifiers (SIDs) can be configured for SQL Server database access accordingly.

The following two diagrams show how the security context will be configured for a particular user group/identity.

The first diagram, shown as follows, highlights "User Group A" with service contexts as well as the persistence store called "Store A":

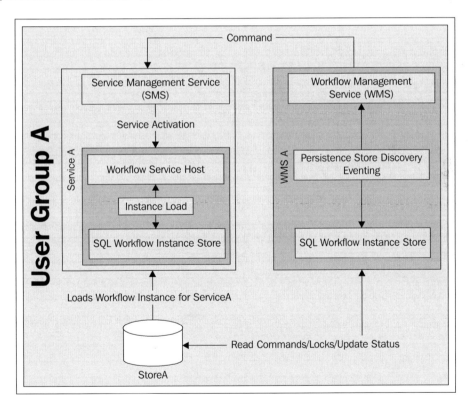

Likewise, the following diagram highlights the second user group, called "User Group B", with its one persistence store titled "Store B":

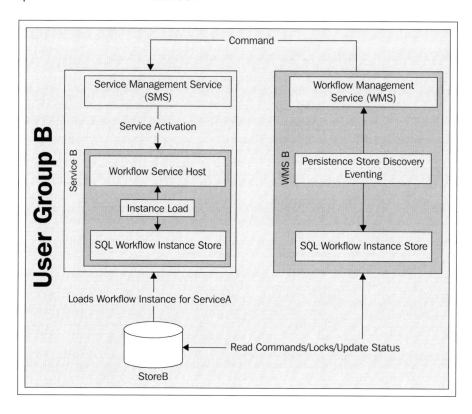

How to do it...

We will start with adding users to SQL Server roles for each service so that the access control is segregated. Then we will set up multiple instances of WMS (one for each instance store). Towards the end of the recipe we will update the configuration for ICE, WMS, and SME to use the newly created user groups.

1. Add `UserA` to the `InstanceStoreUsers` role of `StoreA` database. This can also be achieved by adding `UserA` to a Windows group `UserGroupA` and adding `UserGroupA` to the `InstanceStoreUsers` role of the `StoreA` database.

2. Likewise, add `ReaderA` or `ReaderGroupA`, a Windows group that `ReaderA` is a member of, to the `InstanceStoreObservers` role of the `StoreA` database.

3. Add `AdminA` or `AdminGroupA`, a Windows group that `AdminA` is a member of, to the `WorkflowAdminstrators` role of the `StoreA` database.

4. Repeat steps 1 to 3 for all the stores, assigning `UserX`, `ReaderX`, and `AdminX` to `InstanceStoreUsers`, `InstanceStoreObservers`, and `WorkfowAdministrators` respectively for all stores. (Where X represents the workflow service with a configured corresponding persistence store.)

5. Now add the `WMS-SIDA` (WMS SID for Service A) to the Windows Group `WMSGroupA` and add `WMSGroupA` to the workflow administration related SQL Server roles, that is, `WorkflowActivationUsers` and `WorkflowManagementServiceUsers`.

6. Likewise add WMS-SIDB (WMS SID for Service B) to the Windows Group `WMSGroupA` and add `WMSGroupA` to the `WorkflowActivationUsers` and `WorkflowManagementServiceUsers` of SQL Server roles.

7. Update the Instance Control EndPoint (ICE) of the services that persist to `storeA` to reflect the relevant Windows Group, that is, `WMSGroupA`. Your service `ServiceBehavior` configuration element should look as follows:

```
<system.serviceModel>
        <behaviors>
            <serviceBehaviors>
                <behavior name="myServiceBehavior">
                    <workflowInstanceManagement
                    authorizedWindowsGroup="WMSGroupA" />
                </behavior>
            </serviceBehaviors >
        </behaviors>
</system.serviceModel>
```

 This configuration change with WMSGroupA should only be applied to services that store their workflows to `StoreA`. Likewise, similar changes should be made for the services that persist their workflows to `StoreB`.

8. Similarly, the following configuration changes should be made for all SMEs that persist workflows to `StoreA`:

```
<configuration>
    <microsoft.applicationServer>
        <hosting>
            <serviceManagement enabled="true"
            authorizedWindowsGroup="WMSGroupA"
            endpointConfiguration=
            "ServiceManagementNetPipeEndpoint" />
        </hosting>
    </microsoft.applicationServer>
</configuration>
```

9. Configure each WMS to monitor the persistence store individually:

```
<configuration>
    <microsoft.applicationServer>
        <persistence>
            <workflowManagement>
                <workflowManagementServiceInstances>
                    <workflowManagementServiceInstance name=
                    "WMSA">
                        <instanceStores>
                            <instanceStore name="StoreA" location=
                            "[root, SiteName or VPath]" />
                        </instanceStores>
                    </workflowManagementServiceInstance>
                    <workflowManagementServiceInstance name=
                    "WMSB">
                        <instanceStores>
                            <instanceStore name="StoreB" location=
                            "[root, SiteName or VPath]" />
                        </instanceStores>
                    </workflowManagementServiceInstance>
                </workflowManagementServiceInstances>
            </workflowManagement>
        </persistence>
    </microsoft.applicationServer>
</configuration>
```

How it works...

Securing the Windows Server AppFabric persistence store is all about securing the underlying configuration and persistence store. The persistence store, being SQL Server, mostly concerns securing the SQL Server database using SQL Server roles and adding relevant Windows Groups or Windows Users to it.

After setting up SQL Server database roles with Windows Groups/Users, we updated configuration files so that they reflect the access rules that only allow configured Windows Groups/Users to access the underlying persistence stores.

The following is a brief outline of the SQL Server roles that we have used in this recipe:

▶ **InstanceStoreUsers**: InstanceStoreUsers role (defined as System. Activities.DurableInstancing.InstanceStoreUsers in SQL Server) allows members of this role to load and save to/from the configured SqlWorkflowInstanceStore (which in turn reads from/writes to the SQL Server database). This implies that the application that uses WorkflowApplication or the WorkflowServiceHost to host services should run under an identity that is part of this role.

▶ **InstanceStoreObservers**: The `InstanceStoreObservers` role (defined as `System.Activities.DurableInstancing.InstanceStoreObservers`) allows its members to query persisted workflow instances from the configured `SqlWorkflowInstanceStore`. Just like for the `InstanceStoreUsers` role, any application that uses `WorkflowServiceHost` or `WorkflowApplication` to host services for persistence should run under an identity that is a member of this role.

▶ **WorkflowAdministrators**: Members of the `WorkflowAdministrators` role (defined as `Microsoft.ApplicationServer.DurableInstancing.WorkflowAdministrators` in SQL Server) are allowed to enqueue commands for `SqlWorkflowInstanceStore`.

▶ **WorkflowActivationUsers**: As the name implies, members of the `WorkflowActivationUsers` role are allowed to query for activatable workflow instances. As Workflow Management Service (WMS) is responsible for activating workflow instances, it should run under the identity that is part of the `WorkflowActivationUsers` role.

▶ **WorkflowManagementServiceUsers**: Members of the `WorkflowManagementServiceUsers` role (defined as `System.Activities.DurableInstancing.WorkflowActivationUsers` in SQL Server) are allowed to dequeue the control command from the command queue in the `SqlWorkflowInstanceStore`. The WMS must run under an identity that is part of this `WorkflowManagementServiceUsers` role.

There's more...

The security model for Windows Server AppFabric caching enforces secure communication between the server and the clients. By default, the communication between the server and clients needs to be rewritten.

Securing Windows Server AppFabric's monitoring store

Applications and services may sometimes emit sensitive and confidential monitoring related data, including but not limited to PII (Personally Identifiable Information). Considering the nature of the data, this calls for securing all the avenues involved in the whole workflow of capturing and storing monitoring related information in Windows Server AppFabric.

To understand what needs to be secured we need to understand the architecture of Windows Server AppFabric's monitoring subsystem. The following diagram provides a high-level overview of how the Windows Server AppFabric captures and stores monitoring information. Highlighted areas show the components and the subsystems that enable Windows Server AppFabric's monitoring capabilities.

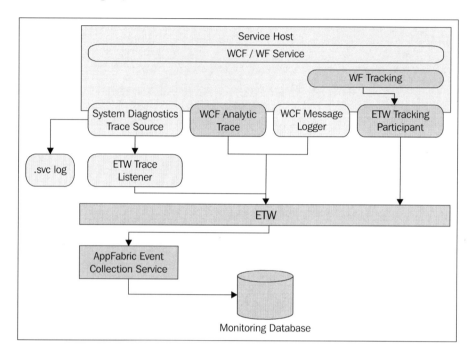

In this recipe, we will focus on securing two important parts of the monitoring subsystem of Windows Server AppFabric:

- Using isolated instances of the monitoring database/store
- Controlling the amount of information that is being stored in the monitoring store

 AppFabric Event Collection Service runs as `NT_AUTHORITY\LOCAL SERVICE` by default. The SID (Security Identifier) specific to AppFabric's Event Collection Service is added to the `AS_Administrators` group. As `AS_Administrators` is part of the SQL Server Role, that is `ASMonitoringDBAdmin`, it enables access for AppFabric's Event Collection Service to read and write to/from the monitoring database.

Getting ready

Before we begin, consider creating additional monitoring databases so that they can be configured as different monitoring stores for different services (rather than using one monitoring store for all services).

How to do it...

We will use a similar approach to that used in the preceding recipe (*Setting up security for persistence stores*) to register multiple monitoring stores with Windows Server AppFabric. Then, we will use two different services and configure them to use these two different monitoring stores.

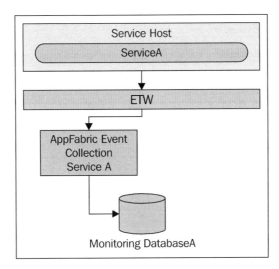

Towards the end, we will use IIS Manager Extensions for AppFabric to control the level of information that we want to persist in the particular monitoring database.

1. Launch the **AppFabric Server Configuration Wizard**.

2. Click on **Next** to go to **Configure Hosting Screen**.

3. Select the **Set monitoring configuration** checkbox.

4. Under **Monitoring provider**, select **sqlStoreProvider** and then click on **Configure**.

5. Select **Initialize monitoring store** and provide the **Server** and **Database** name (this is the name of the new database that we want to create), under **Connection String**:

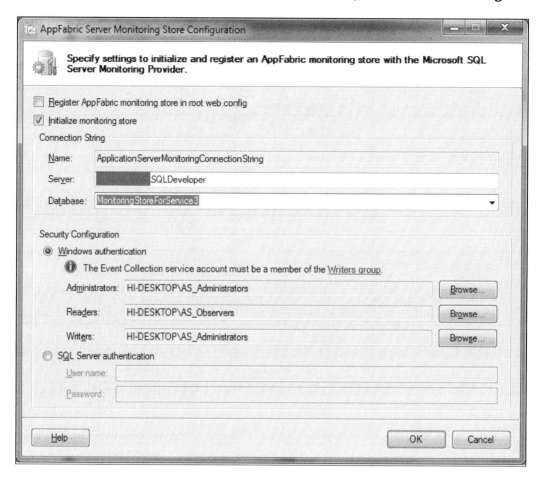

6. Click on **OK** and the **AppFabric Server Configuration Wizard** will ask for confirmation:

7. Click on **Yes** to continue. AppFabric Server will display a confirmation dialog as shown in the following screenshot:

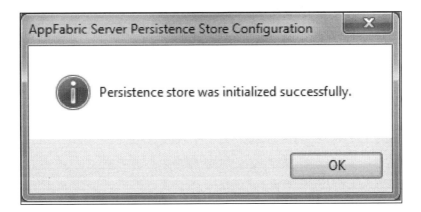

 Instead of using a configuration wizard, we can also use the following AppFabric PowerShell cmdlet to create and initialize a new monitoring store for Windows Server AppFabric:
`Initialize-ASMonitoringSqlDatabase`

For more details on this command, please visit `http://msdn.microsoft.com/en-us/library/ ff428206(v=ws.10).aspx`.

8. Now that the monitoring database has been created, we will need to register this in the `Web.config` file. To do that open the `Web.config` file, and add the following line under the `connectionStrings` XML element:

```
<add connectionString="Data Source= YourSQLServer;Initial
Catalog=MonitoringStoreForService3;Integrated Security=True"
name="ASMonitoringStore"/>
```

9. Now launch **Internet Information Services (IIS) Manager**, select the service for which we want to change the monitoring database for security reasons, then under **Manage WCF and WF** click on **Configure**.

10. On the **Configure WCF and WF** screen select **Monitoring**. Under the **Connection String** drop down select the database that we have created and registered in the previous steps (in this case, I have it registered as **ASMonitoringStore**). Your screen should look as follows:

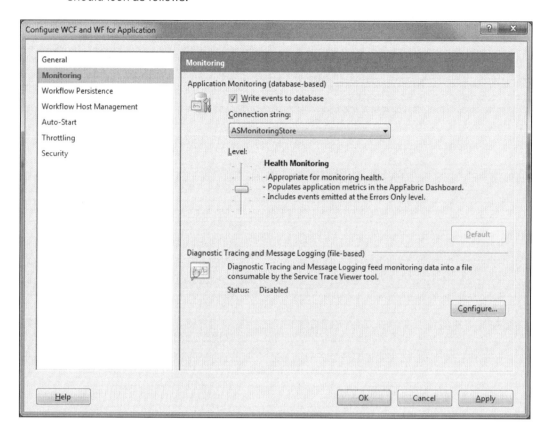

11. Now that the monitoring store is registered with the service, we can control the amount of information that gets written to the monitoring database by selecting the appropriate level. The default is the **Health Monitoring** level, which captures errors as well as relevant health information emitted by a service.

 To learn more about monitoring levels (and other aspects of Windows Server AppFabric monitoring) refer to *Chapter 7, Monitoring Windows Server AppFabric Deployment.*

12. Just as with the persistence store (as highlighted in the preceding recipe) we can create the appropriate users (or in the case of Domain environments, use Domain users) and add them to predefined Windows Server AppFabric roles such as AS_Administrators, AS_Observers, and AS_Administrators.

How it works...

Windows Server AppFabric is highly configurable and enables the use of multiple data stores for persisting monitoring related data. By running an AppFabric PowerShell cmdlet or Windows Server AppFabric's Configuration Wizard we can easily create and initialize a new database that can be used to store monitoring related data emitted by services running on Windows Server AppFabric. After adding new connection string definition in the relevant `web.config` (or `machine.config` depending on the scope of change) we can easily configure a service in IIS Manager to use a newly created and registered monitoring store.

Windows Server AppFabric, by allowing selection of different levels of monitoring information, enables finer level control of what gets persisted in the monitoring store.

Windows Server AppFabric uses the following three SQL Server database roles to control access to the monitoring sub system:

- **ASMonitoringDbAdmin**: The `ASMonitoringDbAdmin` role is mapped to Windows's `AS_Administrators` group. This role allows its members to read data from event views, write to the staging table, as well as providing the ability to archive, purge, and invoke stored procedures.

- **ASMonitoringDbReader**: The `ASMonitoringDbReader` role is mapped to Windows's `AS_Administrators` and `AS_Observer` groups. This role, as the name implies, provides the access to monitoring data via event views.

- **ASMonitoringDbWriter**: The `ASMonitoringDbWriter` role is mapped to the Windows `AS_Administrators` group. This role allows invoking stored procedures and the ability to write the data to the staging table.

There's more...

Apart from access control and data isolation, monitoring data can further be secured by using encryption (to secure data at rest). Using SQL Server's Transparent Database Encryption technology monitoring data can be encrypted such that even if the physical media (hard disk drive and so on) containing monitoring information is compromised, the data cannot be read without the security key.

 Discussion on Data Security architecture and practices is beyond the scope of this book.

In this recipe, we have focused only on the monitoring store part of Windows Server AppFabric's monitoring subsystem. In the following recipe, we will talk about how to secure the Event Collection Service, which is responsible for reading the data from the ETW session and writing it to the monitoring store.

Securing the Event Collection service

Windows Server AppFabric writes emitted data from applications and services to ETW. The emitted data is then further captured from the ETW session by Windows Server AppFabric's Event Collection service and gets written to the monitoring store.

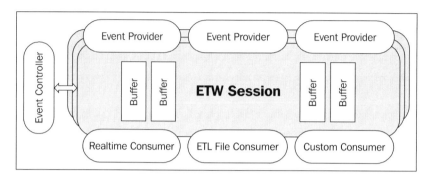

Event Tracing for Windows (ETW) is a high-speed tracing facility that provides a tracing mechanism for events raised by applications (as well as kernel-mode drivers). ETW can be broken down into three distinct components:

- ▶ Controller is responsible for starting and stopping event tracing sessions (without having to restart the application)

- ▶ Provider emits events that go in to ETW session

- ▶ Consumer reads events off the ETW session and consumes the event data based on the consumer logic

The following diagram shows how the WCF/WF events emitted by a Windows Server AppFabric hosted service are written to the monitoring database:

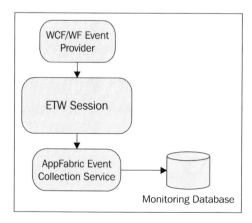

In this recipe, we will get to know how we can secure the following two important parts of the monitoring subsystem of Windows Server AppFabric:

- ▶ Event access control
- ▶ Event collection service

We will learn how to specify an identity for the services that run on Windows Server AppFabric (that is, IIS application pool identities) which are responsible for writing events to the ETW session. We will also see how to change the identity of the Event Collection service such that it is still able to read events of the ETW session and write them to the configured monitoring store.

Getting ready

We will isolate the monitoring subsystem that different services use by assigning them specific identities. These identities must be configured properly such that they have proper access to resources such as the ETW session and monitoring store. To get started with this recipe, we will need to have the following two identities in place so that we can provide them appropriate access rights:

- ▶ IIS AppPool identity
- ▶ AppFabric Event Collection service identity

How to do it...

We will start of by setting up a new IIS AppPool identity that can be used for Windows Server AppFabric services to write emitted data on an ETW session. We will then follow it up with a new identity under which we can run AppFabric the Event Collection service.

1. Launch the Computer Management Console by typing `compmgmt.msc` in the Window's **Search** box and hit *Enter*.

2. Under **Local Users and Groups**, select **Users** and create a new user and call it `AppMonitorIdentity`; provide the rest of the details as shown in the following screenshot. Click on **Create** to complete the user creation:

 You will most likely already have an (Domain) identity available to you for production and staging environments. If that's the case then you can skip steps 1 and 2.

3. Create a new IIS Application Pool and call it `AppFabricMonitoring`. Your new Application Pool should look like the following screenshot. (Or use an existing one if you have it available already and skip this step.)

4. Under **Advanced settings** for the newly created `AppFabricMonitoring` pool, specify the identity of the newly created (or existing) ID as shown in the following screenshot:

 You may want to assign a low privilege identity like Machine\MyUser with the AppPool to log events to a trace session.

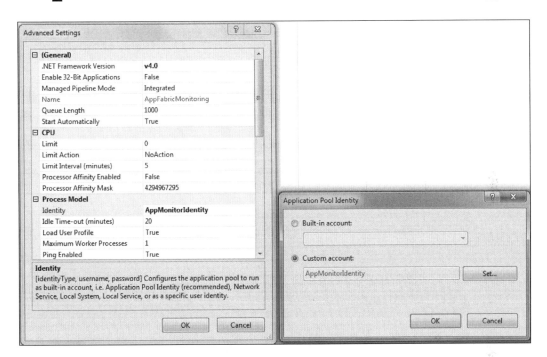

5. Now to enable this AppPool identity to have write access to the ETW session, launch the **Windows Reliability and Performance Monitor** tool by typing `perfmon.msc` in the Window's search box and pressing _Enter_.

6. Under **Data Collector Sets**, select **Event Trace Sessions**. Right-click on **AppFabric Event Collector Session** and launch its properties dialogue box:

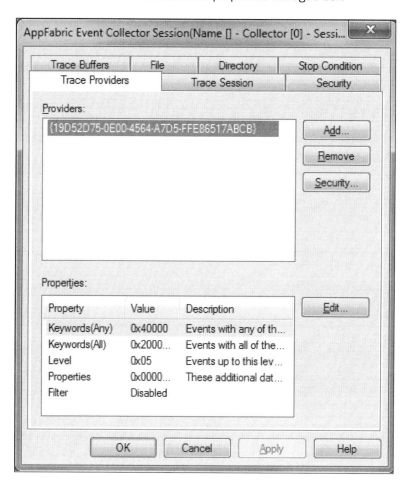

7. Select the **Security** tab and add the identity and ensure that it has access to TRACE_LOG_EVENT enabled, as shown in the following screenshot:

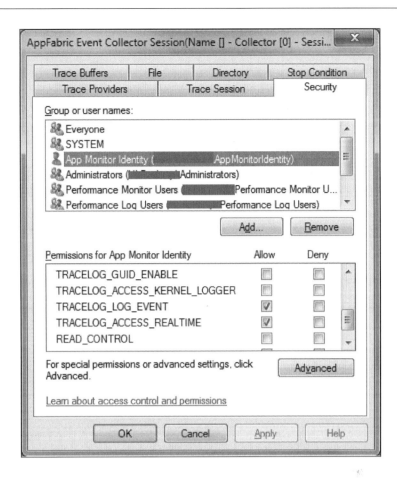

 Another way of allowing the newly created identity (for IIS AppPool) to be able to write to the ETW session is via the following Win32 API call.

```
ULONG EventAccessControl(
    __in   LPGUID Guid,
    __in   ULONG Operation,
    __in   PSID Sid,
    __in   ULONG Rights,
    __in   BOOLEAN AllowOrDeny
);
```

PowerShell provides great support for COM automation, .NET classes, and text processing amongst other things. However, it does not provide a facility to invoke Win32 API directly. Having said that, there is a workaround that can be used by utilizing .NET's support for invoking Win32 APIs. For more details, visit `http://blogs.msdn.com/b/powershell/archive/2006/04/25/583236.aspx`. Follow steps 1 and 2 to create a new identity called `AppFabricEventClctr`, or use an existing Domain account if you have one already.

8. Add the `AppFabricEventClctr` identity to the `Performance Log Users` Windows Group.

 Adding the newly created identity to the `Performance Log Users` Windows Groups sets it up with appropriate ACLs for accessing and reading events data from an ETW session.

9. Add the `AppFabricEventClctr` identity to the `AS_Administrators` Windows Group so that it can read and write the data from/to the AppFabric monitoring store.

 As we learned in the previous recipe, we can also add `AppFabric EventClctr` to the individual SQL Server database roles, called `ASMonitoringDbReader` and `ASMonitoringDbWriter`.

10. Grant `AppFabricEventClctr` read permission on the `web.config` file of the service or application being monitored via Windows Server AppFabric.

 Once `AppFabricEventClctr` is added to the `AS_Administrators` Windows Group it gets read access to the root `Web.Config` file (available at `Root$\Windows\system32\inetserv\config`).

11. To allow `AppFabricEventClctr` to run as a service, use the Local Security Policy tool. `AppFabricEventClctr` must be part of "Log on as a service" policy. For more details on how to add the "Log on as a service" account, visit `http://technet.microsoft.com/en-us/library/cc739424(WS.10).aspx`.

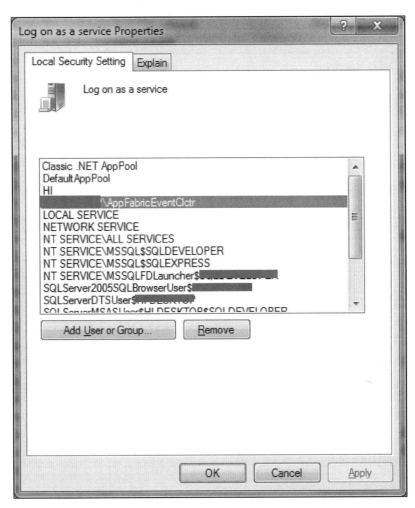

12. Launch the `services.msc` and set `AppFabricEventClctr` (and enter the password) as a Log on account for the AppFabric Event Collection service. Your properties tab should look as follows:

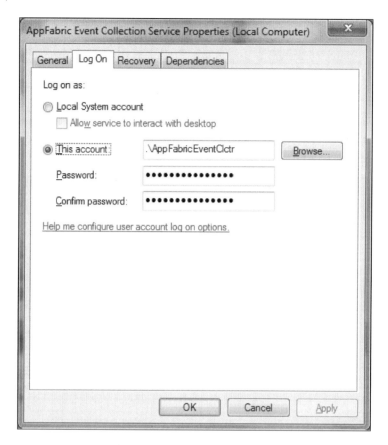

13. Restart the service to reflect the identity change.

How it works...

By isolating the identities of IIS App Pool and the AppFabric Event Collection service, we get to control the security of the application as well as the management part of the monitoring subsystem of Windows Server AppFabric.

With specific identities assigned to IIS App Pools running on Window Server AppFabric we can control application level access to ETW sessions. By assigning these IIS App Pool identities to the Domain level conceptual groups and granting these groups access to ETW session, we have finer level control over who is allowed to access ETW sessions. This can also be done by following the same process as highlighted in this recipe at the local level for the scenarios where we have a standalone host running Windows Server AppFabric.

Likewise, by assigning a new (preferably, Domain level identity) to AppFabric's Event Collection service we get to control the identities that are allowed to read the events from ETW session and write them to the configured monitoring store.

This, when coupled with the SQL Server database roles involved with Windows Server AppFabric's monitoring database, gives a fairly comprehensive security control for monitoring scenarios. This is more appealing as all of the work is based on familiar security practices on the Windows platform.

There's more...

To learn more about Windows Server AppFabric monitoring, read *Chapter 7, Monitoring Windows Server AppFabric Deployment*.

Index

Thank you for buying
Microsoft Windows Server AppFabric Cookbook

About Packt Publishing

Packt, pronounced 'packed', published its first book "*Mastering phpMyAdmin for Effective MySQL Management*" in April 2004 and subsequently continued to specialize in publishing highly focused books on specific technologies and solutions.

Our books and publications share the experiences of your fellow IT professionals in adapting and customizing today's systems, applications, and frameworks. Our solution-based books give you the knowledge and power to customize the software and technologies you're using to get the job done. Packt books are more specific and less general than the IT books you have seen in the past. Our unique business model allows us to bring you more focused information, giving you more of what you need to know, and less of what you don't.

Packt is a modern, yet unique publishing company, which focuses on producing quality, cutting-edge books for communities of developers, administrators, and newbies alike. For more information, please visit our website: www.PacktPub.com.

About Packt Enterprise

In 2010, Packt launched two new brands, Packt Enterprise and Packt Open Source, in order to continue its focus on specialization. This book is part of the Packt Enterprise brand, home to books published on enterprise software – software created by major vendors, including (but not limited to) IBM, Microsoft and Oracle, often for use in other corporations. Its titles will offer information relevant to a range of users of this software, including administrators, developers, architects, and end users.

Writing for Packt

We welcome all inquiries from people who are interested in authoring. Book proposals should be sent to author@packtpub.com. If your book idea is still at an early stage and you would like to discuss it first before writing a formal book proposal, contact us; one of our commissioning editors will get in touch with you.

We're not just looking for published authors; if you have strong technical skills but no writing experience, our experienced editors can help you develop a writing career, or simply get some additional reward for your expertise.

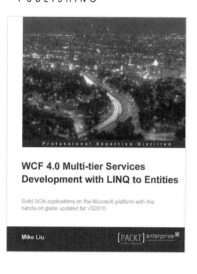

WCF 4.0 Multi-tier Services Development with LINQ to Entities

ISBN: 978-1-849681-14-8   Paperback: 348 pages

Build SOA applications on the Microsoft platform with this hands-on guide updated for VS2010

1. Master WCF and LINQ to Entities concepts by completing practical examples and applying them to your real-world assignments

2. The first and only book to combine WCF and LINQ to Entities in a multi-tier real-world WCF service

3. Ideal for beginners who want to build scalable, powerful, easy-to-maintain WCF services

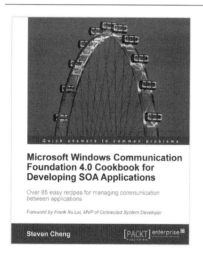

Microsoft Windows Communication Foundation 4.0 Cookbook for Developing SOA Applications

ISBN: 978-1-849680-76-9   Paperback: 316 pages

Over 85 easy recipes for managing communication between applications

1. Master WCF concepts and implement them in real-world environments

2. An example-packed guide with clear explanations and screenshots to enable communication between applications and services and make robust SOA applications

3. Resolve frequently encountered issues effectively with simple and handy recipes

4. Explore the new features of the latest .NET 4.0 framework/Visual Studio 2010

Please check **www.PacktPub.com** for information on our titles

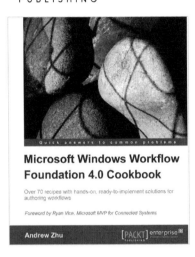

Microsoft Windows Workflow Foundation 4.0 Cookbook

ISBN: 978-1-849680-78-3   Paperback: 255 pages

Over 70 recipes with hands-on, ready-to-implement solutions for authoring workflows

1. Customize Windows Workflow 4.0 applications to suit your needs

2. A hands-on guide with real-world illustrations, screenshots, and step-by-step instructions

3. Explore various functions that you can perform using WF 4.0 with running code examples

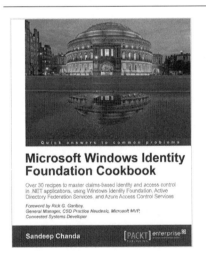

Microsoft Windows Identity Foundation Cookbook

ISBN: 978-1-849686-20-4   Paperback: 294 pages

Over 30 recipes to master claims-based identity and access control in .NET applications, using Windows Identity Foundation, Active Directory Federation Services, and Azure Access Control Services

1. Gain a firm understanding of Microsoft's Identity and Access Control paradigm with real world scenarios and hands-on solutions.

2. Apply your existing .NET skills to build claims-enabled applications.

3. Includes step-by-step recipes on easy-to-implement examples and practical advice on real world scenarios.

Please check **www.PacktPub.com** for information on our titles